T0331423

A MONETARY THEORY OF EMPLOYMENT

STUDIES IN INSTITUTIONAL ECONOMICS

GARDINER C. MEANS
INSTITUTIONALIST AND POST KEYNESIAN
Warren J. Samuels and Steven G. Medema

THE HETERODOX ECONOMICS OF GARDINER C. MEANS
A COLLECTION
Frederic S. Lee and Warren J. Samuels, editors

UNDERGROUND ECONOMICS
A DECADE OF INSTITUTIONALIST DISSENT
William M. Dugger

THE STRATIFIED STATE
RADICAL INSTITUTIONALIST THEORIES OF
PARTICIPATION AND DUALITY
William M. Dugger and William T. Waller, Jr., editors

A VEBLEN TREASURY
FROM LEISURE CLASS TO WAR,
PRICE, AND CAPITALISM
Rick Tilman, editor

ACTIVIST UNIONISM
THE INSTITUTIONAL ECONOMICS OF SOLOMON BARKIN
Donald R. Stabile

BEYOND DISSENT
ESSAYS IN INSTITUTIONAL ECONOMICS
Philip A. Klein

THE UNITED NATIONS AT THE CROSSROADS OF REFORM
Wendell Gordon

A MONETARY THEORY OF EMPLOYMENT
Gardiner C. Means
Warren J. Samuels and Frederic S. Lee, editors

A
MONETARY
THEORY OF
EMPLOYMENT

GARDINER C. MEANS

WARREN J. SAMUELS and
FREDERIC S. LEE
Editors

Routledge
Taylor & Francis Group

LONDON AND NEW YORK

First published 1994 by M.E. Sharpe

Published 2015 by Routledge
2 Park Square, Milton Park, Abingdon, Oxon OX14 4RN
711 Third Avenue, New York, NY 10017, USA

Routledge is an imprint of the Taylor & Francis Group, an informa business

Library of Congress Cataloging-in-Publication Data

Means, Gardiner Coit, 1896–1988
A monetary theory of employment / Gardiner C. Means: edited by
Warren J. Samuels, Frederic S. Lee
p. cm. — (Institutional economics)
Includes bibliographical references and index.
ISBN 1-56324-477-2. — ISBN 1-56324-478-0
1. Employment (Economic theory)
2. Monetary policy.
I. Samuels, Warren J., 1933–
II. Lee, Frederic S., 1949–
III. Title.
IV. Series: Studies in institutional economics.
HD5701.5.M43   1994
331—dc20   94-26135
CIP

ISBN 13: 9781563244780 (pbk)
ISBN 13: 9781563244773 (hbk)

Contents

List of Tables and Figures

Introduction

Warren J. Samuels

The manuscript presented here was, according to dates indicated on the first pages of several chapters, completed during March and April 1947. It has not been published previously.

The manuscript is significant with regard to (1) the development of Gardiner Means's analysis of the economy and his reaction to John Maynard Keynes's *General Theory* (1936); (2) the state of monetary and macroeconomic thinking in the mid-1940s; (3) it being an example of a mode of reasoning alternative to both the quantity theory of money and Keynesian macroeconomics; and (4) Means's serious attention to the limits of his work, including testing.

Means called his analysis a *monetary* theory of employment. The matter calls for explication.

Historically, monetary theory dealt with, and attempted to explain, the demand and supply of money, interest rates, and price level. The quantity theory of money attempted to treat changes in the price level as a more or less purely monetary phenomenon, some writers going so far as to *define* inflation as an increase in the supply of money (and vice versa for deflation), rather than as an increase (decrease) in the general price level; that is, building into the definition of the phenomenon a particular theory of its causation.

Moreover, when the quantity theory was combined with an analysis such as that of Say's law, it could be used to rule out of analytical bounds changes in the demand for money and in output and employment, because such analysis effectively meant that the economy was operating at full employment. In such cases, an increase in the supply of money could only generate an increase in the price level.

In the 1920s another version of the quantity theory was formulated. It too focused on explaining the price level, but it also considered motives for holding money (thereby no longer assuming that money was only a medium of exchange; now it could also serve as a store of value, or buying power—that is, serve as a means of deferring the decision to spend, satisfying a desire to hold purchasing power). Contemporaneous developments included recognition that a hiatus could exist between saving and investment. These developments were considered in the context of monetary theory; macroeconomics as a recognized field with a particular central problem—the determination of the levels of income, output and employment—did not exist. Thus, Keynes's *Treatise on Money* (1930) treated the motives for holding money, and so on, in an essentially monetary theory context.

During the 1930s and beyond, two other lines of reasoning also developed, aspects of which had been around earlier: the real balance effect and portfolio balancing. According to the real balance effect, changes in the level of prices (say, deflation associated with a recession or depression) increased the real balances represented by any particular holding of cash balances. Such changes in the level of prices, and therefore in real balances, could lead, indeed would likely lead, it was thought, to changes in spending, in order to adjust the level of nominal balances to the desired level of real balances. In the case of a fall in prices, spending would exhaust the excess nominal balances, and vice versa with inflation.

Portfolio balancing, or rebalancing, involved changes in the management of assets, especially with regard to their liquidity. Three kinds of assets are particularly involved: money (cash and demand deposit accounts and perhaps some other forms easily converted into cash and/or demand deposits); securities, such as equity stock, bonds, and other loan instruments; and plant or equipment (capital, or investment, goods). Changes in liquidity preference could bring about shifts in the form in which assets were held (insofar as these assets were due to saving, shifts in the form in which saving was held). Movements into and out of plant and equipment represented changes in spending, and therefore changes in income, output, and employment.

One of the important consequences of Keynes's *General Theory* was that economists could no longer assume that equilibrium was necessarily at the full employment level. The determination of the level of employment, and with it the levels of output and income, was now something to be determined. Another result was that the income–expenditure, or saving–investment model could be used as an alternative to the quantity theory to explain changes in the general price level.

Money and interest rates continued to enter into theory but they were no longer quite so central. Whereas the quantity of money (money supply) was critical to the quantity theory and the determination of the price level, it now was limited to the determination of interest rates. The possibility still existed that a contrived increase in the supply of money could directly lead to inflation (at less than or, especially, at full employment), but such was not the center of attention. Also, the interest rate was no longer seen as equating saving and investment (at the full employment level). In Keynes's model, the interest rate now was limited to the determination of the level of investment (and also, but less centrally, consumer durables), and therefore only indirectly the determination of the level of income. In the IS-LM model of John R. Hicks and Alvin Hansen, the interest rate served as a connector of the goods and money markets, somewhat more directly than in Keynes's model, determining the level of income (but by no means as critically as in Say's law).

Means's *monetary* theory of employment is an attempt to use real balance effect, wealth effect, and portfolio-balancing lines of reasoning to provide a monetary explanation of employment centering on the demand for and supply of money. Not surprisingly, it does so through emphasis on the line of reasoning that has become so deeply connected with his name: the role of insensitive (administered) prices. Indeed, one feature of the manuscript (part II) is Means's relatively comprehensive presentation of the sources of price insensitivity (inflexibility) within business and business decision making.

In the case of the quantity theory, flexible prices of goods and inputs were assumed to be ubiquitous. In the case of Keynes's *General Theory,* the argument centered on the determination of effective demand. Keynes did not use price inflexibility as a critical basis for departures from full employment. For Means, price inflexibility over large segments of the U.S. economy meant the failure to achieve full employment—a failure pursued analytically in terms of the demand for and supply of money, hence, a *monetary theory of employment and unemployment.*

Notice that Means's monetary theory does not attribute fundamental causal determinacy to the demand and supply of money, such as the quantity theory tends to do for the supply of money. In Means's monetary theory, the stress on "monetary" has to do with the demand and supply of money constituting an adjustment mechanism. The causal forces are not the demand and supply of money per se but decisions about liquidity, and so on, which have their impact on the relation of the demand for money to the supply of money. The decisions centering on liquidity govern the working out of the real balance, wealth, and portfolio-balancing effects.

Apropos of the respects in which this manuscript is significant, the reader must take care in considering what it says, what it does not say, the way it conducts its analysis, and also precisely why the manuscript is of interest. The reader could evaluate what Means wrote on the basis of whether or not he was correct; that is, whether or not the reader agrees with Means. Such an objective is not irrelevant, but the manuscript is of greater historical interest than providing something to criticize or to praise. And, of course, judgments as to correctness will tend to depend on the critical standpoint established by the choice of a correct theory. But the manuscript is significant for other reasons. The manuscript may be surprising for its monetary analysis in the light of Means's general emphasis on inflexible prices. The manuscript is significant in providing insight into the state of monetary–macroeconomic thinking during the mid-1940s and into how both monetary and macroeconomics could have developed quite differently than they did in subsequent decades.

Another respect in which the manuscript is suggestive, if not significant, concerns the treatment accorded Means by mainstream economists.[1] The manuscript shows Means not only understood but accepted much of the reasoning of mainstream neoclassical economics, including its welfare–economic reasoning. The reader will see this for him- or herself. It involves both Means's understanding of how markets work and his reliance on monetary economics. Means had a justly acquired reputation for heterodoxy, stemming from his emphasis on the separation of ownership and control, price inflexibility, and the critique of neoclassical economics. Yet he accepted much of the neoclassical mode of reasoning, given his deviations from it.

Means's analysis is also suggestive in several lesser technical matters. For example, Means embraces a number of lines of reasoning, such as the critique of the gold standard in chapter 18, to make them a part of his monetary theory of employment, whereas these lines of reasoning could and indeed have been readily absorbed into other monetary–macroeconomic theories.

Means's situation is somewhat reminiscent of that of Henry George. George was considered a radical by many economists for his drawing the implication of unearned increment from the Ricardian theory of land rent, and for further eliciting the policy recommendation of a "single tax" on unimproved land based on that implication, which was seen by many as a threat to the institution of private property. Yet George was quite conventional in his adoption of much of the rest of classical economics. Indeed, he was otherwise quite conservative in his advocacy of systemic values. After all, the idea of taxing the unearned increment is a corollary to the theme that distribution should be in accordance with contribution to production, and was a policy implication not unknown to the classicists themselves.

Both George and Means ran up against the Lakatosian protective belt of a discipline interested in protecting both its analytic core, and its reputation as safe and unthreatening in the larger community among the power elites. Reputations for heterodoxy, even radicalism, accrue on the basis of particular, more or less idiosyncratic ideas. In some cases, the reputation is avoided because the individual is professionally beyond objection and permitted certain deviant ideas; in other cases, individuals, perhaps especially those who are not "insiders," acquire the reputation, whereas in most if not all other respects they are quite orthodox. In the cases of George and Means, each challenged certain fundamental elements of the core belief system about private property and corporate power.

Reading and understanding the manuscript takes some work. First, Means writes with a closer knowledge of business details than do most academic economists. Second, one cannot presume to find his reasoning paralleling, or readily translatable into, that of one or another version of Keynesian macroeconomics. One way in which the manuscript is interesting is precisely that it does differ from the modes or conventions of reasoning that became the heart of macroeconomic training and practice for several decades after World War II. Third, the reasoning is, as already indicated, that of monetary economics rather than the macroeconomics of employment, and, fourth, a somewhat different version of monetary economics than most economists have experienced.

Means's monetary theory of employment is not Keynes's theory but it is an attempt to use monetary theory to explain not the price level but the determination of employment and unemployment. At several points, Means attempts to differentiate his theory from that of Keynes (for example, with regard to liquidity preference); how successfully, the reader will have to assess for him or herself.

The monetary theory, as already indicated, is that of the real balance effect and portfolio balancing. To put that in perspective, consider a middle-brow, or centrist, version of Keynesian macroeconomics (the reader can substitute any preferred alternative version). Income is a function of expenditure. Injections and leakages in the spending flow arise from hoarding and dishoarding, credit creation and destruction, foreign trade, and portfolio rebalancing (as well as changes in consumer expectations and government fiscal and monetary policies), in response to changes in desired money balances (liquidity) and/or expected profits (marginal efficiency of capital) in relation to interest rates. In this context, what Means does in his monetary theory of employment is to concentrate on changes in the demand for and supply of money as brought about by changes in the desired level of real balances, portfolio rebalancing, and the price level, to the exclusion of many other variables and relationships subsequently common to macroeconomics, at least as core elements. In this Meansian world, he advances what he thinks are likely behavioral possibilities, always aware that actual results are likely to be the result of the net effects of competing tendencies; but also in this context he introduces the consequences for economic adjustment and therefore employment and unemployment of price insensitivity or inflexibility. The impact of Keynes is amply evident, but the analysis is quite different.

The manuscript is of interest also with regard to what it has to say about policy. First, the policy analysis is consistent with the *monetary* theory that Means advances in the earlier chapters, largely focusing on changes in liquidity preference relative to the various forms that assets can take. Second, it is in the tradition of U.S. policy pragmatism, typified by the career of Irving Fisher, which has sought policy and institutional adjustments to improve management of the money supply and the monetary system as a whole, within the context of the monetary and banking theory used by the policy analyst. Third, it too reflects Means's close understanding of how markets, especially security and money markets, work. Fourth, Means says that he is more interested in exploring the further implications of the monetary theory in regard to policy than in laying an immediate basis for policy, a rather restrained and diffident position.

The manuscript, the original of which is at the Franklin Delano Roosevelt Library at Hyde Park, New York, is presented here substantially as Means left it. Only minor editing has been undertaken. Editorial insertions are indicated by square brackets. Three figures in chapter 12 from other sources have been added in accordance with notations on the manuscript. Several others, and a mathematical appendix which Means left to be constructed, have not been added; however, statements of his general plans for these have been retained. The reader will appreciate that Means left the manuscript unfinished. The impact of this incompleteness on the substance and coherence of his argument, however, is minimal. Typographical corrections have been made and only relatively slight stylistic changes have been introduced, changes to which I am confident Means would have agreed (including gender-neutral language).

We are indebted to the late Caroline Ware for her help in this and other regards.

Fred Lee and I wish to thank Christine Florie for her splendid editorial work and Richard Bartel for his interest and support.

Note

1. Samuels, Warren J., and Steven G. Medema. *Gardiner C. Means: Institutionalist and Post Keynesian.* Armonk, NY: M.E. Sharpe, 1990.

Introduction: Means and the Making of an Anti-Keynesian Monetary Theory of Employment

Frederic S. Lee

In August 1934, Gardiner Means wrote a paper entitled "NRA and AAA and the Reorganization of Industrial Policy Making," in which he discussed the intra-industry problems of prices and production that emerge when business enterprises, through setting their own prices and level of output, can make their own business policy.[1] In it, he argued that the problem of making policy for an industry as a whole, insofar as it concerned the National Recovery Administration (NRA) and the Agricultural Adjustment Administration (AAA) lay in finding the "key decisions for each industry, which, if made right, would so condition the other elements of industrial policy that the latter could be left to the actions of individuals and the operation of the market" (Means, 1934, p. 5). He then delineated four possible mechanisms through which the key decisions could be made, but added the warning that whatever mechanism was adopted must be congruous with the existing situation and American political and economic traditions if it was to work adequately. In spite of the narrow focus of the paper, it was clear to Means at the time that many of the most important key decisions would concern interindustry relationships and could be made right only in terms of interindustry balance. In addition, he also realized that in a more general paper he would have discussed the importance of interindustry relationships, staff planning, and organization for ensuring interindustry balance, and emphasized that the key decisions were in part intraindustry, and in part interindustry, and had to be made within the context of the national economy. Thus, he soon found that the NRA, AAA, and other specific recovery programs could not repair the poorly functioning economy, and that partial planning in general, whether done by business enterprises or by public institutions, would likely make matters worse rather than better. Moreover, because of the criticisms he received with respect to his suggestions of how industrial policy could be made, Means began to doubt whether an administrative committee approach to the making of industrial policy, even if the committee consisted of all major interest groups, could be employed without at the same time undermining the essential features of democracy and of American institutions.

Shortly after writing the paper, Means shifted his position, now feeling that the process of creating a plan or series of plans for the economy should be entrusted to experts, while the acceptance and implementation of any particular plan should be left in the hands of the community, its elected officials, and the various interest groups that make it up. Thus, given his interest in national economic planning and his new view on the planning process, Means accepted Rexford Tugwell's suggestion that he go to work for a little-known New Deal planning agency, the National Resources Board. Being concerned with national planning of the nation's resources within the context of a free market and democratic society, the Board and its successors, the National Resources Committee (NRC) and the National Resources Planning Board (NRPB), was a natural home for Means. Here he used his knowledge of industry planning derived from his work with the NRA and AAA, his skills as an economist, and his theory of the cause of the depression to construct a multi-industry model of the American economy for use in national economic planning.

In February 1935, after reading H. Loeb's book, *The Chart of Plenty,* Means revived an old idea of his of modeling the American economy in terms of both production and consumption. With such a model, he argued, it would be possible to construct production–consumption patterns that would reflect the economical use of resources to serve human requirements under a variety of possible conditions. The National Resources Committee accepted his argument, so in May 1935, Means initiated research projects on industrial capacity and consumption and thus was on his way to developing a series of production–consumption patterns, or a model of the American economy that could then be used for national economic planning. In November 1936, Means wrote a memorandum on national economic planning in which he argued that one of the concerns of a federal planning organization should be to bring about and maintain effective overall balance of the use of the nation's resources. This implied that his production–consumption projects had to be expanded to include an investigation into the forces that affected the coordination and organization of economic activity, and hence the overall balance of the economy. Thus, Means suggested to the NRC that it initiate a study of the structure of industry that would (1) be concerned primarily with the administrative or controlling units through which industry is now carried on; (2) consider the present and possible roles of competition and administration of economic activity; (3) be concerned particularly with corporations, trade associations, labor unions, farms, and consumer organizations; (4) be concerned with possible techniques for coordinating economic activity with the minimum concentration of power; and (5) result in recommendations as to the structure of planning and acting for overall balance toward which this country should work. The NRC accepted Means's suggestion in July 1937, permitting Means to develop a comprehensive multi-industry model of the American economy. The research undertaken by Means and his colleagues was published in 1938 and 1939. In particular, Means used the model in *Patterns of Resource Use* (Means 1938a) to determine the pattern of consumption, resource use, and labor employment at three different levels of consumer income, including the full-employment level. And, in 1939 Means's work on the structure of industry was published under the title *The Structure of the American Economy Part I: Basic Characteristics* (Lee 1990; Lee and Samuels 1992a).

Administered Prices, Money, and Economic Activity

In his writings, Means argued that if a balanced economy, with a balanced structure of market and administered prices, suffered a decline in aggregate demand due to, for example, a deficiency of buying because consumers and enterprises decided to increase their money balances, the immediate result would be an unbalancing of both the economy and the price structure. On the one hand, prices in the market sector would decline, thus maintaining production and employment, while production and employment in the administered sector would decline in the face of relatively stable administered prices. Because of this asymmetrical response, the level of economic activity in the economy would decline further due to the decline in demand caused by the existence of unemployed workers combined with relatively stable administered prices, resulting in a still further deflation in market prices and decline in production in the administered sector. This process would end when prices in both the market and administered sectors fell far enough to increase real money balances of consumers and enterprises to where they held a redundancy of money. They would then spend the extra money and thus increase aggregate demand so as to bring the downward spiral to an end; however, this new stable position would be accompanied by idle machines and workers. Hence with the existence of administered prices, the coordination of economic activity so as to maintain a fully employed, balanced economy with a balanced price structure was completely undermined. Instead of the business cycle being solely the "dance-of-prices," administered prices had made it both a price and a production and employment phenomenon.

The role of money in Means's explanation for the downturn of the business cycle was initially presented in terms of the failure of the banking system to supply the right amount of money. That is, working from a quantity theory of money perspective, Means argued that in a flexible price economy, changes in the volume of money would result in corresponding changes in prices with the end result that production and employment would remain unchanged. In such an economy, the volume of money was always the right amount. However, in an economy with flexible and inflexible prices, if the volume of money was reduced or the community's need to hold money and not spend it increased, prices in the market sector would decline while production remained constant, and in the administered sector, production and employment would decline while prices remained constant. These latter changes would push the economy from a recession into a depression. Thus, Means concluded that in an economy dominated by inflexible prices, a depression could be caused solely by monetary changes. Consequently, the way out of the economic decline would be for the banking sector to increase the liquidity of individuals by increasing the supply of money since, by doing so, individuals would increase spending on all products with the consequence that market prices would reflate (along with production) and be brought back into balance with the administered prices, and the production of administered price goods would be brought back into balance with the production of market sector goods. However, the banking system, as currently organized in the United States, was unable to carry out this function. Hence, it was necessary to establish an appropriate monetary policy that would keep the flexible prices as a group approximately in line with inflexible prices as a group, and this would require (1) that a technique should be established for keeping close track of prices of varying degrees of flexibility and particularly their relation to each other as an indication of appropriate policy; and (2) that control over the volume of money should be in some central body, presumably the federal government (Means 1935a, 1935b, and 1935c).

Means continued his work on the relationship between the money supply, administered prices, and economic activity in his study on the structure of the American economy at the NRC. Specifically, he argued that transactions in a modern corporate economy were money transactions (as opposed to barter/nonmoney transactions), since prices were stated in terms of money and the organizing and coordination of economic activity took place through series of money transactions based on money prices. Means also noted that besides the negative impact administered prices had on the extent to which money transactions could adequately perform their role of organizing and coordinating economic activity, the various circuits of money flows, such as the money flow from producers to consumers in the form of money income and the money flow from consumers to producers in the form of savings for investment, which tied the economy together, would also have a significant impact on the organizing and coordinating of economic activity. Consequently, those factors that could affect the money flows, such as changes in the total supply of money, the building up or depleting of money balances held by particular economic groups, and shifts in the relative flow of funds into current consumption and capital formations, could also affect the level of economic activity.

Means defined the money supply as currency and demand deposits, and then noted that large variations in the money supply do occur within relatively short periods of time, which necessarily alter the buying power of individuals and institutions. That is, Means argued, since bank credit was the most important contributor to the money supply, increasing bank credit through extending additional loans and investments increased both the buying power of individuals, enterprises, and government units, and the money supply. Thus, variations in bank credit, hence the supply of money, necessarily affected the flow of money and economic activity.[2] Means also argued that, for a given quantity of money, changes in the money balances held by individuals, enterprises, and government could have much the same effect on money flows and on production as have changes in the money supply.[3] For example, if there was a general increase in the holding of money, a deficiency of buying by both consumers and enterprises would result, and this would have an effect on the money flows. Finally, Means argued that the direction of money flows as between consumption and capital formation was significant to the structure of production, because it channeled the volume of productive activity going on, respectively, into the supply of goods currently consumed and into new plant, equipment, and inventory. One result Means derived from his study of the various money flows was that there existed a tendency for the volume of new savings to increase at such a rate with an increase in national income as to suggest the very real possibility of oversaving in relation to current consumption. Another result was that consumers, who account for the bulk of production-stimulating purchases, had relatively small money holdings and therefore could not on their own produce a recovery by simply depleting their money holdings.

The structure study only indicated the importance of money flows to the functioning of production, and suggested a kind of analysis of money flows that would clarify the structure of production and throw light on the behavior of the American economy; but the study could not say how the flows could be changed so as to have a specific impact on the economy. Thus, Means could not say precisely how money flows operated on the economy and therefore could not say how they could be subject to policy making. However, he did believe that government monetary, tax, and budgetary policies, and that dividend policies of corporations, could affect money flows and thus could be used to compensate for any deficiencies in buying power that might arise. Such a compensating policy, he felt, might be limited to the activity of the federal government, or it might be possible to develop a more comprehensive financial program that interrelated the financial policies of the federal government, the major state and municipal governments, and the larger corporations. The more scope involved in such a program, the greater the compensating influence that could be exercised (Means 1939a, 1939c, and 1940f).

Means, Keynes, and the Keynesians

For Means's model of the American economy to be useful for national economic planning, it was necessary that the structure study be followed up by a study of government and corporate operating policies. Such a study, in Means's view, would be oriented toward the problem of effective use of resources, and thus be concerned with how government monetary, fiscal, industrial, saving–investment, and other economic policies came into existence; with the coordination of the economic policies pursued by the different branches of the federal government; and with the focal points of control of the determinants of the money supply, the flow of investment funds and capital creation, government spending and taxes, and the price and production policies of the corporate enterprise. Although Means requested in 1936 and again in 1937 and 1938 that such a study be undertaken, it was never commissioned by the NRC. This lack of support for the policy study was due in part to the committee's rejection of any study that promoted a plan for economic intervention in the economy with regard to the price and production policies of specific industries. It was also due to the committee's gradual acceptance of Keynesian economics and the particular national policy perspective it promoted. Means acknowledged this shift in interest and even suggested that the NRC carry out a study of monetary and fiscal policies. However, the approach to the issue of unemployment became increasingly viewed in Keynesian terms—that is, in terms of a Keynesian model of the economy and the planning of the levels of aggregate variables, such as government expenditures, private investment, and interest and tax rates. Means had much to dislike about the Keynesian approach, partly because it ignored nearly all of his previous work on economic planning and unemployment, and partly because he simply did not believe that compensatory fiscal policy, that is, government spending, by itself would eliminate cyclical fluctuations and generate continuous full employment:

I am convinced that such a fiscal policy is essential to full use of resources but it cannot handle the whole job, and the problem is to insure the operation of other factors in such a way that the magnitude of the unbalance in purchasing power, which needs to be compensated by fiscal policy, is not so great as to make such a policy ineffective over any prolonged period. (Means 1938b)

His disagreement with it was not with what the policy ignored, but that it was theoretically flawed and thus could not account for unemployment, much less suggest ways to eliminate it. Means reached this conclusion after an intense interchange with Keynes during the summer of 1939 (Lee 1990).

Before July 1939, Means believed that Keynes's theory of unemployment might possibly rest on a variant of price rigidity, namely, wage rate inflexibility. This, he felt, would make Keynes's theory and his own similarly characterized by institutional rigidity, each closely paralleling the other, and hence reinforcing each other's point as to the need for government to support aggregate demand. Preparatory to his July 1939 meeting with Keynes, Means wrote him a memorandum in which he outlined his own explanation of unemployment and its possible relationship to Keynes's theory. One conclusion he reached in the memo was that given price inflexibility, a lack of balance between savings and investment would be worked out through reductions in output and employment until a lower level of employment equilibrium was reached. That end result was similar to Keynes's unemployment equilibrium, but it stemmed from the assumption of inflexible prices, whereas Keynes's theory appeared to assume either perfect competition and flexibility of prices or the inflexibility of wage rates. If the latter was the case, then, Means argued, his explanation and Keynes's theory were similar, but if the former was the case, then they were quite different. Thus, Means prefaced the memorandum with a letter to Keynes in which he posed three questions to which, when he met him, he would like to have definite answers: (1) "Does your general theory, and, particularly, your interest theory, depend on an assumption of flexible money–wage rates?"; (2) "Does your analysis depend at any point on an assumption of inflexible goods prices?"; and (3) "Is the tendency toward oversaving the only major cause of involuntary unemployment?" (Means 1939e); [Rosenof 1994; Means 1939d, 1978a].

Means's interview with Keynes centered on whether Keynes's theory rested on an assumption of inflexible prices or wages, and whether his theory could explain persistent unemployment in an economy of perfectly flexible prices and wages in the context of a given supply of money. Keynes answered the first point with a definite NO. Responding to a second memorandum Means wrote for Keynes a few days after their interview, Keynes noted that his theory makes no assumption about the flexibility or inflexibility of prices: "As you will see from my notes, and as I said before, I regard the [General] Theory as equally applicable to flexible economies, inflexible economies, and intermediate conditions" (Keynes 1939a). Keynes's response to the second point was that even if the assumptions of perfectly flexible prices and wages and a given stock of money were made, his theory would still produce an unemployment equilibrium because of the existence of liquidity preference. However, Means had difficulty accepting the argument, and therefore, in the second memorandum to Keynes, addressed the issue again. Keynes's further comments still left him unconvinced, for, instead of making recourse to liquidity preference, Keynes made reference to expectations as the culprit producing the unemployment equilibrium. Thus, Means came away from his interchange with Keynes with the conviction that their explanations for unemployment were quite different, and that Keynes's theory of employment was fundamentally flawed[4] (Means 1939f, 1971, 1976, and undated; Keynes 1939b).

Following his 1939 visit to Keynes, Means returned to the NRC, where Keynesianism had largely taken over. In this new environment, Means was denied funding to embark upon his projected study of the operating policies of government and business. Consequently, his model of the American economy was never completely developed. Moreover, denied the research he wished to do, combined with his disagreement with Keynesian theory, Means did not fit in with the Keynesian NRC or its successor, the National Resources Planning Board. Thus, Means resigned from the NRPB just a year after his meeting with Keynes (Means 1940a, 1940b, 1951).

Politics and Full Employment, 1940–46

Means left the NRPB for the new Fiscal Division in the Bureau of the Budget; however, differences of opinion with Gerhard Colm, the head of the Fiscal Division, about the impending inflation threat with the coming of war, combined with his failure to shape the Director of the Bureau of the Budget's advice to the President, led him to leave the Bureau by the end of 1941. Later, in 1943, Means became associate director of research for the Committee for Economic Development (CED). The CED was established in 1942 as a business-sponsored, private research group concerned with government policies to assure a full-employment transition to a peacetime economy. The individuals who established the CED sought a middle path between statist formulas for the organization of society and the traditional laissez-faire creed of conservatives. Stressing the importance of expertise and of transforming political decisions into technical ones, they saw private, functionally defined groups as partners with a cooperative state apparatus, where together they would work for an objectively recognizable general interest. To carry out its agenda, the CED established the Research and Policy Committee, which initiated economic studies while the Director of Research and his staff assigned the studies to qualified scholars and oversaw their progress. Because the studies had to be "thoroughly objective in character," the CED used them to define a new, expanded role for the federal government in the pursuit of economic stability (Lee and Samuels 1992a; Goode 1994; Stein 1969; Collins 1981).

While the CED believed that the state had a crucial part to play if U.S. capitalism was to survive, it did not accept the type of national economic planning Means advocated, or the extreme spending policy advocated by Alvin Hansen and the members of the stagnation school.[5] Accepting a Keynesian role for the federal government and the need for occasional deficit spending, the CED sought to harness the new economics for the purpose of ensuring the retention of a private-enterprise political economy. From 1942 to 1948, it developed a fiscal and monetary policy package that integrated the concepts of Keynesian economics with their vision of the American political economy, which meant a fiscal and monetary policy that would be impersonal and leave to the private sector the basic decisions about resource allocation, production, prices, and wages. In the period from 1942 to 1946, the CED downplayed government spending in federal fiscal policy and stressed the role of stable tax rates in automatically stabilizing the economy at high employment, and the use of changes in the tax rate, if necessary, to alter consumer and producer spending so as to move the economy toward a high level of employment without inflation. Later, from 1946 to 1948, after the Federal Reserve had obtained some power to alter short-term interest rates, the CED began stressing the role of an interest rate-based monetary policy. Both of the arguments commended themselves to the CED because they operated impersonally and without any of the direct interference with the details of private business, which was so irksome and inefficient in a free economy [6] (Stein 1969; Collins 1981).

The 1940s and the CED were not hospitable to Meansian national economic planning or to any sort of economic planning that involved the federal government in the economy in a major way. The acrimonious congressional debate over the funding of the National Resources Planning Board in 1943 politically killed off Means's approach to economic planning. And Means acknowledged this verdict five months after the Board's demise when he stated that he was interested in avoiding any necessity for government intervention in the direct operating policies of business enterprises, such as with regard to price and production determination.

By 1945, Keynesian economic planning solely based on government spending had also become politically unviable, as evident in the debate over the full employment bill. Means was not terribly disappointed with this; however, he was not adverse to economic planning if it was seen as government responsibility for maintaining adequate demand via a CED-type of fiscal and monetary policy.[7] Such government planning was necessary, he believed, if under capitalism the individual was to achieve both political and economic freedom.[8] Thus, the dilemma Means faced was the need to develop a theory of employment that was not primarily based on government spending but was still amenable to government responsibility and planning, which was consistent with his vision of a liberal society and politically viable (Reagan 1982; Warken 1979; Rosenof 1994; Bailey 1950; Means 1944).

Working Toward a Monetary Theory of Employment, 1940–46

As his work associated with the structure study came to an end at the close of 1939, Means turned his attention to economic theory. He noted that traditional economics, as set forth in the Walrasian system of equations, assumed prices and wage rates to be perfectly sensitive to even the shortest run fluctuations in supply and demand; however, the evidence that emerged from the structure study showed that prices and wages were not perfectly sensitive. Thus, economic theory would be advanced if it were possible to reformulate the Walrasian system so that it could deal equally well with sensitive and insensitive prices and wages. This would be highly desirable, Means argued, because

> (1) it would undoubtedly help to bridge the gap in thinking of between traditional economic analysis and our actual economic behavior, and (2) it would provide a tool for developing carefully formulated hypotheses as to economic *operations* which could be tested statistically. (Means 1940c)

His work on reformulating the Walrasian system, however, came to a dead end. While Means was able to reformulate the system and get a determinate solution for an economy made up of two individuals, of two goods, and with fixed prices, he could not get a determinate solution when the economy was made up of three individuals and three goods.[9] Therefore, he concluded that no simple reformulation of the Walrasian system of equations for a complex economy seemed possible.

Although it was not possible to reformulate the Walrasian system, Means still believed that it was important to develop an analysis of an economy in which prices and wages were assumed to be fixed for periods of time and to indicate the conditions under which such an economy could be expected to run reasonably well. Until this had been done, he argued, it would not be possible to develop a system of national policies with respect to the use of resources that would produce a well-functioning economy. Therefore, Means embarked upon a mission to develop a theory of employment—which he believed was the most important single problem Americans faced—that was based on a conception of an economy where insensitive prices and wages were pervasive. This involved not only developing his own theory of employment, but also explaining why competing theories were "wrong" in their explanation of unemployment. Consequently, from 1940 to 1946, Means divided his time between these two activities, and the end result was his manuscript, *A Monetary Theory of Employment* (Means 1940d).

Means characterized neoclassical (or traditional) theory (as mathematized by Walras) as a nineteenth century conception of a competitive economy where full employment and perfectly sensitive prices and wages prevailed. In such an economy, any initial shock that decreased demand would, given a constant supply of money, work itself out only in terms of lower prices and wages. The linchpin in his argument was a modified Pigou effect, which came into play as a result of the fall in prices and wages. That is, a fall in prices and wages would increase the real buying power of the given money supply. This meant that individuals had more money on hand than they wished to keep and so they spent it on goods, thereby increasing demand.[10] Means found no fault with this mechanism of adjustment, which he called the Classical Theory of Employment (see chapter 4), that always ensured full employment.[11] However, he did note that the conception of a competitive economy on which it was based had no correspondence to the corporate American economy of the twentieth century, and therefore could be summarily ignored[12] (Means 1939c, 1939–40, 1940e, 1940f, 1944, 1957).

Means also developed a critique of what he called the Keynesian saving–investment theory of employment. Although starting with the same conception of the economy as did the neoclassical economists, including perfectly flexible prices and wages, the level of employment in the saving–investment theory was controlled by the level of income and production at which savings out of current income and investment at the current level of income were equal. Essential to the theory, Means argued, was that in equilibrium, savings and investment were defined as equal, that the saving–income and investment–income schedules were positively sloped, that the propensity to save was greater than the propensity to invest, and that unemployment could not generate forces that would cause the two schedules to shift to a full employment equilibrium. Explanations regarding this last point varied among economists; however, Means was mainly concerned with Keynes's explanation since he was his immediate opponent.[13] In the case of Keynes's theory of employment, Means argued (see chapter 2) that it was based on a new theory of the determination of the interest rate (which was based on the existing money stock and the demand for money as a store of value) combined with the existence of the liquidity trap. More specifically, Means argued that Keynes accepted the neoclassical assumption that investment was inversely related to the interest rate, but introduced a new assumption of savings being positively related to income (and not at all directly related to the savings rate). Thus, the lower the interest rate the higher investment, employment, income, and hence savings. In the context of unemployment and perfectly flexible prices and wage rates, there would be a fall in prices that would increase the real buying power of the outstanding money stock. This, in turn, would make the community more liquid and thus more willing to make loans, which would drive down the interest rate to a point where the desire to hold money as a store of value was again equal to the real value of the outstanding money stock. This fall would stimulate investment, hence increasing employment and savings. However, this process would not result in full employment because of the existence of an interest rate floor (i.e., the liquidity trap), which prevented increases in the real stock of money due to falling prices to push the interest rate lower. Thus, an unemployment equilibrium would exist in spite of perfectly flexible prices and wages, and the only way out was to have some external force, such as government, act directly on investment, such as instituting a spending program. In this case, monetary policy vis-à-vis acting on the interest rate would not be capable of guaranteeing full employment.

Means criticized Keynes's theory of employment (see chapter 3) on the grounds that changes in the real stock of money had a direct effect on savings and investment, as well as an indirect effect via the interest rate.[14] That is, although Means accepted Keynes's view that the interest rate adjusted to a level at which the community was just satisfied to hold the outstanding stock of money rather than make additional loans, he did not accept that the interest rate was the price that solely equilibrated the desire to hold wealth in the form of money with the existing supply of money. Rather, what he argued was that the interest rate and the level of income were both important for the equilibration process. Thus, the interest rate would tend to adjust so that the community would rather hold money than make further loans, and income would tend to adjust so that the community would rather hold money than spend at a greater rate on consumption or investment goods. So, in a situation in which unemployment existed, wages and prices would fall, increasing real money balances. One effect of this would be to prompt individuals to make more loans, which would drive down the interest rate with the corresponding increase in investment, while the second effect would be to encourage individuals and business enterprises to spend more on consumption and investment goods.[15] As long as unemployment existed, prices and wage rates would fall, increasing real money balances, with the resulting positive impact on investment and spending until full employment was reached. Thus, as long as the neoclassical assumptions of perfect flexibility of prices and wage rates were maintained, Means argued, the saving–investment theory of employment could not account for unemployment. Hence, the problem with Keynes's theory of employment was that he did not depart sufficiently far enough from the assumptions underlying neoclassical economics.[16]

Means's work on developing an alternative theory of employment had two phases. The first was to establish that insensitive prices and wages were inherent in and dominated the American economy, and then that such an economy, when faced with a decline in aggregate demand, would adjust to it partially through price and wage reductions and partially through output and employment reductions; the second was to develop an explanation of how a decline in aggregate demand could happen. Drawing on his previous work on prices, corporate concentration, and the business enterprise, Means established (see chapters 6 and 7) that insensitive prices and wages dominated the American economy and that they were a product of imperfectly competitive conditions. His previous work also enabled him to describe how an economy dominated by insensitive prices and wages adjusted to a decline in aggregate demand (see chapter 7). That is, a decline in demand would cause prices in the market sector to decline, thus maintaining production and employment, while production and employment in the administered sector would decline in the face of relatively stable administered prices. Because of this asymmetrical response, the level of economic activity in the economy would decline further, due to the decline in demand caused by the existence of unemployed workers combined with relatively stable administered prices, resulting in a still further deflation in market prices and a decline in production in the administered sector. This adjustment process would end when prices in both the market and administered sectors fell far enough to increase real money balances of consumers and enterprises to where they held a redundancy of money. They would then spend the extra money, thus increasing aggregate demand so as to bring the downward spiral to an end; however, this new stable position would be accompanied by idle machines and workers. Means denoted this adjustment process as the "insensitive-price theory of economic adjustment."[17] Thus, for Means, the existence of insensitive prices and wages rather than the liquidity trap was the basic cause of unemployment:

> My thinking about unemployment revolves around 1) the extensive existence of prices which are relatively insensitive to changes in demand and 2) the belief that this insensitivity is inherent in our present system. (Means 1946; see also Means 1957, 1971, 1976)

Drawing upon his previous excursions into monetary theory, Means developed a monetary theory of aggregate demand that could explain how a decline in demand could occur. The foundation of his theory consisted of the following propositions:

1. There was a given volume or supply of money.
2. Business enterprises and individuals held money balances and these money balances constituted their demand for money (all denoted in real terms).
3. Real money balances, hence the real demand for money, were a function of real income and real assets.
4. If the economic agent found itself holding real money balances that were larger than desired, given its real income and assets, it would try to reduce the balances, and hence its demand for money, by spending the surplus or redundant money on investment and consumption goods.
5. The larger the given supply of money vis-à-vis desired money balances, the greater would be the propensity to spend on consumption and investment goods.
6. The greater the real assets held by economic agents, the more likely that they wanted to reduce money balances and spend the redundant money on consumption and investment goods.

The propositions provided the basis for the two basic assumptions that underlie Means's monetary theory of aggregate demand: (1) that the propensities to consume and invest were higher with a larger real supply of money than with a smaller real supply of money (see chapter 8); (2) that the propensities to consume and to invest were higher with a high real value of assets than with a lower real value of assets (see chapter 9).

Given the two assumptions, Means argued that the demand for money and the given supply of money were the central determinants of aggregate demand (see chapter 10). More specifically, assuming an initial position where, given money incomes, assets, and a given supply of money, the money balances desired by each individual and business enterprise were such that the total demand for money equalled the supply. Now, if the economic agents desired to increase their money balances out of income, then there would be an increase in the demand for money vis-à-vis the given supply of money. The effort to save and build up money balances would lead to an increase in interest rates, reduce security prices, and reduce the demand for both consumption and investment goods.[18] The fall in the value of securities would also depress expenditure on both consumption and investment goods. The new equilibrium position would occur when interest rates had so fallen that the economic agents in the aggregate would rather hold the total stock of money outstanding than reduce further their making of loans; when security prices had fallen to the point that they would rather hold the stock of money than reduce further their purchase of securities; and when incomes had so declined that the agents would rather hold the outstanding stock of money than reduce further their expenditure on goods for consumption and investment—that is, equilibrium would be reached only when the aggregate demand for money was equal to the given supply of money. In this situation, Means argued, the economic agents in aggregate would be wanting to spend just the amount of their current income on goods, and there would be no tendency for aggregate demand to change except as the demand for money or the given supply of money were altered. This explanation of how changes in demand would occur and how they would work out in the economy he denoted as a monetary theory of aggregate demand.

Monetary Theory of Employment

Means combined his monetary theory of aggregate demand with his insensitive-price theory of economic adjustment to produce his monetary theory of employment. That is, starting from an equilibrium situation where the demand for money was equal to the given supply of money, if economic agents desired to increase their money balances, then the demand for money would be greater than the given supply, with the result that aggregate demand would fall according to the monetary theory of aggregate demand, and the economic adjustment in response to the decline in demand would work itself out in lower output and employment.[19] Thus, the agents' desire for money balances and the given supply of money were, Means felt, the independently

given forces that governed the level of economic activity and employment in the economy.[20] Since both forces could be altered by the
action of the banking system or by non-spending government activities, which would not directly affect the behavior of the economic
agents in any specific way, Means's monetary theory of employment
provided a liberal, politically acceptable rationale for the government
to become responsible for planning and putting into action economic
policies that would produce and maintain full employment.

Notes

1. The paper was later published as *Industrial Prices and Their Relative Inflexibility* (Means 1935a).
2. Although Means's position might sound like an adherent to I. Fisher's
quantity theory of money equation, this would be incorrect. Rather, Means argued
that it was conceivable to measure the quantity of money outstanding and the
dollar quantity of sales that took place at any point in time; however, he did not
see how it was possible to measure the velocity of money as an independently
measurable factor so long as one included deposits as part of the money supply.
That is, Means argued, it was conceivable that one could measure the number of
times a particular dollar bill changed hands in a given time period, but this was
not possible when demand deposits were utilized as a medium of exchange. Thus,
he concluded that there was no reality to velocity of circulation, and hence no
theoretical validity to Fisher's quantity theory of money equation:

> It becomes an abstraction arrived at by taking the total transactions and dividing
> by the total volume of money. This is an artificial abstraction and not a reflection
> of real behavior. Likewise, this means that in equation $MV = PT$ there is no basis
> for conceiving of an *independent* measurement of V. It can only be arrived at by
> dividing dollar sales (S) by M. Fisher's equation thus becomes $M(S/M) = PT$,
> while T can only be measured by dividing sales by P. This is one of the reasons
> why I generally fight the use of the terms velocity and stick to the concepts of
> total money supply and total sales. (Means 1939b, 7; also see Means 1953)

3. It should be noted that in his later work, Means centered most of his
monetary analysis of employment on money balances—why people and enterprises hold money balances and what would happen if they decided to change
them. It is the possession and passing on of the liquid store of value property of
money that is significant to Means in his monetary analysis of employment
(Means 1953).
4. One reason why Means had difficulty coming to grips with Keynes's General Theory was that he habitually conceived of it in terms of a Walrasian system
of equations, whereas Keynes did not. Consequently, what was meant by equilibrium and the forces that produce unemployment equilibrium would be different
(Keynes 1939b).
5. The CED objection to federal spending as a way to achieve full employment came out quite clear in its objection to the 1945 Full Employment Bill—see
Bailey (1950).

6. The view that monetary policy leaves the internal workings of the market system unaffected was held by many economists, and was strongly pushed by Hayek in his book *The Road to Serfdom*. Hayek's book was well known to many in the CED.

7. Means's belief in the "goodness" of economic planning comes out quite clearly in his comments on Hayek's book, *The Road to Serfdom*. He had read the first fifty pages of the book and found it repulsive. Means objected to Hayek's conceptions of totalitarianism and of a competitive capitalist system. Regarding the latter, Means complained that the concept of a market economy that Hayek used in his critique of planning existed in the 19th century and did not include mass production, power, or insensitive prices and wages that were clearly prevalent in America's 20th century corporate economy. Thus, he concluded that Hayek's critique of planning was not worth paying attention to and was simply a vicious smear on all economic planning, including that advocated by the CED (Means 1944).

8. Means held the view that the individual should be the source of value, and individual self-development in society should be the objective of social institutions. This, he asserted, was the "basis of any liberal philosophy. Its fulfillment requires both political and economic freedom. In most situations free enterprise operating within appropriate rules and regulations and assistances can contribute to this end" (Means 1944).

9. Means's comments on the indeterminacy of the solution is of interest:

> We also established to our own satisfaction that for three individuals and three commodities, there would be no single determinate solution, but rather several possible solutions, the actual solution depending on what the economist would call non-economic factors such as which individual made the first offer and which accepted the offer when two individuals were both ready to do so. Beyond the point of three individuals and three commodities, it seems probable that the number of possible solutions multiplies rapidly and our best efforts failed to harness these possibilities into any systematic form. (Means 1940c, 2)

10. Means realized that it was not strictly necessary to assume a constant supply of money for his adjustment mechanism to work. If the money supply contracted as demand fell, then prices would have to decline faster than if the money supply had remained constant, in order for real buying power to increase. On the other hand, a price decline that would cause a more than proportionate contraction in the money supply, so that real buying power fell, was dismissed outright as being unrealistic (Means 1940e, 1943a).

11. Means first articulated this mechanism in 1939–40, and claimed it was the mechanism implicitly envisaged by classical and neoclassical economists that ended to move the economy toward full employment. The reason for this, he felt, was that economists had devoted little time to articulating the adjustment mechanism by which a competitive, perfectly flexible price–wage economy always tended toward full employment. Yet, Means did cite J.S. Mill (see chapter 4) and I. Fisher's doctoral thesis (Fisher, 1925) as support for his argument. It was not until Patinkin (1948) described a similar adjustment mechanism and christened it the Pigou effect that Means began citing contemporary neoclassical economists, such as Pigou and Friedman, for support. Although articulated in 1940, Means did

not further elaborate his adjustment mechanism until the 1950s (Means 1939c, 1939–40, 1940e, 1940f, 1948, 1957).

12. Means's critical view of neoclassical theory comes out quite clearly in his comments on O. Lange's manuscript *Price Flexibility and Employment*:

> . . . the question of how an economy could be expected to work if prices were really flexible seems pretty academic. It is consistent with 19th century theorizing, but bears little relation to the modern economy in which the bulk of prices (including wage rates) are very far from being flexible. Granted that it is possible to create a logical picture of what could be expected to happen in an hypothetical economy of flexible prices, the results would have little direct bearing on current problems. The conclusion reached could neither be tested by the evidence of our actual economy nor could they throw much light on public policy. (Means 1943a)

13. Means also dealt with Hansen's version of the saving–investment theory—see chapters 2 and 3.

14. Means repeatedly stated, when asked, that he rejected Keynes's explanation of employment because he failed to take account of the direct effect of money—see Means 1957, 1971, 1976, 1977, and 1978b.

15. Of the two impacts, Means believed that the direct impact of money on investment and employment was more powerful than the impact via the interest rate. This was because he believed that investment was primarily a function of past sales rather than the interest rate (Means 1938c).

16. Means believed without reservation that the assumption of perfectly flexible prices and wage rates would always ensure a full employment equilibrium; and if an argument was advanced in which this was not the case, Means countered by claiming that the "conditions under which unemployment would not tend to be automatically corrected appear on analysis to be either incompatible with his economy of flexible prices or capable of producing results quite different from those he indicates—results tending to correct the unemployment" (Means 1943a). Thus, the moment when Keynes stated that his theory of employment was consistent with flexible prices and wages, Means concluded that his theory was faulty.

17. Means had first articulated this adjustment process in 1940, and further developed it with regard to international trade in 1943 (Means 1939–40, 1940f, 1943b).

18. Although the interest rate does have a role in Means's monetary theory of aggregate demand, it is a minor one because the evidence of the 1930s indicated to him that low interest rates did not prompt business enterprises to borrow money for investment purposes (Means 1953).

19. As Means himself noted many times, his monetary theory of employment was anti-Keynesian in two respects: first, because it was the direct impact of money via the desire of economic agents to alter their money balances, rather than the interest rate, which had the greatest impact on aggregate demand; second, because it was insensitive prices and wages rather than the liquidity trap that produced unemployment and idle machines (Means 1946, 1957, 1971).

20. Because of the important role of money balances in his monetary theory of employment, Means has devoted much effort to explaining why economic agents hold money balances—see Means (1953).

References

Bailey, Stephen K. 1950. *Congress Makes a Law: The Story Behind the Employment Act of 1946*. New York: Columbia University Press.

Collins, Robert M. 1981. *The Business Response to Keynes, 1929–1964*. New York: Columbia University Press.

Fisher, Irving. 1925. *Mathematical Investigations in the Theory of Value and Price*. New Haven: Yale University Press.

Goode, Richard. 1994. "Gardiner Means on Administered Prices and Administrative Inflation." *Journal of Economic Issues* 28 (March): 173–186.

Hayek, Friedrich A. 1944. *The Road to Serfdom*. London: Routledge & Kegan Paul.

Keynes, John Maynard. 1939a. Letter to G.C. Means. August 10. G.C. Means Papers, Series VI B, John M. Keynes. Franklin D. Roosevelt Library.

———. 1939b. Keynes's annotated copy of Means's "Second Memorandum on: Effect on Economic Activity of Shifts in Propensity to Consume and in Liquidity Preference." G.C. Means Papers, Series VI B, John M. Keynes. Franklin D. Roosevelt Library.

Lee, Frederic S. 1990. "From Multi-Industry Planning to Keynesian Planning: Gardiner Means, the American Keynesians, and National Economic Planning at the National Resources Committee." *Journal of Policy History* 2: 186–212.

Lee, Frederic S. and Samuels, Warren J. 1992a. "Introduction: Gardiner C. Means, 1896–1988." In *The Heterodox Economics of Gardiner C. Means: A Collection*, eds. Frederic S. Lee and Warren J. Samuels, xv–xxxiii. Armonk, NY: M.E. Sharpe, 1992.

Lee, Frederic S. and Samuels, Warren J. (eds.). 1992b. *The Heterodox Economics of Gardiner C. Means: A Collection*. Armonk, NY: M.E. Sharpe.

Means, Gardiner C. 1934. "NRA and AAA and the Reorganization of Industrial Policy Making." Washington, D.C.: August 29.

———. 1935a. *Industrial Prices and Their Relative Inflexibility*. Senate Document No. 13. 74th Cong., 1st sess. Washington, D.C.: GPO. Reprinted in Lee and Samuels (1992b).

———. 1935b. "The Major Causes of the Depression." In *The Heterodox Economics of Gardiner C. Means: A Collection*, eds. Frederic S. Lee and Warren J. Samuels, 73–92. Armonk, NY: M.E. Sharpe, 1992.

———. 1935c. "Price Inflexibility and the Requirements of a Stabilizing Monetary Policy." *Journal of the American Statistical Association* 30 (June): 401–413.

———. 1938a. *Patterns of Resource Use*. Washington, D.C.: GPO.

———. 1938b. Letter to Beardsley Ruml. October 18. National Archives: Central Office Records of the National Resources Planning Board (RG 187), 751.

———. 1938c. "Incentive to Capital Creation." In *The Heterodox Economics of Gardiner C. Means: A Collection*, eds. Frederic S. Lee and Warren J. Samuels, 110–112. Armonk, NY: M. E. Sharpe, 1992.

———. 1939a. *The Structure of the American Economy. Part I: Basic Characteristics*. Washington, D.C.: GPO.

———. 1939b. Memorandum to Dr. John D. Summer. October 11. G.C. Means Papers, Series II, Price Rigidity. Franklin D. Roosevelt Library.

————. 1939c. "Conclusion." National Archives: Central Office Records of the National Resources Planning Board (RG 187), 751.

————. 1939d. "Effect on Economic Activity of Shifts in Propensity to Consume and in Liquidity Preference." July 16. G.C. Means Papers, Series II, Economics-General. Franklin D. Roosevelt Library.

————. 1939e. Letter to J.M. Keynes. July 16. G.C. Means Papers, Series VI A, John M. Keynes. Franklin D. Roosevelt Library.

————. 1939f. "Second Memorandum on: Effect on Economic Activity of Shifts in Propensity to Consume and in Liquidity Preference." July 22. G.C. Means Papers, Series II, Economics-General. Franklin D. Roosevelt Library.

————. 1939–40. "Big Business, Administered Prices, and the Problem of Full Employment." *Journal of Marketing* 4 (April): 370–381.

————. 1940a. Memorandum on Arrangements for Future Work. May 31. C.E. Merriam Papers, Box 217, Folder 13. University of Chicago.

————. 1940b. Memorandum to C.E. Merriam. June 29. C.E. Merriam Papers, Box 217, Folder 13. University of Chicago.

————. 1940c. Progress Report. May 18. C.E. Merriam Papers, Box 222, Folder 8. University of Chicago.

————. 1940d. Letter to D. Wallace. April 13. National Archives: Central Office Records of the National Resources Planning Board (RG 187), 751.

————. 1940e. Letter to C. Edwards. February 9. G.C. Means Papers, Series II, Correspondence. Franklin D. Roosevelt Library.

————. 1940f. "The Controversy over the Problem of Full Employment." In *The Structure of the American Economy. Part II: Toward Full Use of Resources*, 9–17. Washington, D.C.: GPO.

————. 1943a. Letter to J.T. McNeill. July 7. G.C. Means Papers, Series IV, Chicago University. Franklin D. Roosevelt Library.

————. 1943b. "An Insensitive-Price Mechanism of International Trade Adjustment and Its Policy Implications." In *The Heterodox Economics of Gardiner C. Means: A Collection*, Frederic S. Lee and Warren J. Samuels, eds. 129–40. Armonk, NY: M.E. Sharpe, 1992.

————. 1944. Letter to W. Benton. December 28. G.C. Means Papers, Series IV, Correspondence—Benton. Franklin D. Roosevelt Library.

————. 1946. Letter to J.M. Clark. March 28. G.C. Means Papers, Series IV, Correspondence—Clark. Franklin D. Roosevelt Library.

————. 1948. "Further Consideration of Price Flexibility and Full Employment." November 23. G.C. Means Papers, Series IV, Prices–General (2). Franklin D. Roosevelt Library.

————. 1951. Letter to H.J. Kennedy. November 13. G.C. Means Papers, Series IV, Correspondence I–K. Franklin D. Roosevelt Library.

————. 1953. "Monetary Policy and Depression." January 21. G.C. Means Papers, Series IV, Monetary Policy and Depression. Franklin D. Roosevelt Library.

————. 1957. Letter to B.C. Hallowell. April 22. G.C. Means Papers, Series IV, Correspondence: G–H. Franklin D. Roosevelt Library.

————. 1971. Letter to Abba P. Lerner. February 17. G.C. Means Papers, Series V, Abba P. Lerner. Franklin D. Roosevelt University Library.

————. 1976. "Which Was the True Keynesian Theory of Employment?" In *The*

Heterodox Economics of Gardiner C. Means: A Collection, eds. Frederic S. Lee and Warren J. Samuels, 313–317. Armonk, NY: M.E. Sharpe, 1992.

————. 1977. Letter to W.C. Peterson. June 14. G.C. Means Papers, Series V, P. Franklin D. Roosevelt Library.

————. 1978a. Letter to J.H. Hotson. March 30. G.C. Means Papers, Series V, H. Franklin D. Roosevelt Library.

————. 1978b. Letter to A.S. Eichner. October 18. G.C. Means Papers, Series V, Eichner, A.S. Franklin D. Roosevelt Library.

————. n.d. "An Interview with Keynes." G.C. Means Papers, Series VI B, John M. Keynes. Franklin D. Roosevelt Library.

Patinkin, Don. 1948. "Price Flexibility and Full Employment." *American Economic Review* 38 (September): 543–564.

Reagan, Patrick D. 1982. "The Architects of Modern American National Planning." Ph.D. Thesis, Ohio State University.

Rosenof, Theodore. 1994. "Economics in the Long-Run: The New Deal and Its Legacies, 1930s–1990s." Unpublished.

Stein, Herbert 1969. *The Fiscal Revolution in America.* Chicago: The University of Chicago Press.

Warken, Philip W. 1979. *A History of the National Resource Planning Board, 1933–1943.* New York: Garland Publishing.

A
MONETARY
THEORY OF
EMPLOYMENT

1

Introduction

This book is concerned with the maintenance of full employment. It examines certain existing theories of employment; presents a general theory which can account for mass unemployment under modern industrial conditions; indicates ways in which this theory can be tested by appeal to statistical evidence; points to the type of measures which the theory indicates would be effective in maintaining employment at approximately the optimum level; and on the basis of the theory, outlines a series of concrete steps aimed at maintaining optimum employment in the United States.

Any general theory of employment presented today must take into account three sets of general theory already existing and each widely held by one or another group of advocates. On the one hand there is the classical theory of Adam Smith, Mill, and Marshall which holds that, in a competitive society, there are forces which automatically tend to bring employment to the optimum. This theory points to a policy of laissez-faire. At the opposite extreme is the Marxian theory of employment which explains unemployment in terms of the accumulation of capital and private control over the instruments of production and points to the rejection of a free enterprise system. Intermediate lies the Keynesian saving–investment theory which explains the level of employment in terms of the relation between saving and investment and points to a policy of compensation rather than one of laissez-faire or of rejection.

The theory presented in this book, like the saving–investment theory, lies intermediate between the Classical and Marxian theories. Like the Keynesian theory it rejects both the Marxian and the laissez-faire conclusions and aims to make a free enterprise system work effectively by using governmental powers over monetary and fiscal policy to offset in some degree the unstabilizing effect of the actions of the millions of separate individuals and enterprises which make up the economy. In many respects the analysis parallels the saving–investment analysis but in other respects it differs. It does not find the explanation of mass unemployment in the peculiarities of interest rates and liquidity preference, but in the insensitivity of prices and wages rates. It places primary emphasis not on a tendency to oversave, but on a tendency to accumulate money balances. The two explanations are significantly different in their implications for policy. The first points to fiscal policy as a major device for reducing unemployment; the latter to monetary measures, the efficacy of which the oversaving explanation would deny.

The biggest single difference underlying the analysis in this book as compared with that of the saving–investment analysis is the emphasis placed on the buying power of assets. It is assumed that real consumption, saving and investment are a direct function of the buying power of assets as well as a direct function of the buying power of income. It is this assumption applied to the outstanding stock of money which invalidates the saving–investment theory. It is this assumption which brings monetary policy into the foreground in an insensitive-price economy. And it is this emphasis on money which furnishes the name by which it is proposed to distinguish the present theory from the saving–investment theory of employment.

As compared with the classical theory implicit in Say's law,[1] the fundamental difference in assumption is the insensitivity of goods prices and wage rates. It is this assumption which makes Say's law untenable. With respect to the Marxian theory of employment, there would appear to be a fundamental difference as to both the reasons for unemployment and the possibilities of maintaining full employment in a modern free society.

Because of the close parallel between the theory presented here and the saving–investment theory, it will be convenient to start this book with an examination of the saving–investment theory and the reasons for questioning it. Then the Classical and Marxian theories will be sketched and reasons for rejecting them will be indicated. Finally a monetary theory of employment will be developed and its implications for policy discussed.

This theory will be presented in equilibrium terms. This does not mean that it is a static theory. A moving equilibrium can take account of changing conditions provided the *rate of change* is not so rapid as to generate important effects which change alone would not produce. A rapid price rise is likely to generate a wave of speculation which a slower price rise of the same magnitude would not. The application of any theory to problems of policy must take account of dynamic forces as well as equilibrium forces. Dynamic forces are discussed in considering the problems of corrective action. But they are excluded from the main presentation of the theory because of the author's belief that the central problem of unemployment is an equilibrium problem and not a product of dynamic forces.

Finally, the monetary theory of employment presented here is not a complete theory of economics. Full employment or, more technically, optimum employment is a basic objective of economic policy. But there are other objectives. One could have the optimum amount of employment and yet have a poorly working economy, either because resources were ineffectively used, or because the distribution of income was inequitable. Monopoly on the part of business or labor or farmer or consumer, or faulty regulation on the part of government could mean both ineffective use of resources and inequitable distribution of income, but not necessarily general unemployment.

Most of general Classical theory was concerned with the way the price system operated to shift resources from one use into another so as to increase the real values created and reward the factors of production according to their presumed contribution. This is explicitly true of Alfred Marshall's great classic, *The Principles of Economics,* which concerns itself solely with this subject.[2] This is quite a different focus of study from that of the level of employment and the forces which cause employment to be high or low.

In the present book no attempt will be made to cover the vitally important fields of resource use or income distribution. Optimum employment is not used to mean optimum use of resources. It has to do with the amount of employment, not the direction of employment. Problems of direction of use and of income distribution will be touched on only as they are believed to affect the level of employment.

This discrimination rests on two beliefs: (1) that the two sets of problems, optimum employment and optimum use, are reasonably separable; and (2) that the first has to be close to solution before the second can be effectively tackled. Obviously, how each problem is solved will affect the practical solution of the other. But the central problem of optimum employment has to be tackled for an economy as a whole as a single integrated problem, whereas the problem of optimum use can be tackled piecemeal, with improvement first in one area and then in another. Furthermore, the existence of mass unemployment greatly complicates, if it does not make impossible, the solution of nearly every other economic problem. Until a satisfactory solution can be found to the problem of optimum employment, all other economic problems are secondary.

Notes

1. That general overproduction was impossible because the supplying of goods constitutes an equivalent demand. Translated into modern terms, this meant that the only condition of equilibrium would be one of optimum employment.

2. It should be remembered that Marshall's *Principles* was only the first of three books on the fundamentals of economics which he planned but only one of which he wrote. He made it clear, though not in the terms now current, that his first volume assumed full or optimum employment and that in a subsequent volume he would take up business fluctuations.

Part I
Theories of Employment

2

The Saving–Investment Theory of Employment

The saving–investment theory of employment is built around one central idea, namely that within the limits of productive capacity, the level of employment is controlled by the level of income and production at which the saving that would be made out of current income and the investment in goods that would be made at the current level of income are just equal.

This conclusion is based on four main logical steps:

1. Saving and investment are so defined that in any real situation they must be equal.
2. It is assumed that the higher the real income of a community, the more the community would save. This assumption can be represented as a schedule, showing the amount of saving that a community would make at each possible level of real income.
3. It is assumed that, at any given time, the desire to invest in goods would differ less at different possible levels of real income than saving. This means that a schedule of real investments at each possible level of real income would rise less steeply than that representing the real propensity to save.
4. It is held that the two schedules are so determined that, at least under some conditions, general unemployment would not cause an alteration in them that would lead to the elimination of general unemployment.

So long as the potential saving and the potential investment at each possible level of income are given, the first three assumptions are sufficient to make the level of income and employment determinate.[1] Income must be that at which potential saving and potential investment are just equal. At any higher level of real income, potential saving would exceed potential investment and force a lower level of income and employment. At any lower level of income, potential investment would exceed potential saving and force income and employment upward. If one grants these three steps and *the determinateness of the two schedules,* the basic conclusion of the saving–investment theory would seem to be sound.

The several variants of the saving–investment theory differ primarily in the reasons given for believing that the schedules of saving and investment are determinate, and would not tend to shift in such a way as to raise the point of intersection if general unemployment developed. To appraise the significance of the basic line of reasoning, it is necessary to examine the reasons given on this point in the two major variants of the theory, that by Keynes and that by Hansen.

Keynes's General Theory

Keynes, in the theory of employment presented in *The General Theory of Employment, Interest and Money,* builds his case for the determinateness of the saving and investment schedules almost entirely on a new theory of interest.[2] Indeed, Keynes's *General Theory* can be broken down into two separate theories—a theory of interest and a theory of employment based on his theory of interest. The new theory of interest therefore needs to be understood as a background for the theory of employment.

Keynes's Theory of Interest

Keynes's theory of interest is a direct repudiation of the supposedly classical theory that interest is the factor that brings the demand for investment and the willingness to save into equilibrium with one another. Instead, he concludes that interest is the factor that brings into equilibrium the willingness to hold savings in the form of money and the existing stock of money.

This conclusion grows out of the importance of liquidity in the calculation of any prospective investor. Keynes points out that an individual can hold his or her savings in various forms, some more, some

Figure 2.1 **[Saving and Investment]**

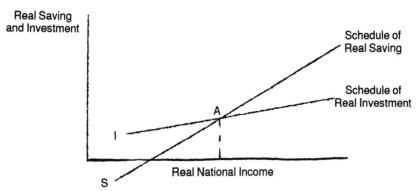

Schedule S represents the propensity to save and rises sharply with higher real income. Schedule I represents potential investment in the light of existing investment opportunities and interest rates, and rises less rapidly than schedule S. Since, by definition, the only possible real situation is one in which saving and investment are equal, the level of income and employment would have to be that at which the two schedules intersect.

Source: These crude drawings are reproduced from Gardiner C. Means' original manuscript.

less liquid. He or she may hold savings in the very liquid form of money and obtain no income from them, or savings may be held in the form of earning assets—loans or securities or capital goods—which are as a rule less liquid and involve more risk. In deciding between these possibilities, he must balance the advantages of more liquidity with the prospect of more return. Usually an individual with any considerable volume of savings will distribute them between money and other assets of various degrees of liquidity, risk, and earning prospect so as to establish a rough balance between greater liquidity, greater return, and greater risk.

A change in the prospect of return for a given risk would tend to alter the most desirable combination of money and earning assets. If interest rates rose, there would be more advantage in putting money out at loan almost as fast as it accumulated, and individuals would tend to get along with smaller holdings of money even though it meant being somewhat less liquid. On the other hand, very low interest rates would lead people to let their balances of money accumulate, since the prospect of a very small return would not overweigh the risk and loss of liquidity involved in making a loan. Therefore, with a given volume of assets and of income, the amount of savings that a community would seek to hold in the form of money would be greater the lower the level of interest rates. From this Keynes concludes that interest is a return "for parting with liquidity for a specified period of time,"[3] and that the level of interest rates is therefore determined by the relation between the desire to hold savings in the form of money and the existing stock of money.

This position is vividly summarized in Keynes's own words when he says:

> Thus the rate of interest at any time, being the reward for parting with liquidity, is a measure of the unwillingness of those who possess money to part with their liquid control over it. The rate of interest is not the "price" which brings into equilibrium the demand for resources to invest with the readiness to abstain from present consumption. It is the "price" which equilibrates the desire to hold wealth in the form of cash with the available quantity of cash;—which implies that if the rate of interest were lower, i.e., if the reward for parting with cash were diminished, the aggregate amount of cash which the public would wish to hold would exceed the available supply, and that if the rate of interest were raised, there would be a surplus of cash which no one would be willing to hold.[4]

Not only is the level of interest rates determined by the relation between the preference for liquidity and the outstanding stock of money, but, according to Keynes, there is a limit appreciably above a zero rate of interest below which long-term interest rates will not fall no matter how much the stock of money may increase. This limit arises from the existence of uncertainty as to the amount that could be obtained from selling or discounting a loan before it matured, and is so crucial to Keynes's theory of employment that it needs to be closely examined.

As Keynes indicates, if bonds as safe as money could be purchased, which could be redeemed at any time at the purchase price and would pay a positive interest in the meantime, it would always pay to store savings in such bonds rather than in money except for such money as was needed for current transactions. If the purchaser needed money at any time prior to the maturity of the bonds, the bonds could always be redeemed and the individual would have as much money as he or she started with plus any interest that the bonds had paid. The individual would be better off by the amount of this interest than if his or her savings had been kept in cash.

However, most bonds and loans are not redeemable at a moment's notice and an effort to realize on them before maturity may involve a loss because of a rise in the level of interest rates and a resultant fall in the market value of the security. Even in the case of a bond whose interest and principal are regarded as *certain* to be paid, the prospective buyer knows that if he or she should want to realize on the bonds before maturity, the risk is run of having to sell at a loss. A rise in the level of interest rates could force the current market value of an individual's bonds below the price that was paid for them, and the loss in principal might more than absorb the gains from interest that had been made. If this should happen, and individuals needed their money before maturity, they would be worse off from their bond purchase than if they had kept their assets in the form of money. Therefore, in making an initial choice between buying bonds or holding money, the prospective buyer would have to take this chance of loss into account as well as the corollary chance of gain.

It might be thought that the chance of a gain in market value because of a fall in the level of interest rates would compensate for the chance of loss due to a rise of interest rates, but such compensation would usually occur only when interest rates were already well above a zero rate, while at very low interest rates, the chance of loss would outweigh the chance of gain. For example, if the yield on a first grade bond maturing in twenty years was currently 1 percent, a drop in the level of comparable interest rates to zero percent could not induce an increase in the price of the bond of more than 20 percent—equal to the twenty years of 1 percent yield. A chance of such a drop in interest rates could be offset by the chance of a rise to approximately 2 percent. A rate of interest below zero is not likely to occur, whereas a rise of interest rates from a 1 percent to a 3 or 4 percent level long before maturity is a possibility not to be disregarded. Thus, at very low interest rates or yields, the chances of loss from a fall in the market prices of bonds would tend to outweigh the chances of gain from a rise in values. This greater chance of loss must be compensated for by the interest payments themselves. As a result, a bond, as safe as money so far as the payment of interest and principal are concerned, must still pay an appreciable rate of interest to make up for this greater risk of loss, unless it is *certain* that the funds tied up in the bond will not be wanted before its maturity. Under ordinary circumstances money would be a better store of value than *an equally safe* long-term bond or loan that paid only 1 percent interest, since the very low interest could offset only a very small rise in interest rates. Keynes believes that this fact "is perhaps the chief obstacle to a fall in the rate of interest to a very low level."[5]

A further ground for preferring to hold money rather than loans at low rates of interest would occur, as Keynes points out, whenever there was a general belief that interests rates were temporarily below the level that was likely to be maintained.[6] Thus, if central bank policy brought a reduction in interest rates that forced up the prices of long-term bonds to a level that an individual investor regarded as temporary, the investor would prefer to hold his or her funds in cash rather than in such bonds unless the yield to maturity on the bonds at the higher prices would more than compensate for the prospect of lower prices before maturity. According to Keynes, a monetary policy aimed at reducing long-term interest rates, which was regarded as temporary and likely to be reversed, might operate so as to increase the demand for money as a store of buying power "almost without limit" while interest rates were very low.

On the basis of this analysis, Keynes concludes that, while interest rates can be reduced either by an expansion in the stock of money or by a fall in goods prices and wage rates, which increases the real buying-power of the existing money stock, they cannot be reduced below some limiting point. Thus, he says, in discussing the determinants of interest rates:

> Thirdly, we come to what is the most fundamental consideration in this context, namely the characteristics of money which satisfy liquidity-preference. For in certain circumstances such as will often occur, these will cause the rate of interest to be insensitive, particularly below a certain figure, even to a substantial increase in the quantity of money in proportion to other forms of wealth.[7]

Below this "certain figure," expanding the stock of money or increasing its buying power will not further reduce interest rates, since the holders would prefer to hold any amount of money rather than loan it at lower rates of interest. As to the magnitude of this "certain figure," Keynes suggests that:

. . . unless reasons are believed to exist why future experience will be very different from past experience, a long-term rate of interest of, say, 2 per cent leaves more to fear than to hope, and offers, at the same time, a running yield which is only sufficient to offset a very small measure of fear.[8]

In this summary of the Keynesian theory of interest, we need not concern ourselves with the exact level of interest rates at which further increase in the amount or the buying power of the money stock ceases to bring further reductions in the rates of interest. The essentials of the theory stand clear — that interest rates are determined at the point at which the existing stock of money can just and only just satisfy the demand for money as a store of buying power; and that, because very low current interest rates greatly expand the desirability of holding money as compared with bonds or long-term loans, there is a limit below which long-term interest rates will not go regardless of how much the quantity or the real buying-power of the money stock is expanded.

Keynes's Theory of Employment

Once Keynes's theory of interest is clearly understood, it is easy to follow the basic logic of his theory of employment. Since interest rates cannot operate to equate saving and investment, some other mechanism must be at work, and Keynes finds that mechanism in adjustments in the level of real income, production, and employment.

In spelling out this mechanism, Keynes accepts the classical assumption that real investment is a function of the level of interest rates, so that the lower the rates of interest, the greater the real investment that would be made at each possible level of real income.[9]

Keynes also recognizes that other factors than income and interest rates influence the volume of investment in goods, but for purposes of his theory of employment, they can be treated as "given." Thus, an expectation that goods prices will rise can be expected to increase the opportunities to invest. Similarly, an expectation of higher interest rates can stimulate investment. Finally, the state of confidence can be expected to affect the volume of investment. These factors play an important role in Keynes's explanation of business fluctuations but in his basic analysis the state of expectation and of confidence can be assumed as given just as resources, technology, and tastes are assumed as given. This leaves real income and the rate of interest as the variables that determine the volume of real investment.

With respect to saving, Keynes suggests that the principal variable determining the amount of real saving is the level of real income. If real incomes are high, a larger real amount of the total income will be saved than if real incomes are lower.[10] Keynes regards the effect of interest rates on the rate of saving out of a given income as "open to a good deal of doubt."[11] So far as the usual types of short-period fluctuations in rates of interest are concerned, he regards them as not likely to have much *direct* influence on saving, either to stimulate or to damp it.[12] He points out that "there are not many people who will alter their way of living because the rate of interest has fallen from 5 to 4 percent, if their aggregate income is the same as before."[13] To the extent that changes in interest rates result in "windfall" gains or losses, the latter, like windfall gains or losses from other sources, might affect saving somewhat. So also changes in government fiscal policies could have a significant effect on income disposal, but for purposes of practical analysis, Keynes regards the aggregate real income as the principal variable upon which the volume of real saving depends.[14] He concludes that the relation between real saving and real income may be considered a fairly stable function that can be represented as a single schedule showing the volume of saving that would take place at each possible level of real income.

With these two Keynesian assumptions accepted, it is easy to see that the rate of interest would determine the level of real income.[15] The interest rate would determine the schedule of real investment at each possible level of real income and the actual level of real income, and employment would be that at which the community sought to save a real amount just equal to its real investment. If real income were greater, potential saving would exceed potential investment; if real income were less, the reverse would be the case. In either case, income would adjust so that at the given interest rate, potential saving and potential investment would just be equal. If the labor force were employed at this level of real income, this level would be stable.

However, if there were general unemployment at this level of income and prices and wage rates were sensitive, a fall in interest rates would bring up the level of real income and employment. The adjustments would take the following form:

1. The pressure of unused resources and low demand involved in unemployment would tend to force down both prices and wage rates.

2. A general fall in prices would have the effect of increasing the real buying power of the outstanding stock of money.

3. This increase in the real stock of money would make money redundant; that is, the increase in the real value of money would make the community more liquid than its members desired to be at the current rates of interest.

4. With the excess holdings of money, they would be more willing to make loans and their effort to do so would force down interest rates to a point where the desire to hold money as a store of real value was again just equal to the real value of the outstanding stock of money.

Thus, with no change in the total units of money outstanding, a fall in the price–wage level would bring about a fall in interest rates. Such a fall in interest rates would, in turn, stimulate potential investment at each possible level of real income, and since the propensity to save at each possible level of real income is assumed to be constant, saving and investment would be equal only at a higher level of real income. If there were still general unemployment at this higher level of income, wage rates and prices would continue to fall, thereby increasing the real value of the money stock and forcing down the level of interest rates. The resulting increase in investment would bring about a further increase in the level of real national income.

If there were no limit to this adjustment of interest rates, Keynes would simply be presenting a mechanism whereby general unemployment would tend to be eliminated in a sensitive price economy. General unemployment would force down the price–wage level until interest rates were so low that investment would absorb all the saving that would take place at full employment. This would not explain continued unemployment.

At this point the second main element in Keynes's interest theory comes into play—that beyond a "certain point," well above a zero rate of interest, expansion in the real stock of money will not further reduce the level of interest rates. This, in fact, is the key to his explanation of long continued unemployment. So long as interest rates are relatively high, a fall in the price–wage level can bring them down and thereby increase the level of real income and employment. But once a low level is reached, a further fall in the price–wage level would have no effect on interest rates, and, therefore, no effect on real income and employment.[16] If there were still general unemployment at this limiting level of interest rates, there would, according to Keynes, be no automatic forces at work in the system tending to increase employment.[17] Thus, even though prices and wage rates were perfectly sensitive, general unemployment might continue over a long period. Here is a logically consistent explanation of continued unemployment.

Keynes carries the implications of this story one step further. He holds that when unemployment develops to such a point that a reduction in the price–wage level cannot stimulate employment, unemployment has also reached a point where it cannot be reduced through monetary policy. While interest rates are high, a central bank can force them down by expanding the outstanding stock of money. Thus, up to a point, direct monetary expansion could take the place of a fall in the price-wage level in stimulating employment. But, according to Keynes, beyond a point, monetary expansion could not force a further reduction in interest rates, and, therefore, could not stimulate employment. Beyond this point, both the automatic corrective of a falling price–wage level and the planned corrective of monetary expansion would be ineffective.

If this is the true explanation of continued general unemployment, it is clear that some outside force, acting not on interest rates, but directly on the propensity to save or on the volume of investment, would be necessary to increase employment. It is this conclusion that has led to the emphasis on net investment or spending by government and on investment abroad as ways of reducing or eliminating mass unemployment. The validity of this conclusion will be examined in the next section. But before turning to this question it will be useful to consider certain modifications in Keynes's theories, which have been introduced in Hansen's *Fiscal Policy and Business Cycles,* and in Hicks's *Interpretation* [sic] of Keynes.[18]

Hansen's Variant of the Saving–Investment Theory

Hansen's general theory of employment closely parallels that of Keynes in many respects, but it differs in two significant ways. It differs in the influence that interest rates are assumed to have on investment, and it differs in that it builds a business cycle theory and a mature economy theory on the basis of its theory of employment. The cycle and mature economy theory lie outside the immediate discussion.

All that needs to be pointed out here is that since they depend on Hansen's employment theory, they are undermined if the latter is found to be invalid. This leaves, as the only immediately significant difference between the Hansen and the Keynes theory of employment, the effect of interest rates on investment.

Hansen accepts Keynes's position that interest rates have relatively little net effect on the volume of saving, but also concludes that they can have relatively little effect on investment. According to Hansen, "The fact seems to be that with respect to short-lived goods, such as machinery, the rate of interest within realizable limits, of say, 2 to 7 percent, is not an important consideration,"[19] and, "in a world of high risk, a low rate of interest is relatively ineffective as a stimulant to long-term fixed investment."[20] Having minimized the role of interest, Hansen says, "This is not to say that a low rate of interest achieved through monetary policy has no effect upon the volume of investment—the low rate of interest might in certain areas bring about an expansion of investment."[21] But on the whole, Hansen takes the position that a decline in the rates of interest can neither stimulate investment in goods nor curb saving to an extent sufficient to have an important effect in equalizing the efforts to save and to invest in goods.

Hansen's virtual elimination of low interest rates as a stimulant to investment means that he does not need to rely, as does Keynes, on some limiting figure below which long-term interest rates cannot be forced. He can explain chronic unemployment simply on the grounds that (1) saving is a function of the level of income and not significantly affected by the level of interest rates; (2) net investment in goods is determined by fixed or outside factors and is not significantly affected by the level of interest rates; and (3) saving and investment must be equal. Under these conditions, income would have to adjust to the point where saving was just equal to the independently determined volume of investment. If the volume of investment demand was not sufficient to absorb the savings that would be made out of an income corresponding to full employment, then an equilibrium at less than full employment would result.[22] For the purposes of the present discussion, it makes little difference whether an equilibrium at less than full employment is explained by the impotency of interest rates to affect saving and investment in a sufficient degree, or by the existence of a limit below which long-term interest rates cannot fall. Each represents a variant of a "Saving–Investment Theory of Employment."

Hicks's Proposed Variant

J.R. Hicks has suggested a third variant of the saving–investment theory, which he regards as a more general version of the Keynes theory. He indicates that the investment opportunities are likely to increase with an increase in production and income so that investment should be treated as both a function of interest rates and of income (as has been done in Figures 2.1 and 2.2). He also points out that the Keynesian theory can still explain equilibrium at less than full employment even if savings are affected by interest rates. Finally, he suggests generalizing the theory so as to recognize that the demand for money is a function not only of interest rates but also of the level of income. These three modifications of the theory give it greater generality without reducing in any way its ability to explain unemployment.

Two Major Characteristics of the Saving–Investment Theory

Before the reasons for questioning the saving–investment theory are set forth, there are two characteristics of the theory that need to be emphasized, the first having to do with the sensitivity of prices and wage rates and the second with the role of monetary policy.

No variant of the theory depends on any assumption of insensitive prices or wage rates. Each variant could explain chronic unemployment in a *perfectly* sensitive price system just as readily as in an insensitive system such as actually exists. Hansen is explicit about this point, though his statements with respect to it occur in conjunction with his discussion of a static economy. Thus he says:

> A perfectly flexible price system, undisturbed by technical change, will always tend toward an equilibrium position in which there is no net investment. *But there is nothing in the functioning of a perfectly flexible competitive price system that yields a distribution of income which will insure a consumption function which makes this condition compatible with full employment.*[23]

And in another part of his book he says:

> The classicals were quite right when they argued that without technological progress the price system, including the rate of interest, would

progressively drive the economy to the point at which there would be no net investment. They were wrong in assuming that the price system could also insure a propensity to consume compatible with this investment situation so as to provide full employment.[24]

While the above passages, so far as prices are concerned, apply to an economy without technological change, it is clear from Hansen's analysis that they would apply equally to an economy in which technological change occurs. According to his theory, if there were a tendency to save more than could be invested at a given level of prices and wage rates, unemployment would result, and no amount of general price and wage adjustment would operate to eliminate this unemployment. General unemployment would, therefore, continue whether prices and wage rates were perfectly sensitive or relatively insensitive.

Keynes's analysis is not so explicit on this point. His central reasoning is first developed for a case in which money wage rates and other factor costs are assumed to be constant. However, he goes on to say, "but this simplification, with which we shall dispense later, is introduced solely to facilitate the exposition. The essential character of the argument is precisely the same whether or not money-wages, etc., are liable to change."[25] In his book, this is as close as he comes to saying that his theory of employment does not depend on price or wage insensitivity.[26] Some passages in his book even suggest that he might be relying on the insensitivity of prices or wage rates to explain unemployment. However, the theory presented, like Hansen's and Hicks's, is just as capable of explaining equilibrium at less than full employment under a perfectly sensitive price–wage system as under an insensitive price–wage system. This will be crucial in considering the validity of the theory in the next chapter.

The second characteristic of importance is the conclusion that chronic unemployment cannot be significantly reduced or eliminated through monetary expansion. It has already been shown that, in Keynes's analysis, when interest rates are initially high, monetary expansion can bring them down and thereby expand investment and employment. But, once interest rates have reached their lower limit, monetary expansion cannot reduce them further, and, therefore, according to his theory, cannot bring about an expansion of employment. In Hansen's view, "monetary policy is an important weapon which we cannot afford to dispense with in cyclical compensatory policy,"[27] but it can contribute to the correction of chronic unemployment only to a minor degree. His skepticism as to the stimulating effect of a reduction of interest rates brought about by monetary policy has already been indicated. In his view, "after the requirements of trade and the desire for liquidity have been reasonably satisfied, no useful purpose is served by a continued multiplication of the money supply . . . "[28] It would simply create an artificial degree of liquidity. The same conclusion is implicit in Hicks's generalized version of the theory. Thus, according to each of these variants, monetary expansion is a very limited instrument of employment expansion. This is a most important conclusion and will be challenged in later chapters of this book.

Notes

1. This thesis is clearly indicated in Figure 2.1.

2. John Maynard Keynes, *The General Theory of Employment, Interest and Money.* New York: Harcourt, Brace and Company, 1936.

3. Ibid., p. 167. It is obvious from the context that the above statement intentionally excludes the risk factor involved in the payment of interest and principal, but does include the risk factor with respect to the value of the security prior to maturity. For any specific interest rate, Keynes would presumably regard the actual interest as a return in part for "parting with liquidity" and in part for taking risk as to interest and principal.

4. Ibid., p. 167. It should be noted that in the above statement, Keynes is using the term "rate of interest" to cover the complex of interest rates and discounts that actually exist. See, for example, his footnote, p. 137.

5. Ibid., p. 202.

6. Ibid., p. 203.

7. Ibid., p. 233. It is clear from the context that in the term "increase in the quantity of money" in the above quotation, Keynes is referring to an increase in real buying power due to lower goods prices and wage rates as well as to an increase in the nominal quantity.

8. Ibid., p. 202.

9. In the presentation above, all reference to or reliance on Keynes's conception of the "marginal efficiency of capital" has been carefully avoided. Keynes's use of his schedule of the marginal efficiency of capital rests on his statement that "it is obvious that the actual rate of current investment will be pushed to the point where there is no longer any class of capital-asset of which the marginal efficiency exceeds the current rate of interest" (p. 136). There is too much concrete evidence contradicting this position to make it tenable. Also, the new researches into the theory of imperfect competition seem destined to make the above conclusion unlikely on theoretical grounds. Since it is not essential to Keynes's theory of employment that *all* the investment that would promise to yield more than the current rate of interest would be undertaken, but only that more investment would

Figure 2.2 [Saving, Investment, and Interest Rates]

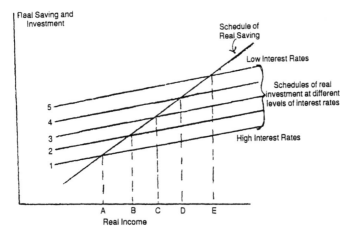

Source: These crude drawings are reproduced from Gardner C. Means' original manuscript.

be undertaken at a current rate of 4 percent than one of 6 percent, the particular marginal-efficiency ·of-capital refinement in his theory is omitted as nonessential.

10. It is to be noted that Keynes actually analyzes the factors determining saving by indirectly analyzing the factors determining consumption, treating saving as a residual obtained by deducting consumption from income. This procedure, though not incorrect, involves serious pitfalls in statistical practice. Since the essence of the oversaving problem is the adjustments by which the efforts to save and the efforts to invest in goods are kept equal, the direct approach is adopted above.

11. Ibid., p. 93.

12. Keynes's theory of employment is not in any way dependent on this conclusion. Even though lower interest rates seriously discouraged saving, his theory would be unaffected so long as there was a "certain point" below which interest rates could not fall.

13. Ibid., p. 94.

14. It should be noted that Keynes habitually uses a standard wage rate that he calls the "wage unit" as the divisor in deflating money terms into "real" terms. The *essential* elements in his explanation of unemployment would be the same whether an index of goods prices or Keynes's "wage unit" is used, so long as consistency is maintained.

15. This thesis is exemplified in Figure 2.2.

Each of the parallel lines above shows the volume of real investment that could be expected with a given rate of interest at each possible level of real income. The successive lines from top to bottom show the investment schedules at successively higher rates of interest. These schedules slope up to the right, thus reflecting the greater investment at higher levels of income than at lower levels, an assumption not explicit in Keynes's analysis but consistent with it. With the schedule of real saving shown above and interest rates such as to give the volume of investment represented by, say, schedule # 2, the only possible level of real income would be that indicated by the intersection of the two schedules—the real income represented by B. This would be the level of real income at which saving and investment would be equal, and would also involve a level of interest rates at which the community was just willing to hold the outstanding stock of money.

If this level of real income did not involve full employment, and interest rates fell as a result of a fall in the price–wage level and a consequent increase in the real value of the stock of money, the schedule of investment would rise, say, to schedule # 3, and income would rise to the level C corresponding to the new intersection. Falling interest rates would increase real income until either full employment prevented any further price fall, or interest rates had reached their minimum level. If the latter occurred, before full employment was reached, there would be nothing, according to the Keynesian theory, that would increase employment, unless new factors came into play altering the saving or the investment schedule.

16. Provided, of course, that there is not an equal or greater fall in the stock of money outstanding.

17. Keynes does not indicate what would happen to the price–wage level at this point, but only that a further drop would not operate to increase employment.

18. Alvin H. Hansen, *Fiscal Policy and Business Cycles*. New York: W.W. Norton, 1941. John R. Hicks [presumably "Mr. Keynes and the 'Classics'," *Econometrica*, vol. 5, April 1937, pp. 147–59].

19. Hansen, ibid., p. 330.

20. Ibid., p. 332.

21. Ibid., p. 330.

22. This condition would be represented by Figure 2.2 if all but one of the parallel lines were removed.

23. Ibid., p. 334. Italics added.

24. Ibid., p. 288.

25. Keynes, note 2, p. 27.

26. Keynes did explicitly take this position, in personal conversation with the author in the summer of 1939.

27. Hansen, note 25, p. 261.

28. Ibid., p. 184.

3

A Challenge to the
Saving–Investment Theory

In spite of its logical coherence, the saving–investment theory of employment involves one basic assumption that is subject to serious question. The theory clearly indicates that *interest rates* cannot be depended upon to bring saving and investment into equality at full employment. Therefore, an increase in the real stock of money either through a general fall in the price–wage level or through monetary expansion cannot reduce chronic unemployment *through its effect on interest rates*. But the basic conclusions of the saving–investment theory rest on the assumption that it is *only* through interest rates that saving and investment can be significantly affected by a change in the real stock of money. It is this assumption that will be challenged here.

In this chapter, reasons will be given for believing that a change in the real stock of money can be expected to have a direct effect on saving and investment. This is an effect quite apart from any effect that may result from changes in interest rates. It is an effect so potent that, in a sensitive-price economy, the only condition of adjustment would be one of full or optimum employment. The conclusion is therefore reached that the saving–investment theory does not depart sufficiently from the classical assumptions to provide an explanation for continued unemployment.

This challenge to the saving–investment theory rests on a partial but not complete repudiation of the role which that theory assigns to interest rates. It is reasonable to accept Keynes's thesis that interest is, in part, a reward for surrendering liquidity, and that therefore interest rates tend to adjust to a level at which the community is just satisfied to hold the outstanding stock of money *rather than make additional loans.* But Keynes goes further and claims that *the rate of interest "is the 'price' which equilibrates the desire to hold wealth in the form of cash with the available quantity of cash."*[1] If this were true, there would seem to be no reason to question the saving–investment theory. Actually, interest rates would seem to be only one of the factors that equilibrate the desire to hold wealth in the form of money with the outstanding stock of money.

Hicks has already suggested that the demand for money is a function not only of interest rates but also of income. Below it will be shown that the level of real money holdings is likely to affect both the desire to save and the desire to invest. The larger the real money holdings of the individual (the real value of other assets and income being the same) the greater his protection against the future and the larger the part of his income he can spend on consumption without a threat to his security. Likewise, the more liquid an enterprise, the more risks it can take. This means that saving and investment expenditure must also adjust so that the community is just and only just satisfied to hold the outstanding stock of money *rather than make additional expenditures on consumption or capital goods.*

If this position were accepted, then both interest rates and the level of income would play a part in maintaining monetary adjustment. Interest rates would tend to adjust so that the community would rather hold money than make further loans and *income would tend to adjust so that the community would rather hold money than spend at a greater rate on consumption or investment goods.* In later chapters, other factors contributing to monetary adjustment will be introduced, but for the present discussion it will be sufficient to deal only with interest rates and income. The immediate problem is, therefore, to show how these two factors both enter into the monetary adjustment.

Monetary Adjustment

The combined effect of interest rates and income in establishing monetary adjustment can most easily be followed by taking a case of initial unbalance and tracing through the adjustments that could be expected.[2] Take, for example, a case in which there was more money in circulation than the community found it desirable, or convenient, to hold at the initial level of interest rates and the initial level of income.[3] What adjustments would take place to increase the willingness of the community to hold money?

The Keynesian analysis indicates that interest rates would fall. This would result from the actions of individuals or enterprises who had more money on hand than they wished to hold and who offered to make loans. Provided interest rates were sensitive, they would fall until they were so low that the holders of money would prefer liquidity to the smaller return from making loans. At this level of interest rates, monetary equilibrium would be established *insofar as loans were concerned.* Whether or not the lower interest rates would affect saving and investment is not important here and so, for simplicity, it will be assumed that neither saving nor investment are significantly affected.

But an adjustment of interest rates that made the community willing to hold the whole of the money outstanding rather than make additional loans would not necessarily mean that the community would be willing to hold the money rather than make additional purchases of goods. It is often suggested that, when interest rates are so low that they cannot be driven lower, it necessarily follows that individuals and enterprises are indifferent as to the amount of money they hold. But such a conclusion is not justified. It overlooks the fact that making loans is not the only way of disposing of money. When interest rates have reached their minimum, it presumably follows that individuals and enterprises are indifferent as to the amount of money they hold *as an alternative to making loans.* It does not follow that they are indifferent as to the amount of money they hold in preference to spending more on goods for consumption or investment.[4] A money surplus might be a surplus of money in relation to goods. In this case, some individuals or enterprises with surplus money would seek to spend it on consumption or investment goods. This would mean a net addition to the demand for goods over and above the demand normally arising out of the expenditure of current income. It would increase the total demand for goods without simultaneously increasing the offering of goods. The effect of this would be to increase money incomes, though the way it would affect prices and employment would depend on specific conditions.

If prices and wage rates were sensitive and there was no mass unemployment at the outset, the surplus demand could be expected to cause the whole price–wage level to rise. With no change in production and employment, the increase in the price–wage level would mean an increase in income measured in dollar terms while real income remained constant. The rise in money income would induce or force individuals and enterprises to hold larger cash balances in order to hold the same volume of real buying power. And the rise would come to a halt, and a new balance would be established between money and goods, when money income had reached such a level that the community was just willing to hold the outstanding amount of money *rather than attempt to spend more on goods than they were receiving as income.*

On the other hand, if there was mass unemployment to begin with, the surplus demand could be expected to stimulate production and employment. If there were no increase in prices and wage rates, both real income and money income would go up together. A balance between money and goods might then be reached only when real income was so large that the community was willing to hold the whole of the outstanding stock of money and spend on consumption and investment goods only as much as was being received as income.

It should be noted that, in this adjustment process between money and goods, the surplus demand for goods is not satisfied, but dissipated. The individual can get rid of surplus money by spending it on goods, but the community as a whole cannot do so. Each holder can only pass his or her surplus money on to another holder. If the initial condition is one of full employment and prices are sensitive the extra demand simply pushes prices up. If there is initial unemployment and the extra demand increases production and employment, the process of meeting this demand itself creates income. For the community as a whole, all that can happen is that income goes up to the point where the community *wants* to spend on goods only as much as it is currently receiving as income. As a result of this increase in money incomes, whether from higher prices or higher employment, the stock of money ceases to be excessive.

It is because of the necessity that the community be just and only just induced to hold the outstanding stock of money rather than spend more of it on investment or consumption goods, that interest rates cannot be regarded as the only factor that equilibrates the desire to hold wealth in the form of money and the outstanding stock of money. Clearly, monetary adjustment requires both the proper adjustment of interest rates and the proper adjustment of income so that the community is just and only just willing to hold the existing stock of money rather than make more loans and is also just willing to hold the existing stock of money rather than spend more on goods.

Economic Equilibrium in a
Sensitive-Price Economy

If this more complex monetary adjustment is accepted, it must be apparent that, in a sensitive-price economy, the only condition of economic equilibrium would be one of optimum employment. In such an economy, any general unemployment would lead to a lower price–wage level, and, by thus providing a larger real stock of money, would stimulate employment through a higher rate of expenditure on goods. This would mean that a condition of general unemployment was unstable. For similar reasons, a condition of general overemployment would be unstable, since it would lead to a higher price–wage level and lower employment. It is these adjustments that would make full or optimum employment the only condition of equilibrium in a sensitive-price economy.

The logical steps leading lead to this conclusion are spelled out in more detail below.[5]

1. If general unemployment developed in a sensitive-price economy, prices and wage rates would fall, thereby increasing the real buying-power of the outstanding stock of money.[6]

2. The increased real stock of money would so increase the liquid assets of the community that the offerings of loan funds at the initial level of interest rates would increase and interest rates would fall, until the community was just willing to hold the outstanding stock of money rather than make additional loans. For simplicity, it will be assumed that the fall in interest rates is either limited or for other reasons has insufficient influence on saving or investment to correct the unemployment.

3. The increased real stock of money would at the same time so increase the liquid buying power of individuals and enterprises that some would increase their expenditure on current consumption, while some would increase their expenditure on capital goods. This would result in stepping up the level of income and employment to a point where, because of the higher real income, the community was willing to hold a larger real stock of money rather than seek to spend on

capital or consumption goods more than their current income.

4. So long as general unemployment continued, the price–wage level would continue to fall, increasing the real stock of money and stimulating employment so that an equilibrium would only be reached when optimum employment was reached. At this point of equilibrium, the real value of the money stock would have so increased that a real income corresponding to optimum employment was necessary to induce the community to want to hold just and only just as much money as was outstanding and to want to spend on capital and consumption goods an amount just equal to their incomes. Interest rates would fall to the point that the community was just willing to hold the resulting real stock of money rather than make additional loans in excess of those financed out of their current income.

The validity of the above analysis turns on the validity of the assumption that if individuals and enterprises had enough more real buying power in the form of money, they would seek to spend more on consumption or capital goods than if their other real assets and real income were the same and their real money holdings were less.

That this is a reasonable assumption should be clear. Suppose that interest rates have already fallen so low or have so little effect on saving and investment, that unemployment continues to force down the price–wage level, and that prices drop 50 percent while the outstanding stock of money remains constant. The effect on each holder of money would be somewhat similar to giving each a dollar for every dollar he already possessed. Regardless of current interest rates, some holders could be expected to spend a little more on consumption, that is, save less out of their current income, because of their extra buying power. Others could be expected to spend more on capital goods for the same reason.

Consider the case of a man with, say, an initial income of $5,000 and $1,000 worth of money. If the price–wage level dropped 50 percent, and this drop affected him in an average fashion, his money income would fall to $2,500 but he would still have $1,000 in money. His real income would have remained the same but his buying power held in the form of money would have doubled. If the initial balance of 1 to 5 between real buying power in the form of money and real income had been stable, it could be expected that the new balance of 2 to 5 would represent a surplus of money. And even though the rate of interest dropped to the point where he found no advantage in lending the surplus money, it would be surplus in relation to his income. His liquid wealth would be that much greater. He would have more elbow room. And he would need to save less to secure his future. It is likely that he would want to spend at least a part of the surplus for consumption goods.

The increase in the real stock of money could also be expected to stimulate investment. So long as real income remained the same, there would presumably be no increase in the real investment opportunities that would be open, but the power to take advantage of investment opportunities would be increased. Take, for example, the case of a retail storekeeper with part of his working capital in goods and a part in cash. If the buying power of his cash were to double without altering his other real assets, he would be likely to shift part of his cash into a larger inventory. Another man whose real money holdings increased might find that he now had enough money to go into business for himself. A corporate management, finding the real value of its liquid assets increased, would feel freer to expand its activity. Thus, an increase in the real buying-power of the outstanding stock of money could be expected to stimulate both the expenditure on consumption goods and the expenditure on capital goods.

It is important to notice that this stimulation of expenditure is not just a temporary but a continuing increase. It may be that the windfall gain that an individual realizes from the increase in the real value of his or her money would have a temporary stimulating effect on the individual's consumption or investment. But this is not the influence important here. If, after the price drop, a person's $1,000 of cash was more than that person wanted to hold when his or her income was $2,500, he or she as an individual could, of course, spend a part and thereby reduce money holdings. But as has already been indicated, the community as a whole could not, since the spending of the extra money does not make it disappear. If the aforementioned individual were *typical* of the community, his or her income would have to increase until he or she was willing to hold the $1,000 of cash and only spend currently on consumption and investment goods as much as was currently being received as income.

The potency of a general price–wage adjustment in stimulating general employment in a sensitive-price economy can be suggested by an extreme example covering a whole economy. Suppose that optimum employment would be reached at a national income of $150 billion measured at the initial price level; that at this price level there was such a tendency to oversave as to result in a national income of only $100 billion with consequent general unemployment; and finally that there was $50 billion of money outstanding *or the equivalent of half a year's current income.* In these circumstances and with prices and wage rates both sensitive, the price–wage level could be expected to fall. If it dropped 50 percent and the volume of production and employment and the stock of money remained constant, national income measured in money, but at the lower prices, would be only $50 billion, while money holdings would still be $50 billion. Instead of having the equivalent of half a year's income in the form of cash on hand, the community would now have the equivalent of a full year's income. If this increase in real liquid assets did not stimulate spending to the point of full employment, the price–wage level could be expected to drop further. Should it reach 1 percent of its initial level, the community would be holding the equivalent of fifty years' worth of income in the form of liquid buying power. Certainly long before such a huge volume of liquid buying power was reached, an increase in spending would take place. And since the increase in spending would not reduce the stock of money or real buying power outstanding, but would only shift it from hand to hand, it would act as a stimulant to spending for both consumption and investment so long as prices did not rise. As a result, any general unemployment in a sensitive-price economy would set in motion a general price–wage decline whose direct effects on saving and investment would tend to increase employment.

The corollary would also be true that excessive employment would stimulate a price and wage rise that would operate to reduce employment through increasing the propensity to save and reducing the propensity to invest. Thus, in a sensitive-price economy, economic equilibrium would only be reached at optimum employment.[7]

Realistic Objections

There are certain objections to the above thesis that are bound to arise. First, is it reasonable to talk of a *general* fall in the price–wage level? Wouldn't a drop in goods prices and wage rates tend to distort the price structure, as was the case in the 1929–32 price drop, and so produce important effects not covered above? Second, wouldn't the expectation of further price decline lead to the postponement of orders and so postpone or prevent the corrective effect of a price–wage drop?

And third, wouldn't a major price–wage drop lead to general fear and disorganization as in 1932? In each case, the answer appears to turn on whether one is considering a sensitive-price economy or one in which insensitive prices and wage rates play a major role.

In answering these questions, it is important to bear in mind the unreal character of a sensitive-price economy. In our actual economy, a large body of prices and wage rates are administered privately or publicly and tend to be insensitive, at least for short periods of time. The bulk of industry is habituated to administered prices that are revised from time to time. Only in agriculture is there a major field in which the bulk of prices are "made in the market" and are truly sensitive to short-run changes in offerings or demand. In only a few industries, such as the production of standard cotton textiles or the supplying of steel scrap, does anything like the same degree of price sensitivity and the absence of price administration arise. But for purposes of the above analysis, it has been necessary to envisage an economy in which both prices and wage rates for the whole economy were as sensitive as prices in most of agriculture are today.

Traditional economics has had no difficulty in assuming such a sensitive-price economy for purposes of theoretical analysis. Yet in the present day of more realistic analysis, it is difficult to get away from some of the characteristics of our actual economy that derive from its insensitive-price character. On examination it will be found that each of the above questions arises from certain characteristics of our modern economy, which would not be applicable to a sensitive-price economy.

Changes in the Price–Wage Level

It is notable that the whole conception of a general change in price level has been gradually falling into disfavor in recent years. In considerable part this has been due to the recognition of the fact that prices do not tend to move up and down *together*. Rather, when a general index of prices moves down, it is likely that the sensitive prices will fall very much more than the administered prices, with the reverse behavior in the case of a price rise. The whole conception of a general change in price level does not apply to such price behavior. Yet the impediment to general price changes would seem to be the presence of insensitive prices and of price administration. If all prices were "made in the market," and therefore as sensitive as most agricultural prices, the concepts of a price level and of general price changes would be appropriate so long as the constant flux of individual price relationships within the level was recognized. In the same fashion, it is possible to conceive of wage rates that are as sensitive as goods prices and of general changes in the price-wage level, though of course the latter conception is appropriate only to a sensitive-price economy.

Expectations of Price Change

Of greater practical importance is the difference in the effect of *expected* price changes on economic policy where prices are "made in the market" and where they are administered. Where prices are made in the market, the current price is presumed to reflect the balance of expectation as to what the price is likely to be in the future. So long as the stocks of a particular commodity can be stored for reasonable periods of time, and this is the case where the problem of expected price change is most important, a *general* expectation that its price will be higher in the near future cannot long exist. The very fact that the price is expected to be higher will force up the current price. Similarly, a *general* expectation that a price will fall in the near future will cause the current price to fall. In either case, the current price will tend to be one at which those who expect a higher price in the near future and those who expect a lower price will just offset each other. This means that the action of persons or enterprises that are postponing their purchase because the price of an item is expected to go down will be more or less offset by the action of others who expect the price to rise. Therefore, the *expectations* of departures from the current price will have only minor influence on the total volume of a particular good currently produced or consumed, since the current price would have to be one at which the expectations were about equally divided between an expected rise and an expected fall.

The exact opposite is the case with administered prices. A general opinion can develop that an administered price is going to be revised downward in the near future, without this opinion having any immediate effect on the price. Such a general expectation is likely to lead to a fairly general market-wide postponing of orders for the good in question, until it is clear whether or not a reduction is actually made. Take, for example, the prices of standard rolling mill products. It is customary for the big steel mills to set their prices for three months at a time, announcing the prices for the next quarter before the old quarter is finished. With this quarterly revision, steel prices tend to be fairly sensitive as administered prices go. But the current price does not reflect the market's expectations of price change in the next one, two, or more quarters. Steel buyers and users will advance or postpone their buying in the light of their own expectations as to the prices likely to exist in subsequent quarters. And because the current price does not adjust to keep a balance between those expecting lower and higher prices, the bulk of the action due to price expectation may be on one side only, retarding or stimulating production.

Indeed, in the case of a great many administered prices, the action due to expected price changes is most likely to be entirely one-sided. In most cases it is clear that if the administered price does change it will change in a certain direction. Thus, in the case of an administered price, the question is usually not "will the price fall or rise?" but is either "will the price fall or stay the same?" or "will the price rise or stay the same?" When it becomes clear that if the price is revised it will be revised downward, the market is often called a buyer's market; when it becomes clear that if revised, it will be revised upward, it is called a seller's market. In a buyer's market there is a tendency to postpone new orders; in a seller's market, to accelerate new orders. These reactions in turn influence production and employment. But these effects are produced by expectation of price change *where prices are insensitive.* They would not occur where prices are made in the market and are therefore sensitive.

The *market-wide* postponement or acceleration of orders due to expected price changes is so much a part of modern industry that it is often thought of as a characteristic of all types of price movement. It should be clear from the above analysis that while postponement or acceleration is likely on the part of individuals as a result of their expectations as to future price, regardless of the type of price, only in the case of administered prices is market-wide acceleration or postponement likely to occur as a result of expected price changes. Since in the preceding analysis we have been dealing with a sensitive-price economy in which prices are made in the market and not administered, the expectations of price changes that are a part of the process of change in the price–wage level would have no significant accelerating or postponing effect. In particular, a widespread decline or the expectation of a widespread decline in the price–wage level would not produce the serious contraction of production in a sensitive-price economy that could be expected in an economy in which administered prices played a significant role.

Market Demoralization

Finally, there is the possibility that a rapid price decline might instill such lack of confidence in the future that production would be seriously disorganized. Certainly a rapid decline in prices under modern conditions, accompanied by increasing unemployment, seems likely to produce serious lack of confidence. But again, this appears to be closely tied up with the fact that we live in an economy *habituated* to insensitive prices and wage rates. In the only major part of our economy habituated to sensitive prices, namely agriculture, the 1929–32 price decline of 60 percent did not result in a contraction of production. It seems likely that, in an economy in which goods prices and wage rates were sensitive throughout, and in which the community was habituated to this condition, quite important changes in the price–wage level could take place with relatively minor effects on confidence. Indeed, a community with a sensitive-price system might become so habituated to relatively full employment that only minor changes in the price–wage level would be necessary, if sufficiently frequent, to offset changes in the propensity to save or to invest in goods, and to correct any unbalance between the outstanding stock of money and the demand for money. However, such speculations are academic since we have no sensitive-price economy in which to test them. What is important here is that as long as we are trying to analyze the effects of a tendency to oversave in a sensitive-price economy, it seems reasonable to speak of general changes in the price–wage level and to assume that expectation of price changes would tend to cancel out, while the effect of major price movements on confidence can be neglected. Of course, all three of these conclusions are clearly not applicable to the insensitive-price economy in which we actually live.[8]

Effect of Type of Money

A question may also be raised as to whether the preceding analysis would hold for all types of money. If money consisted entirely of the IOUs or notes of individuals, the analysis would presumably not hold.

Some individuals would gain from an increase in the value of their money if prices fell, but the other individuals who issued the notes would lose to an equal extent. At the opposite extreme, if all money consisted of gold coins, the gain in real value to the holders of the coins would not be offset by any recognizable loss to other individuals. In this case the analysis would clearly apply. If money consisted wholly or largely of government debt or bank debt created through the purchase of government obligation(s), the analysis would appear to apply, unless the credit of the government itself came into serious question. The individual's gain from a fall in prices would be offset theoretically by an equal loss to the government, but in practice it would be a specific gain and a generalized loss. It could have an important effect on the current behavior of individuals, but only a minor effect on government behavior provided the integrity of government credit was not seriously involved. The issue is more complicated in the case of money based on commercial credit, but since, in most modern money systems, the bulk of money is backed by metal or government credit, the exact conclusions with respect to this effect of commercial credit is of secondary importance. Provided a sufficiently large part of a country's money is backed by metal or government credit, and provided the prices and wage rates are sensitive, a general fall in the price–wage level can be expected to increase both the propensity to consume and the propensity to invest, and thus increase the level of national income at which saving and investment would be equal.

Particular Application to the Keynesian Analysis

To those not habituated to the Keynesian analysis, the foregoing should be reasonably convincing, but for the followers of Keynes there is still one important hurdle. If it is accepted that the lower the level of interest rates, the larger the amount of money that the community will want to hold, why will the fall in interest rates not absorb the *whole* effect of an increase in the real stock of money? Why will the effect be divided between a fall in interest rates and a rise in the rate of expenditure? The answer to this is that, theoretically, the whole of the effect could be absorbed through a fall in interest rates. Also, theoretically, the whole effect could be absorbed through a change in expenditure and income. But in practice it would be likely to be a combination of both. For example, if the real stock of money were increased through a fall in the price–wage level, the whole of the increase could be absorbed if the level of interest rates fell far enough. But would they fall far enough? Presumably, the level would be established by the interaction of those seeking to borrow and those seeking to loan money. If the whole of the surplus money was surplus in relation to loans, then there would be an increase in the money offered for loan that would force down interest rates until the whole of the surplus money was absorbed. But to the extent that the surplus money was not surplus in relation to loans, it would not be offered for loan and would therefore not have any effect on interest rates. Therefore, though sufficiently lower rates of interest *could* absorb the whole of the extra money, the relations between potential borrowers and potential lenders would not force interest rates down to the necessary extent. The situation is a little like that of three balls in a bowl where no one of them is likely to come to rest at the bottom. Where the surplus in money is partly a surplus in relation to loans and partly in relation to goods, there will be no pressure to force interest rates low enough to absorb all of the surplus.

The Effect of an Increase in the Stock of Money

The preceding analysis has covered only half of the problem raised at the beginning of the chapter—whether a change in the real stock of money could have a significant direct effect on the propensities to save and invest. It has been shown that a change in the real stock of money brought about by a change in the price–wage level could have a significant effect quite apart from interest rates. It remains to be shown that an increase in the real stock of money through an increase in the quantity of money outstanding could also have such a direct effect.

This problem is complicated by the many different ways in which monetary expansion could take place, since the effect to be expected depends in part on the manner in which the expansion is brought about. At one extreme, an expansion that simply placed a quarter in the hands of each holder of money for each dollar already held, could be expected to have somewhat the same direct effect as a 20 percent cut in the price–wage level in a sensitive-price economy. The indirect effects due to such reactions as fear for the integrity of the monetary medium might either magnify the stimulating effect through reducing the general desire to store wealth in the form of money or it might reduce the effect by reducing the propensity to invest. But the effect of such an increase in the real stock of money could not be determined, as Keynes assumes, by considering just the effect of the change in interest rates that it engendered. The effect on the rate of expenditure would also have to be taken into account and would be significant.

At the other extreme, a monetary expansion brought about by replacing with money such government bonds as were in the hands of individuals who were perfectly indifferent as to whether they held bonds or money, could be expected to have no effect on either interest rates or the level of employment.

Between these extremes lie a multitude of situations that will be explored in a later chapter. For the present, it will be sufficient to suggest that when these situations are examined it will be found that in the bulk of cases a direct expansion in the stock of money can be expected to affect both the level of interest rates and the level of national income in ways comparable to those arising from a change in the price–wage level. This conclusion, if substantiated, will be of supreme importance when methods for reducing mass unemployment are considered. It is, however, of secondary importance in this chapter, where the validity of the saving–investment theory of employment as an explanation of mass unemployment is under consideration.

The basic conclusion of this chapter is that, if the above analysis is accepted, the saving–investment theory ceases to be an adequate explanation of mass unemployment. Interest rates are not the only significant way through which a change in the real stock of money can affect the propensity to save or the propensity to invest. And what remains of the Keynesian theory of interest is not sufficient to explain equilibrium at less than optimum employment. It is possible to accept the conclusion that interest rates are in part controlled by liquidity preference, and have to adjust so that the community is willing to hold the outstanding stock of money rather than make loans. But this is not a sufficient departure from the classical assumptions to explain equilibrium at less than full employment. Some other factors must be introduced.

Notes

1. Keynes, chapter 3, *supra,* note 21. Italics added. Quoted in context in chapter 2, at note 3, supra. It is clear that Keynes, in this quotation, is using "the

Figure 3.1 **[Saving, Investment, and Wage Levels]**

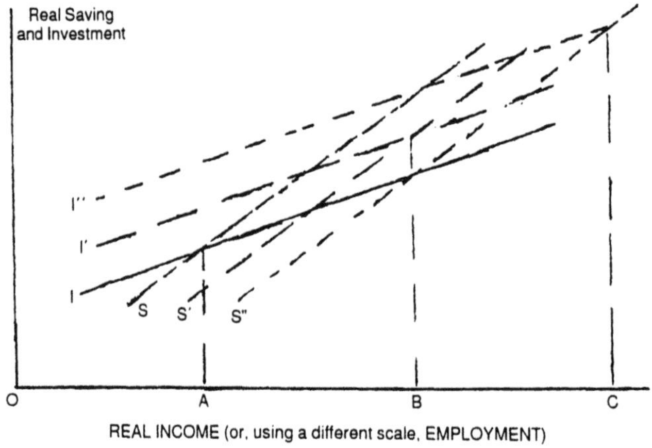

REAL INCOME (or, using a different scale, EMPLOYMENT)

Source: These crude drawings are reproduced from Gardiner C. Means' original manuscript.

interest rate" to represent "the level of interest rates" and that "cash" is used in essentially the same sense as the term "money" in this volume.

2. In order to keep the analysis simple and applicable only to the two adjusting factors, interest rates and national income, it is presumed that enterprise is not carried on by corporations and that there are therefore no equity securities outstanding.

3. This could happen, for example, if a tax were newly placed on money holding, or if uncertainty as to the value of money arose.

4. A little consideration should make it obvious that the indifference arising from low interest rates does not apply to goods. When an individual is surfeited with a particular commodity, say ice cream sodas, it means that he would rather hold any amount of money rather than consume more of it. He is indifferent to the amount of money he holds so far as that commodity is concerned. But this does not mean that he is indifferent with respect to other commodities. Only a surfeit of all commodities would result in such a general indifference to the amount of money held. While lending may not involve the possibility of satiety, the general principle holds that indifference as to how much money is held with respect to one particular use of money does not imply indifference to all uses.

5. For simplicity in exposition, corporate stocks are left out of account. As a result, this analysis can apply only to an economy in which enterprise is not incorporated. However, essentially the same results would be reached if corporate enterprise was included.

6. Assuming no immediate change in the stock of money.

7. The thesis presented here can be set forth in the customary type of saving–investment chart (Figure 3.1). For simplicity, it will be assumed that neither saving nor investment is significantly affected by the level of interest rates and that the outstanding stock of money remains constant.

In Figure 3.1, the solid lines I and S indicate, respectively, the potential real investment and the potential real saving at different possible levels of real income when the price–wage level is presumed to be high. The dashed and dotted lines I′ and I″ indicate that as the price–wage level falls and the real buying power of the money stock increases, the propensity to invest rises. Likewise, the dashed and dotted lines S′ and S″ indicate that as the price–wage level falls, the real buying power of the money stock increases, and the propensity to save also falls. Since, in any real situation, saving and investment must be equal, the level of real income and employment must be that represented by the intersection of the investment and saving lines corresponding to the assumed price–wage level. At a high price–wage level with saving and investment represented by the solid lines, real income (or employment) would be represented by the distance OA. If the price–wage level was somewhat lower, so that saving and investment were represented by the dashed lines, real income (or employment) would be that indicated by OB, and if still lower, that represented by OC.

Under a sensitive-price system, none of these points would represent economic equilibrium unless it also represented optimum employment. If there were general unemployment at say the level of real income represented by A, the price level would fall, thereby decreasing the propensity to save and increasing the propensity to consume, and the level of real income at which saving and investment were equal would be higher. Equilibrium would be reached only when there was no further downward pressure on the price–wage level due to general unemployment. Similarly, if there were general overemployment, the price–wage level would fall [sic] and bring a reduction in the level of real income.

8. It should be noted that the preceding analysis of monetary adjustments does not rely at all on the *dynamic* effects of changes in the price-wage level. It is concerned only with the differences in price–wage level, not the temporary repercussions of a change in level. In particular, it does not depend on the quasi-income of capital gains, or windfall gains. As Keynes points out (Chapter 3, *supra,* note 2), windfall gains from an increase in asset values can stimulate consumption to the extent that these gains are treated by the beneficiaries as if they were to some extent analogous to income. But such effects would be temporary. The *continuing* effect of the possession of assets of a higher real buying power is not covered by Keynes. Only the latter would, of course, contribute to a continuing equilibrium at optimum employment.

4

The Classical Theory
of Employment

Before an effort is made to provide an explanation for general unemployment, it will be useful to examine the classical theory of employment. This theory, summarized in Say's law, is seldom set forth in detail, and its real character and its limitations have been lost to sight.

According to Say's law, the supplying of goods involves an equal demand for goods. This position is well stated by Mill in an attempt to deny the argument that it was possible to have "a deficiency of demand for all commodities, for want of the means of payment." He goes on to say:

> Those who think so cannot have considered what it is which constitutes the means of payment for commodities. It is simply commodities. Each person's means of paying for the production of other people consists of those which he himself possesses. All sellers are inevitably and *ex vi termini* buyers. Could we suddenly double the productive powers of the country, we should double the supply of commodities in every market; but we should, by the same stroke, double the purchasing power. Everything would bring a double demand as well as supply; everybody would be able to buy twice as much, because everyone would have twice as much to offer in exchange.[1]

If one were dealing with a barter economy in which goods could only be exchanged for goods, this position would be clearly tenable. But where goods are exchanged for money, and the money in turn is exchanged for goods, or where labor is hired to produce goods and is paid in money, money intervenes in the process. The offering of goods for money may not be matched by an equal offer of money for goods. As Marshall says after quoting, with approval, the above paragraph from Mill, "though men have the power to purchase, they may not choose to use it."[2] Here is the crux of the problem. Many classical writers repeat Say's law and go no further. Others, recognizing that in absolute terms it can apply only to a barter economy, take the further position that, in a money economy, money acts simply as an intermediary and cancels out so that the net effect on the demand and offering of goods is that to be expected under conditions of barter. However, no classical economist appears to have spelled out in detail the process by which this adjustment would occur.

A close approach to a statement of a mechanism of adjustment is to be found in Mill's statement on the adjustment following a credit crisis. This statement comes almost immediately after the passage quoted above. Having given reasons why general overproduction was theoretically not possible, he goes on in the following words to indicate that in one sense there can be general overproduction, but that this is temporary and will be corrected through a temporary or possibly permanent fall in prices and the restoration of confidence:

> I have already described the state of the markets for commodities which accompanies what is termed a commercial crisis. At such times there is really an excess of all commodities above the money demand: in other words, there is an under-supply of money. From the sudden annihilation of a great mass of credit, everyone dislikes to part with ready money, and many are anxious to procure it at any sacrifice. Almost everybody, therefore, is a seller, and there are scarcely any buyers: so that there may really be, though only while the crisis lasts, an extreme depression of general prices, from what may be indiscriminately called a glut of commodities or a dearth of money.[3]

Mill then goes on to suggest that "the remedy is not a diminution of supply, but the restoration of confidence."[4] However, he adds with respect to the drop in prices, "The fall being solely of money prices, if prices did not rise again no dealer would lose, since the smaller price would be worth as much to him as the larger price was before."[5]

It may be that in this section Mill did not have in mind a fall in the general price level *as a corrective* of "a glut of commodities or a dearth of money." But it is very easy to build, on this type of analysis, a justification for applying Say's law to a money economy, provided prices, including wage rates, are presumed to be sensitive. This is the justification already suggested in the discussion of the preceding chapter. If a glut of commodities or a dearth of money developed at one price level, prices (including wage rates) would fall; this would increase the real value of the stock of money until the dearth of money was dissipated by an expansion of the real stock of money and the glut of commodities disappeared. Such a "mechanism of adjustment" would justify Say's law as an equilibrium law when applied to a sensitive-price economy, since the real value of the stock of money would tend to adjust so that the offering of goods for money and the offering of money for goods were just equal. Under these circumstances, a general lack of demand for goods and general unemployment at one level of price and wage rate would automatically tend to be corrected and the only condition of equilibrium would be one of optimum employment.[6]

This mechanism of adjustment is simple and obvious to anyone who is as habituated to considering equilibrium under conditions of perfect price flexibility as were the later classical writers. It may well be that this was the justification for applying Say's law to a money economy, and that it was so obvious that it was never set down in detail. Since it does justify Say's law for a sensitive-price economy, and since there seems to be no other justification, it will be referred to in what follows as "the Classical Theory of Employment." It explains the classical reliance on automatic adjustments to maintain optimum employment. A small amount of general unemployment could be understood as due to economic friction or lags that prevented perfect equilibrium from being maintained, and wide upheavals could be attributed to temporary credit crises. However, apart from credit crises, automatic forces could be expected to hold total employment quite close to the optimum level.

This classical theory of employment might point to a workable policy if price and wage rates were sufficiently sensitive. Whether or not prices and wage rates are today sufficiently sensitive will be considered in Part II.

Notes

1. John Stuart Mill. *Principles of Political Economy*, Ashley Edition. London: Longmans, Green, 1926, pp. 557–558. Italics in original.

2. Alfred Marshall. *Principles of Economics,* London: Macmillan, 1930 (eighth edition), p. 710.

3. Mill, p. 561.

4. Ibid.

5. Ibid.

6. It should be noted that, if money is introduced into the Walrasian equations, the *level* of prices adjusts so as to produce a solution only at optimum employment.

The Marxian Theory
of Employment

In contrast to the classical theory, the Marxian theory of employment leads to the expectation of increasing unemployment and repeated crises as a result of the historical development of capitalism. According to this theory, under capitalism the level of employment in any period is determined largely by the extent of capital accumulation, but is also influenced by periodic crises that arise from contradictions inherent in the capitalist mode of production. In what follows, an attempt will be made to outline this theory and consider its validity.

The General Law of Capitalist Accumulation

The effect of capital accumulation on employment is determined, according to Marx, by a general law of capitalist accumulation. This law can be broken down into four propositions:

1. The basic drive in the capitalistic mode of production is the accumulation of capital.
2. Capital accumulation, combined with industrial concentration, improved industrial techniques and increased labor productivity, leads to a progressive decline in the ratio of capital invested in wages to the total capital invested in production.
3. The progressive decline in the ratio of capital invested in wages to total capital leads to a progressive fall in the average rate of profit.

4. These developments tend to produce a relative surplus-population and unemployment.

The Accumulation of Capital

The first of these propositions needs no clarification. The growing volume of capital and the increasing role of the machine in modern industry are familiar. Whether this accumulation of capital reflects *the* basic drive of capitalism or only *a* basic drive need not detain us, since Marx's theory of employment is not dependent on which position is accepted. That accumulation of capital has occurred, is one of the generally accepted facts of modern industry.

Capital Invested in Wages versus Total Capital

The cumulative decline in the ratio of capital invested in wages to total capital is a proposition that needs more elaboration. The distinction between capital invested in wages—what Marx calls variable capital— and other capital—what Marx calls constant capital—is of major importance not only to Marx's theory of capital accumulation but also to his conceptions of surplus-value and the exploitation of labor by capital. Here we are concerned only with the significance of this distinction in relation to capital accumulation, and the reasons Marx gives for expecting an accelerated decline in the proportion of total capital invested in wages.

First, it is necessary to have clearly in mind Marx's conception of capital invested in wages—his variable capital—and its relation to total wage payments. In the individual enterprise, money is paid out in wages and recovered in the sale of the product. This means that at any given time an enterprise will have a certain amount of its capital that it has paid out in wages, which has not yet been recovered through the sale of products. This is the capital invested in wages.[1] In any given period the capital invested in wages may be turned over several times, so that total wage payments for the period will exceed the amount of capital invested in wages at any particular time during the period. Thus, the average capital invested in wages will equal the wages paid during a period divided by the number of times the capital is turned over.[2]

Marx's reasons for expecting a progressive decline in the proportion of total capital that is invested in current wages are based, in the first instance, on the changing *technical composition* of capital as production becomes more and more mechanized. Thus, Marx says, "Apart from natural conditions such as fertility of the soil, etc., and from the skill of independent and isolated producers . . . the degree of productivity of labor in a given society, is expressed in the relative extent of the means of production that one laborer, during a given time, with the same tension of labor-power, turns into products," and "The mass of machinery, beasts of burden, mineral manuers [sic], drain pipe, etc. is a condition of the increasing productivity of labor. So also is it with the means of production concentrated in buildings, furnaces, means of transport, etc." Also as a *consequence* of increasing productivity, ". . . more raw material is worked up in the same time, and, therefore, a greater mass of raw material and auxiliary substances enter into the labor-process."[3] The increase in the productiveness of labor "appears, therefore, in the diminution of the mass of labor in proportion to the mass of means of production moved by it, or in a diminution of the subjective factor of the labor process as compared with the objective factor."[4] Thus, with capitalistic development and the mechanization of industry, the physical mass of capital increases faster than the physical mass of labor.

Marx goes on to argue that,

> This change in the technical composition of capital, this growth in the mass of means of production, as compared with the mass of the labor-power that vivifies them, is reflected again in its value-composition, by the increase of the constant constituent of capital at the expense of its variable constituent. These may be, e.g., originally 50 percent of a capital laid out in means of production, and 50 percent in the labor power; later on, with the development of the productivity of labor, 80 percent in means of production, 20 percent in labor-power, and so on.

Thus, according to Marx, the increased technical role of machines, and so on, as compared with labor, results in an increase in the *value of capital* invested in plant, equipment, and materials relative to the *value of capital* invested in current wages.[5]

This relative increase in the value of capital invested in plant, materials, and the like would not, according to Marx, be as great as the relative increase in the physical mass of the means of production.

> With the increasing productivity of labor, not only does the mass of the means of production increase, but their value compared with their mass

diminishes. Their value therefore rises absolutely, but not in proportion to their mass. The increase in the difference between constant and variable capital is, therefore, much less than that of the difference between the mass of the means of production into which the constant, and the mass of the labor-power into which the variable, capital is converted. The former difference increases but in a smaller degree.[6]

Thus, the total capital invested in production can be expected to increase faster than the capital invested in wages.

The Declining Rate of Profit [7]

The third proposition in Marx's argument—that the relative increase in the role of capital invested in plant, materials, and so on will lead to a fall in the average rate of profit—rests on certain assumptions as to (1) the relation between total profits in the economy and total wage payments,[8] and (2) the rate of turnover of capital invested in wages. Marx first assumes that the ratio of total profits to total wages remains constant,[9] and that the rate of turnover of capital invested in wages also remains constant. This means that capital invested in wages increases only as fast as total wages and total profits. If capital invested in plant, materials, and the like increases faster than that invested in wages, and profits only keep pace with the latter, the ratio of total profits to total capital—that is, the average rate of profit—must decline. On this basis Marx concluded that a *relative* decline of the capital invested in wages "must necessarily lead to *a gradual fall in the average rate of profit*," so long as the ratio of total profits to total wages remains the same.[10]

This progressive decline in the average rate of profit could be reduced or eliminated by a progressive increase in the ratio of total profits to total wages—what Marx calls a progressively increasing "degree of labor exploitation"—or by a progressive increase in the rate of turnover of capital invested in current wages. But Marx expects neither of these to prevent "a tendency to a progressive fall" in the average rate of profit. "This progressive tendency of the average rate of profit to fall is, therefore, but a peculiar expression of capitalistic production for the fact that the social productivity of labor is progressively increasing."[11]

The Insufficient Demand for Labor

The fourth proposition in Marx's argument is that the progressive accumulation of capital, the shift in its relative composition, and the tendency for the average rate of profit to fall lead to the development of a surplus-population and unemployment. According to Marx's analysis, "the demand for labor is determined not by the amount of capital as a whole, but by its variable constituent alone."[12] This means that, since the variable constituent of capital increases but only in a constantly diminishing proportion, "an accelerated accumulation of total capital is needed to absorb an additional number of laborers, or even, on account of the constant metamorphosis of old capital to keep employed those already functioning."[13] At the same time, "the accumulation of capital, so far as its value is concerned, is checked by the falling rate of profit." More capital plant and equipment is needed at the high rates of mechanization to maintain employment, while the inducement to invest more capital is dissipated by the declining rate of profit. The process of accumulation may even be carried, according to Marx, to a point where there is both a surplus of capital and a surplus of population. Thus, to Marx *"the real barrier of capitalist production is capital itself."*[14]

The Theory of Crises

In addition to this law of capitalist accumulation, leading to the expectation of a progressively increasing surplus-population, Marx presents a theory of crises, which temporarily increase the unemployment arising from the operation of the law of capitalist accumulation, and the aftereffects of which may temporary reduce the unemployment arising from the working of this law.

According to this theory, crises arise periodically as a result of internal contradictions in the capitalist mode of production. As a result of the working out of the law of capitalist accumulation, a period is reached in industrial development where periodically the conflict arising from these internal contradictions "seeks vent in crises. The crises are always but monetary and forcible solutions of the existing contradictions, violent eruptions which restore the disturbed equilibrium for a while."[15]

> The contradiction, generally speaking, consists in this, that the capitalist mode of production has a tendency to develop the productive forces absolutely, regardless of value and of the surplus-value contained in it and regardless of the social conditions under which capitalist production takes place; while it has on the other hand for its aim the preservation of the existing capital and its self-expansion to the highest limit.

As a result of this contradiction, productive forces expand to the point where there is insufficient room for further profitable accumulation of capital. The resulting crises "restore the disturbed equilibrium for a while" by "a depreciation of the existing capital and a development of the productive forces of labor at the expense of the already created productive forces." This periodical depreciation of capital "is one of the immanent means of capitalist production by which the fall in the rate of profit is checked and the accumulation of capital-value through the formation of new capital promoted."[15] Thus, for a period after a crisis the opportunities for expansion are increased and unemployment can be temporarily reduced until the next crisis approaches.

Appraising the Marxian Theory of Employment

In the Marxian theory of employment outlined above, the weakest link in the reasoning lies in the second proposition that the ratio of capital invested in wages must be expected to decline progressively with increased capital accumulation and increased labor productivity, so that an accelerated rate of capital accumulation would be necessary to maintain full employment. We can accept the proposition that the capitalist mode of production begets the accumulation of capital. We can also accept the idea that the forces of capitalism operate to increase the physical plant, equipment, and materials used per worker, and thereby increase both the physical output per worker and the physical "mass of the means of production" used per worker. And, at first thought, it might seem reasonable to accept the idea that the increase in the physical mass of the means of production per worker would also involve at least some increase in the capital invested in the means of production per unit of capital invested in wages, that is, that the proportion of total capital that is invested in wages would decline. But this last does not necessarily follow. It is important, therefore, to see under what conditions the proportion of total capital that is invested in wages would not decline.

It is often assumed that an increase in the capital employed per worker would be evidence in support of this element in Marx's theory. But the comparison between dollars worth of capital and a number of workers involves a cross between value and physical units. Even if complete adjustment were made for the value of money, the comparison would be between the *value* of capital and the *physical* units of labor. The comparison Marx is making is between the value of capital and the value of capital involved in wages, or between the value of capital and the value of wages paid. The comparison between a value quantity and a physical quantity can throw no light on changes in the proportion of total capital that is invested in wages.

A more appropriate comparison would be between the total capital invested and the wages paid, both valued in the same unit. If, for example, the dollars worth of total capital invested in production increased, while the dollar amount of wages remained the same and the rate of turnover of capital invested in wages was constant, then the proportion of the capital that was invested in wages would decline. On the other hand, if the amount of capital and the amount of wages went up exactly together, then, so long as there was no change in the rate of turnover of capital invested in wages, there would be no change in the proportion of total capital and the capital invested in wages. Thus, in order for the ratio to decline, either the capital measured, say, in dollars per dollar of wages must rise or the rate of turnover of capital invested in wages must rise. If the rate of turnover were relatively constant, as Marx assumes, the crucial problem would be, not whether capital increases relative to the number of workers but whether it increases relative to wage payments.[17]

(Insert paragraph comparing increase in capital per worker and wages per worker—mentioning also decline in hours worked.)

Because the expectation that total capital would increase faster than wage payments is so central to both Marx's law of capitalist accumulation and to his theory of crises, its rejection undermines both elements of his theory of employment. A declining rate of profit could be explained on other grounds, such as the larger volume of savings available for investment when productivity and incomes are high. And a declining rate of profit itself would not lead to unemployment. In Marx's analysis, it is the progressively declining rate of profit in combination with a progressively declining ratio of variable to total capital—a progressively declining ratio of wage payments to total capital that leads to progressively increasing unemployment. And in Marx's analysis the internal contradictions in capitalism that lead to periodic crises grow out of this same tendency for a progressively declining ratio of variable to total capital. What Marx's analysis failed to take into account was the possibility that a part of the dynamic of capitalism might be a rise of wage rates as rapid as the increase in capital per worker, more rapid when the shortening of hours is taken into account.

Notes

1. Marx suggests that in any actual situation, this capital can be estimated by taking the circulating capital of an enterprise or group of enterprises (the total capital less the fixed capital tied up in plant, equipment, etc.) and assuming that the capital invested in wages bears the same relation to the circulating capital as wage payments bear to total operating expenses. (See Marx, *Capital,* Vol. III, pp. 90–92 [Part I, Chapter V]). Marx assumes that the rate of turnover of capital invested in wages is the same as that of capital invested in materials, and so on, since the two are combined and sold as a single product.

2. Much of Marx's analysis runs in terms of a period in which there is just one turnover of capital invested in current wages, so that he can speak interchangeably of his variable capital as an amount of capital invested in current wages or as the amount of wages paid. But when his discussion runs in terms of a longer period, say, a year, he makes total wages paid equal to the capital invested in current wages multiplied by the number of times it has been turned over.

3. Ibid., note 1, Vol. I, pp. 681–682 [part VII, chapter XXV].

4. Ibid., p. 682.

5. Ibid. It should be noted that this is a relative matter. Marx makes it perfectly clear that an increase in the capital invested in current wages would be possible provided the total capital increased at a faster rate. (See ibid, p. 683.)

6. Ibid.

7. It should be noted that Marx presents only propositions 1, 2, and 4 above in his first volume, and presents proposition 3 in his third volume as an outgrowth of propositions 1 and 2. Proposition 3 is presented here before proposition 4 because it appears essential to the understanding of the latter.

8. More exactly, the Marxian assumption has to do with the ratio of the total of surplus-value to the total of wages. While the total of surplus-value is not *necessarily* equal to the total of profits, Marx usually assumes them to be equal. See, for example, ibid., note 1, Vol. III, pp. 247–248 [Part III, Chapter XV]. No distortion of Marx's theory of capitalist accumulation is involved in following Marx's example in this respect.

9. The exact assumption is that there is "the same rate of surplus-value, with the same degree of labor exploitation." Ibid., p. 248. Since the rate of surplus-value, by Marx's definition, is the ratio of surplus-value to wages, in so far as profits equal surplus-value, the assumption is that the ratio of profits to wages remains constant.

10. Ibid. Italics in the original.

11. Ibid., p. 249; see also pp. 257, 272–76.

12. Ibid., Vol. I, p. 690.

13. Ibid., pp. 690–691. The requirement that there be capital accumulation in order to *maintain* employment rests on (1) the assumption that existing capital is constantly being replaced from funds derived from its use, and (2) that in this replacement, the ratio of constant to variable capital steadily increases with improved technology, etc., so that without capital accumulation, the absolute amount of capital invested in current wages would decline.

14. Ibid., Vol. III, p. 293.

15. Ibid., p. 292.

16. Ibid.

17. Marx's assumption of a relatively constant average turnover of capital invested in wages lays his theory *as actually stated in terms of variable capital* (capital invested in wages) open to serious question even within his own frame of reference. However, the question would not undermine Marx's theory if the latter were somewhat differently stated. For this reason the question is not raised in the text. The reasons for questioning the theory *as stated* arise from the effect to be expected from industrial concentration on the rate of turnover of capital invested in wages and the relation of the latter to total capital. They are given below.

Vertical integration, one phase of concentration, tends to reduce the rate of turnover of capital invested in wages and increase that capital relative to total capital, even though the identical labor and physical means of production are used to produce the same output. This can be shown in Table 5.1, which reproduces the figures presented by Marx for a cotton spinning mill (Ibid., Vol. III, pp. 90–92) and adds comparable figures for a weaving mill that is assumed to buy the total yarn output of the first mill as its sole raw material. Calculations are then made for the activity of the two mills, the rate of turnover of capital invested in wages, the proportion of total capital that is invested in wages; and the rate of profit, first on the assumption that the two mills operate independently and then on the assumption that they are consolidated into a single enterprise.

It can be seen from Table 5.1 that, with the same functions performed with the same labor and capital, vertical consolidation decreases the rate of turnover of capital invested in wages and increases in the proportion of total capital that is invested in wages, but does not alter the rate of return on capital. The change in turnover and magnitude of the capital invested in wages arises from the fact that in the combined enterprise, the yarn is never sold or bought. This means that the expenditure for materials is less for the combined enterprise than for the sum of the separate enterprises, and the wages paid out for spinning are not recouped until after the weaving process is completed, so that the *average* turnover of capital invested in wages is reduced and a larger average investment in wages is necessary to maintain a given level of wage payments.

Since Marx's analysis leads him to expect increased concentration of industry, at least some of which would presumably be vertical, he should have expected a progressive decline in the average turnover of his variable capital and an increase in its magnitude, a development which might result in an increase rather than a decline in the proportion of total capital made up of variable capital. It could be argued that, if all production were carried on by one enterprise, *all* capital would be variable capital, since labor would be the only expense; or at the very least, that all circulating capital would be variable capital.

However, these conclusions, while they cast doubt on the theory when stated in terms of variable capital, do not apply to Marx's theory when stated in terms of the relation of *wage payments* to total capital. If total wage payments and total profits maintain a constant ratio and total capital increases relative to wage payments, the average rate of return on capital must fall. When Marx assumes that the rate of turnover of variable capital is constant, it is immaterial whether the theory is stated in terms of variable capital or in terms of total wage payments. But if vertical combination takes place, the theory would continue to hold if stated in terms of total wages but not in terms of variable capital.

Table 5.1

	Spinning mill	Weaving mill	Sum of accounts of both mills	Combination of both mills in one enterprise
Weekly Account Costs				
1. Capital charge (wear and tear)	20	18	38	38
2. Cotton purchased	342	—	342	342
3. Yarn purchased	—	510	510	—
4. Other nonlabor costs	16	16	32	32
5. Wages	52	52	104	104
6. Total operating expenses (2 + 3 + 4 + 5)	410	576	988	478
7. Total costs (1 + 6)	430	596	1,026	516
Revenue				
8. Sale of yarn	510	—	510	—
9. Sale of cloth	—	676	676	676
10. Total revenue (8 + 9)	510	676	1,186	676
11. Total profits (10 − 7)	80	80	160	160
Capital Account				
12. Fixed capital	10,000	8,975	18,975	18,975
13. Circulating capital	2,500	3,525	6,025	6,025
14. Total capital (12 + 13)	12,500	12,500	25,000	25,000
15. Ratio of wages to total operating expense (5 ÷ 6)	.127	.090	.1053	.2175
16. Variable capital ÷ capital invested in wages (13 × 5)	318	318	636	1,310
17. Rate of turnover of variable capital, 52 times turned over per year (5 ÷ 16)	8.5	8.5	8.5	4.1
18. Percent of total capital in variable capital (16 ÷ 14)	2.5%	2.5%	2.5%	5.24%
19. Rate of return on capital 52 (11 ÷ 14)	33.28%	33.28%	33.28%	33.28%

Part II

An Insensitive-Price Theory of Economic Adjustment

6

Insensitive Prices and Wage Rates

That prices and wage rates are, on the whole, insensitive is generally recognized, but just why they are insensitive and what this means for economic adjustment is not so widely understood. Sometimes this insensitivity is regarded simply as a matter of a lag, a product of economic friction, which doesn't seriously affect the workings of a free enterprise system, except to make the expected adjustments approximate rather than perfect. Sometimes it is regarded as a product of monopoly and something that would be eliminated if monopoly were eliminated. In this chapter it will be shown that this insensitivity is neither a matter of lag nor of monopoly. It is essentially a product of imperfect competition, though it is also to be expected in cases of monopoly. And it is not something that time can be expected to correct.

In order to bring out the differences between sensitive and insensitive prices, it will be convenient to present a series of abstract situations that sharpen these differences. No attempt will be made to investigate all the possible formulations that could be developed. Rather, the behavior of each type of price will be considered when there is a general drop in demand, on the assumption that all other prices, wage rates, and other costs are perfectly sensitive. While this assumption of perfect adjustment for the rest of the economy is most unrealistic, it will serve to highlight the differences. The effect of these differences on the working of the economy can then be taken up under more realistic assumptions in a subsequent chapter.

An examination of price behavior can best start by drawing a sharp distinction between three situations that differ in the kind of price policy that an individual producer is in a position to make. A producer may be simply a price-acceptor, with no control over price; he or she may be able to make a price independently of the effect on the price policy of other producers; or the individual may be a price-maker whose own price has to be made in the light of the probable effect on the price action of other producers of the same or similar products.

The case of the price-acceptor is simple and provides the backbone of the general classical analysis. In many concrete situations, particularly likely to arise in agriculture, the individual producer, if he or she wants to sell in the current market, has no choice as to the price at which goods will sell. The producer can either take the current market price or not sell in the current market. If the producer is not satisfied with the current price, he or she can speculate on the possibility that demand will increase relative to supply and, therefore, be able to get a better price in a subsequent market. The individual producer may even set an offered price in the speculative hope that subsequent demand will increase so that he or she gets a price better than the current price. But in either case the producer is "speculating for a rise." If he or she wants to sell currently, the only alternative is to accept the current price.[1] There is no range of alternative prices from which one can choose. The individual can sell the whole or any part of his or her output at the current price, but can sell none in the current market at a price above the current market price. In a very real sense, the individual producer cannot have a price policy. He or she can be a price-acceptor or a speculator, but not a price-maker. Speculation simply postpones in time the price he or she accepts. At no point does the individual·producer make the price.[2]

The situation is quite different where a producer is in a position to choose between a range of possible prices with the expectation of selling more currently if his or her price is set low, but with the expectation of selling some if the price is set higher. Then, unless the producer chooses to sell on an auction basis, he or she has the problem of deciding what price to set. The producer has to *make* price policy. He or she becomes a price-maker, not a price-acceptor.[3]

The price-makers can, in turn, be divided into two groups—those who, in setting or changing their prices, have to take into account the probable counteractions by competitors or others, and those who can disregard such considerations. The first group would include the producer who believes that, if he or she cut prices by 10 percent, the producer's immediate competitors would cut their prices by an equal amount, but that, if he or she did not cut prices, the competitors would not cut theirs. In deciding whether to cut or not, the producer would have to take into account the probable alternative actions by his or her competitors. The second group would include the producers whose product was so differentiated from that of competitors or was subject to so little competition that prices could be set or changed without leading to price changes by competitors. This does not mean that he or she could disregard the prices of competitors in setting or changing his or her own price, but only that a change in price would not lead to a change in competitor prices. Thus, the owners of a small automobile company might have a considerable range within which they could set prices without having to expect that their big competitors would alter their own prices because of what they do. Similarly, a local candy store, the only "homemade" candy story in the region, could sell its homemade candy at any one of a range of prices. In setting its price, it would have to take into account the prices of nationally advertised and priced brands, but it would know that, so long as its sales were localized, it could set its price high or low without inducing a change in the price of the nationally marketed products. Yet in both cases competition would be active. To distinguish between the two groups of price-makers, we can refer to the second as independent price-makers, since they do not have to consider the counteraction of competitors; and refer to the first as dependent price-makers, since their price policy must in part depend on the expected policy reactions of competitors. Often, of course, a price-maker may be an independent price-maker within a certain range of prices and a dependent price-maker beyond this range.

It must be clear that the dividing line drawn above between price-acceptors and price-makers coincides with that drawn in the current literature between perfect and imperfect competition. It cannot, however, be said that the dividing line between the dependent (and independent) price-maker(s) coincides with that drawn in the current literature between imperfect competition and monopoly. The term monopoly has become so much of a political football, that its popular meaning is altogether too narrow to cover all the situations that involve independent price-making. And even at the most technical level, the term "monopoly," originally meaning a single seller, has to be given strained definition to cover all situations in which producers have a range within which they can set their own price.[4] The small auto company and the candy maker cited above would be independent price-makers, but they would not usually be thought of as monopolists. A great many small or specialty manufacturers who would certainly not ordinarily be thought of as monopolists can set their prices without the expectation of immediate counteraction on prices by others. For this reason, it would be wrong to attempt to relate the distinction between dependent and independent price-makers to that between imperfect competition and monopoly, except in some esoteric sense.[5]

The importance of the three categories—price-acceptor, dependent price-maker, and independent price-maker—lies in the difference in price sensitivity that the different types of policy produce. In what follows, the reactions of goods prices to a general drop in demand will be considered under each type of price making. A comparable analysis will then be made for wage rates. Other elements contributing to price insensitivity will then be considered.

The Case of Perfect Competition

If each producer of a particular good could only act as a price-acceptor and had no significant control over price, the adjustment to be expected from a general fall in demand can be shown with the traditional curves of demand and supply. An initial condition of adjustment might be represented by the conventional curves in Figure 6.1, with price OP and quantity of sales OA corresponding to the intersection of the two solid curves. If there were then an increase in the demand for money as a store of buying power, such that it could be satisfied by a 10 percent increase in the real buying power of the outstanding stock of money, and if the relative fall in the demand for goods were *perfectly general,* the demand for each good would fall in such a way that any given quantity would be demanded at 10 percent below the former price. In the case of the good covered above, the new demand schedule could be drawn with prices 10 percent below the initial schedule. If wage rates and other "out-of-pocket" costs fell 10 percent and other prices fell 10 percent, a new supply schedule could be drawn with prices 10 percent below the initial supply schedule. Such new demand and supply schedules are represented by the dotted lines in Figure 6.1. Since both schedules are exactly 10 percent below their former levels, their new intersection is at a price 10 percent below the initial price, but the

Figure 6.1 **Supply and Demand Curves**

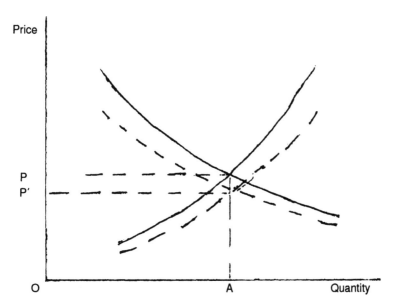

Source: These crude drawings are reproduced from Gardner C. Means' original manuscript.

quantity of sales would remain the same—OA. Thus, regardless of the elasticity of demand or the slope of the supply schedule, the general fall in demand relative to the initial price level and money stock would involve simply a fall in price and no change in production, *provided, of course, that other goods prices and wage rates fell in the same proportion.* What would happen to such a competitive price if other goods prices or wage rates were insensitive will be discussed later. So far as prices made under conditions of price acceptance are concerned, there is nothing to suggest any lack of price sensitivity.

The Case of Independent Price-Making

The same type of analysis can be made for prices set by an independent price-maker, and at first appearance would seem to suggest that such prices should be equally sensitive. In this case, the average cost schedule of the price-maker takes the place of the market supply schedule, and the significant calculation would be made in terms of

Figure 6.2 **[Costs and Revenue]**

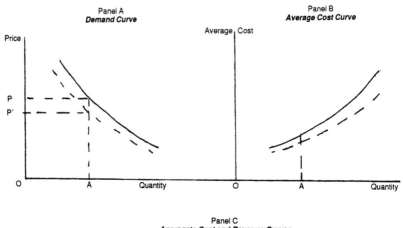

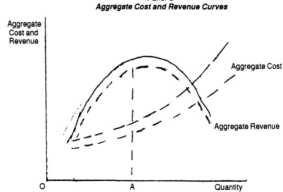

Source: These crude drawings are reproduced from Gardner C. Means' original manuscript.

aggregate revenue and aggregate costs. Let the price-maker believe that the initial schedules of demand and of average costs are those represented by the solid curves in the first two panels of Figure 6.2. The aggregate revenue and the aggregate costs would then be those represented by the solid curves in the third panel. The difference between the two curves would represent the aggregate gross profit (or loss) to be obtained at each possible volume of production. In this case, profit would reach a maximum at a price corresponding to the volume of production OA, and this is the price the independent price-maker is usually presumed to set.

Under these conditions, if the same general drop in demand and costs occurred as in the case of the perfectly competitive good, the maximum profit would be made with the same physical quantity of sales, but at a price 10 percent lower. The demand for a given quantity would be the same as before, at a 10 percent lower price so that the money revenue to be expected for each volume of production (and sales) would be 10 percent lower. Also, if wage rates and other out-of-pocket costs fell 10 percent, the aggregate cost at each volume would be 10 percent less.[6] The new curves of aggregate revenue and cost are represented by the dotted lines in Panel C. Because the two curves have both fallen 10 percent, the point of maximum aggregate profit would still be reached at a price corresponding to the volume OA. As is indicated in the first panel, the new profit-maximizing price would be 10 percent below the initial maximizing price.

Actual Pricing

If prices set by the independent price-makers were *really* made in the fashion indicated above, they could be classed as sensitive, and the buying power adjustment could follow the lines already indicated for a sensitive-price economy, so far as independently made prices are concerned. In such a case, the presence of independently made prices would in no way interfere with the general price and wage drop that could correct a tendency to oversave or an attempt to build up money balances. This would justify Say's law as an equilibrium law for a sensitive-price economy, regardless of whether there was a monopoly of only competition.

But even a very casual examination of industrial prices will show that the independent price-maker seldom makes prices in this fashion. He or she does not adjust prices quickly to short-run changes in demand or costs, but is likely to keep prices constant for considerable periods of time, and when changes are made they are likely to be adjusted only partially to short-run changes in demand or costs. In practice, independently made prices tend to be insensitive.

Causes of Insensitivity

There are three major factors which, in combination, could account for the insensitivity of goods prices set by independent price-makers, apart from any insensitivity of wage rates or other costs: (1) the range of possible prices that will yield essentially the same profit; (2) the uncertainty of demand and costs; and (3) the economic advantages of administered prices. Each of these will be examined separately before their combined effect on price policy is considered.

The Range of Profitable Prices

The price that the independent price-maker would adopt is by no means as rigidly determined as is often suggested in economic writings. In the case of a perfectly competitive price, the curves of supply and demand are presumed to slope in opposite directions, and to intersect at a point such that a price slightly above would involve a surplus in supply that would force the price down, while a slightly lower price would involve a surplus in demand that would force the price up. As a result, the price would be relatively determinate, and any significant departure would create a large pressure toward its own elimination.

In the case of an independently determined price, the reverse is the case. With the demand and costs both given, a very considerable departure from the *most* profitable price could develop without developing any large pressure for price revision. This is due to the fact that in the immediate vicinity of the most profitable price, the curves of aggregate revenue and aggregate costs tend to be roughly parallel. That this must be so can be seen in Figure 6.3, showing the aggregate costs and revenues for different possible volumes of production and sales. If there is a price that will give the maximum profit, this means that the difference between the curve of aggregate revenue and the curve of aggregate costs must reach a maximum at some point as quantity is increased. At this quantity, which corresponds to the most profitable price, the two curves must be exactly parallel to each other.[7] On either side, the curves are likely to be approaching each other only slowly. In the example given above, the price could be 10 percent above or below the maximum-profit price without reducing aggregate profits as much as 3 percent. There would, therefore, be a price range of 20 percent within which there would be less than 3 percent difference in the profits to be expected. In this particular case, the independent price setter would be largely indifferent, *so far as profits are concerned,* just where between 90 and 110 the price might be set.

Just how wide this range of relative indifference might be would, of course, depend on circumstances. In the above example, it has been made fairly wide so as to emphasize the point under discussion. It is, however, difficult to imagine a realistic situation in which there would

Figure 6.3 **Aggregate Costs and Revenues**

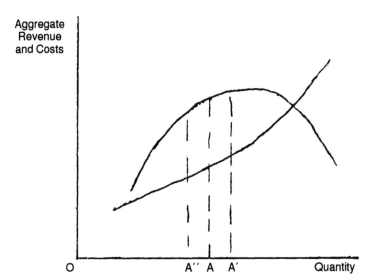

Source: These crude drawings are reproduced from Gardner C. Means' original manuscript.

not be some range. The very fact that volume of sales can be expected to be greater with lower prices means that *if the price were initially at the point of maximum profit,* a fall in prices would not at first greatly reduce *aggregate* profits even though profits *per unit* were significantly reduced. This range of relative indifference might not be important in itself. It might still be worth the while of the producer to set the exact price that would maximize profits, *if he or she knew what that point was* and if there were no cost involved in changing prices.

The Uncertainty of Demand and Costs

Actually, the producer cannot know the point of maximum profits. In the above analysis of independent price-making, curves representing demand and marginal cost were glibly presented, and from them it was easy to see what price would bring the largest aggregate profit, just as in the competitive case the intersection of the curves of supply and demand indicate the price to be expected. This analysis would suggest that the prices in the two cases would be equally determinate. Actually, the two analyses are of quite a different kind. The crossed lines of supply and demand involve data that *nobody needs to know* in order for price to be reached at the point of intersection. Nobody sets the perfectly competitive prices. But, in the case of the price-maker, the curves of demand and marginal cost are not impersonal curves, but rather the subjective curves that the producer must construct in order to determine the price that would maximize profit. The two curves represent, not facts, but forecasts, and as such they are subject to grave uncertainty.

Take the demand for a commodity, say for the coming month. Can the sales that would occur in a single month at different possible prices be forecast with an accuracy of 3 percent, 5 percent, 10 percent? It may be possible to forecast *fairly* accurately the sales that would occur for a standard product, if it has been selling at a constant price and that price is continued. But what of the sales if the price were 5 percent or 10 percent or 20 percent higher—5, 10, or 20 percent lower? And what if the price were being set, not for a single month, but for three months or six months at a time? Even the most refined and reliable market analysis could not provide more than a very approximate demand schedule, and most producers have to rely on very much less reliable estimates of demand.

The range within which actual demand would be likely to lie would be narrower under some conditions than others. For standard products with a relatively stable demand, the range might be relatively narrow, but much wider for less standard and less staple products. It is likely to be narrower in the area of recent prices than for higher or lower prices. It is likely to be narrower for moderately short forecasts than for longer ones. But seldom will the range be so narrow that a single curve can represent the schedule of demand. In the typical case, the demand schedule would have to be drawn thus (Figure 6.4): with OP representing the past price, the outside lines representing the limits within which there is, say, a two-out-of-three chance that actual demand lies, and the center line representing the average chance. Even the future demand at the past price would usually involve a significant range.

A somewhat similar situation would arise with respect to costs. A particular producer may be able to estimate the physical work force and raw materials necessary to produce different volumes of output fairly accurately, but, to estimate the corresponding out-of-pocket costs, forecasts must be made as to what he or she will have to pay for the different raw materials and for labor. The less sensitive these might be, the narrower the range of these estimates of cost, but seldom would

Figure 6.4 **Forecast of Demand**

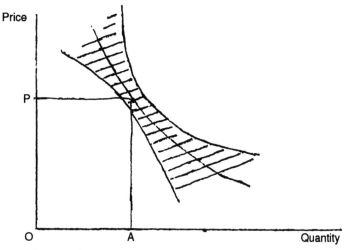

Source: These crude drawings are reproduced from Gardiner C. Means' original manuscript.

there be no range.[8] In the case of most larger producers, the problem of joint costs also contributes in a serious degree to making the costs for a particular product indeterminate. Costs may be more reliably estimated than demand, but here also a considerable range is almost inevitable.

With both demand and costs represented by a range rather than by single lines, the price that will produce the maximum profit becomes more realistically a *price range* within which the most profitable price is likely to lie. As a result, the producer cannot point to a particular price and say, "this will produce the maximum profit." All a producer can do is to say, "Here is a series of prices, any one of which may produce the maximum profit." If no other factors intervened, the producer could be expected to adopt a price somewhere in the middle of the range. However, when this uncertainty is combined with the zone of relative indifference as to price, the *exact* price becomes a matter of less importance than the usual analysis would suggest.

The Economic Advantages of Administered Prices

In considering the price policy of the independent price-maker, it is important to have in mind not only the range within which any price is about equally satisfactory, but also that, once a price has been set, there are very real advantages in not changing it, at least for a considerable period of time. Prices that are perfectly rigid and open to all comers for periods of time—what have elsewhere been referred to as "administered prices"—are so much a matter of everyday life in America that they are taken for granted, and little study has been given to the reasons that lead to their adoption or to the forces that bring about changes in them.[9] Yet they bear little relation to the "higgling and bargaining" of classical economics, or to the streamlined commodity or security markets of the present day. In many parts of the world, administered prices are the unusual, not the usual. Traditionally in cities of Asia Minor it has been necessary to be sure when you started to buy in a store whether the store was doing business on an administered-price basis or on a bargaining basis. In the first type of store, the first price asked was the only price and the customer could take it or leave it. In the second type, by far the most frequent, the first price asked was more likely to be double, or even triple the price at which the item could finally be bought. Stores of the first type, though increasingly numerous, were so infrequent that they were apt to advertise "Fixed Prices," "Continental Prices," or "American Prices" to indicate the price basis on which they operated. In the absence of such signs, they were presumed to operate on the basis of bargained prices.

To anyone who has attempted to make purchases in an Oriental bazaar, the economic efficiency of administered prices is obvious. Both the buyer and the seller save time. And because no bargaining ability is needed by the seller, it is possible to delegate the actual selling to a much greater extent to persons of limited skill. The efficiency of the modern department store would be simply impossible if the price of each sale necessitated a bargaining process between the sales person and the customer. Mail-order selling would be practically impossible. The great bulk of retail distribution in the United States is carried on through administered prices.

Similar efficiencies result from the use of administered prices in industry. The producer of standard products who is in a position to adopt either an administered-price or a bargained-price system of selling will almost invariably adopt the former because of its time-saving and skill-saving character.[10] He or she may have different prices for different categories of customers or for different quantities of products. But for each category there will be a single price. Bargaining may develop over unusually large quantities or over off-standard lots, but the great bulk of standard manufactures are sold on the basis of administered prices. This one-price system is as essential to modern mass production and distribution as are modern machines and the corporate form of doing business.[11]

The Stability of Administered Prices

Once the administered-price system of selling has been adopted by a particular business, there are very real advantages in not changing a price after it has been set. These advantages are numerous and likely to vary more or less from situation to situation.

A change in price may involve significant costs. Thus, a mail-order house issuing comprehensive catalogues only once every six months cannot easily change the bulk of its prices at shorter intervals. It can publish special catalogues from time to time covering a few items, but the expense of this for a larger number of items is almost prohibitive. In the field of manufacturing, the "trade" has to be notified of a change in established prices; new printed matter may have to be prepared, and other costs, minor in themselves, help to provide a barrier to price change.

More important is the disorganizing effect both of an expectation of price change and of an actual price change. Once an administered price has been established, if a belief arises "in the trade" that a price reduction is due, there may be a serious postponement of buying in order to take advantage of the subsequent lower price. Similarly, an expectation of a subsequent price rise may lead to excessive stocking up. To minimize the effects of this, the price must be either highly sensitive or changed very infrequently. When an established price is changed, comparable difficulties arise. If dealers have stocked up at the old price and the price is reduced, either they will be forced to take a loss and the producer will lose some of their good will, or the producer will have to make an adjustment. To a lesser extent, a rise in price could cause friction with dealers who had not stocked up. In the automobile industry, such price-change difficulties are minimized by the annual-model technique, which tends both to eliminate inventory speculation and to keep inventories to a minimum at the time of the price change. But it does this by a device that makes price change *within* the model year unlikely, except under the greatest pressure.

Another important reason for not changing a price once set has to do directly with short-run changes in demand or costs. It is well recognized that in many industries more ill will is engendered *by an upward* revision of an administered price than good will by an equivalent downward revision. Therefore, a change in demand or in cost that is thought to be temporary or cyclical may lead to a constant price, rather than a reduction with an expectation of a subsequent return to the initial level.[12] This alone would be sufficient in many cases to prevent a price adjustment until long after the change in demand or costs would have justified a price change, if current profits alone were considered. This reason for not changing a price applies, however, only to changes in demand or cost that are believed to be transitory.[13] A technological change reducing costs would allow a price reduction without any expectation of a subsequent price rise. Similarly, a change in demand that was believed to be permanent would not involve the net cost of an equal movement up and then down, or the reverse.

Other impediments to a change in an established price could be cited. Sheer inertia, the administrative effort involved in making the decision to set a new price, particularly in a big corporate enterprise, and other impediments, each minor in itself, combine with those already mentioned to place a barrier to the change in a price, once it has been established. There are thus real advantages not only in the adoption of administered prices, but in keeping them constant for very considerable periods of time.

The Effect of a General Drop in Demand

When the advantages of a constant price and the "range of indifference," within which the price can lie with approximately the same expectation of profit are both taken into account, it is at once apparent why an independent price-maker is likely to keep prices constant in spite of a considerable fall in general demand. This can be brought out most clearly by assuming at the outset that there is no ambiguity as to the schedule of demand or the schedule of costs.

Let the solid lines in Figure 6.5 represent the aggregate revenue and the aggregate costs of producing and selling different amounts of an independent price-maker's product under the initial conditions of demand and costs.[14] The price corresponding to the quantity OA would then maximize his or her aggregate profits. If revenue and costs for

Figure 6.5 **Aggregate Revenues and Cost**

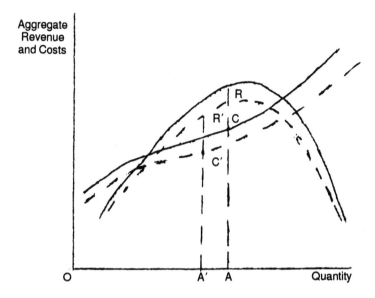

Source: These crude drawings are reproduced from Gardner C. Means' original manuscript.

each quantity were then reduced by 10 percent as a result of a general fall in demand, the new revenue and cost schedules would be represented by the dotted lines and the new point of maximum profit would be the *new* price corresponding to the quantity OA, a price 10 percent below the initial price. On the other hand, if he or she stuck to the initial price, the quantity would fall to the amount represented by OA′ in the specific example, some 12 percent below the initial quantity. However, his or her aggregate profits, though less than before the change in demand and costs, would be almost the same whether he or she cut the price by 10 percent or stuck to the initial price. These profits, the difference between aggregate revenue and costs, are represented by the distance RC for the 10 percent price reduction and the distance R′C′ at the initial price. The latter, in this particular case, is only 5 percent less than the former. If the producer thought the drop in demand would last only a year and the advantages of no change had a greater value than 5 percent of his or her expected profits, the producer would not reduce the price *at all.* In this particular case, a drop in expected revenue and cost of 10 percent for each level of production and sales, would not lead to a price reduction if the advantages of avoiding a price change outweighed the 5 percent reduction in current profits over what they would be if the appropriate price reduction were made.

When the uncertainty as to what price would maximize profits is added in this situation, the likelihood of a price reduction with a given drop in demand and costs is further reduced. The independent price-maker never *knows* that the reduction in price would increase profits. It may be that initially he or she had the price too low to obtain the maximum profits and that, after the 10 percent fall in demand and costs, the initial price becomes the price to yield maximum profits. This possibility is not wholly outweighed by the reverse possibility that his or her initial price was itself too high. The uncertainty that he or she would increase profits by lowering the price, combined with the advantages of no change and the relatively small addition to profits, even if his or her estimates of revenue and cost were reliable, would tend to discourage a price reduction. The typical independent price-maker could be expected to let sleeping dogs lie, unless very considerably greater profits could be expected from a price reduction. For this reason, administered prices set by individual producers who do not have to consider the counteractions of parallel producers to their price action are not likely to be lowered as a result of temporary reductions in demand or costs. And since, with the exception of technical changes that alter costs and seasonal changes, the producer cannot easily distinguish between a temporary and a continuing reduction in demand or costs, he or she is likely to meet any general drop in demand without changing prices until the reduction in demand shows clear signs of being permanent or of considerable duration.

The Magnitude of Price Change

Even when the independent price-maker is finally driven to make a price change, it is unlikely that he or she will reduce the price in proportion to the reduction in demand and costs for the product when he or she believes there is an important chance that it is a general drop in demand that will be reversed. On the basis of historical experience, the producer knows that a general depression is likely to pass, so that the general decline in demand and costs is likely to be followed by an increase in demand and costs. This means that any reduction in price is

Figure 6.6 **Behavior of a Typical Independently Determined Price in Depression and Recovery**

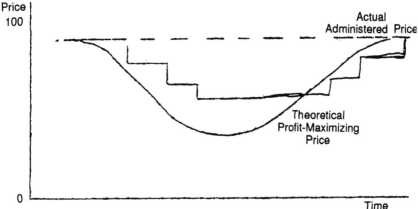

Source: These crude drawings are reproduced from Gardiner C. Means' original manuscript.

likely to have to be reversed.[15] He or she is, therefore, under pressure to keep the reduction to a minimum. If the initial price was in the middle of the initial range of indifference, then, when demand and costs had declined sufficiently to induce him or her to change the price, the price-maker would not drop it to the *middle* of the new range of indifference, but only toward its upper end, with the likelihood that it would be closer to the upper limit, the greater the temporary fall in demand and costs. If a 10 percent drop in demand and costs were sufficient to induce the independent producer to reduce prices, so long as he or she believed the depression to be temporary, prices might be reduced by only, say, 5 percent. This might be sufficient to eliminate *all* the pressure on the individual to reduce his or her price, except as demand and costs dropped still further. Even though he or she reduced the price, the individual would not reduce it in *proportion* to the reduction in demand and costs. In the presence of a general fall and recovery in demand, the price, instead of paralleling that of market prices as the more abstract analysis of profit-maximizing price would suggest, could be expected to diverge in the manner suggested in Figure 6.6.

There are two characteristics of this price behavior that deserve to be emphasized. First, the analysis so far applies only to the price policy of a producer able to set or change prices without having to take account of the possible counteraction that parallel producers might take—the price policy of an independent price-maker. Second, it has been assumed that the prices of his or her raw materials, wage rates, and other costs fall exactly in proportion to the fall in the demand for the individual's product. This would be a reasonable assumption if all other goods prices, wage rates, and other costs were perfectly sensitive. But, if some of the producer's costs were insensitive, a more realistic assumption, this would contribute to the insensitivity of his or her price. What has been important in the analysis is that the insensitivity of the individual's price does not *depend* on the insensitivity of any element in his or her costs. The important conclusion is that, regardless of whether the individual's costs are sensitive or not, the price administered by an independent price-maker in an otherwise free market is likely to be insensitive to a general change in demand, both in terms of frequency and in terms of magnitude of price change.

Dependent Price-Making

The third type of price-making remains to be considered, that of the dependent price-maker. In a great many industries prices are administered, but subject to such a degree of competition that each price-maker has to take into his or her calculations the counteraction on prices that competitors are likely to take. We cannot here go into the details of the semi-competitive process by which prices are likely to be determined in such circumstances. It will be sufficient for present purposes to consider two separate cases, one in which competitive conditions are such that all producers are likely to adjust their prices so as to maintain identical prices, and a second in which, because of minor differences in product, geographical differences, differences in the size of competitors, or some other factors, differences in price among the different producers are likely to survive for considerable periods.

Dependent Identical Price-Making

Under certain circumstances, several dependent price-makers, acting without collusion, could be expected to arrive at identical prices. This would be the case, for example, if there were only three producers making a given product and they were located in the same place and were of equal size, and if their output were perfectly interchangeable, so far as consumers are concerned. Each would know that if his or her price were above that of the others he or she would make few, if any, sales, whereas if it were below that of the others, both of the others

Figure 6.7 **[Profit Maximization]**

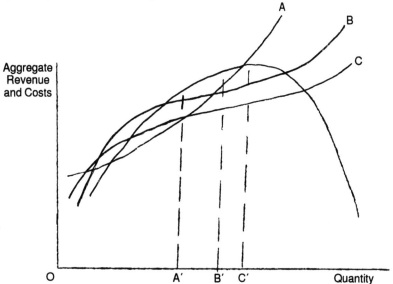

Source: These crude drawings are reproduced from Gardner C. Means' original manuscript.

would then have to come down to his or her level. Each producer could then go about solving the problem of price policy on the assumption that each will finally set the same price and that, whatever price is finally arrived at, the total market would be divided up between them in a fairly determinate proportion.[16] As a first step, an individual could treat his or her *share* of the market as if it were fixed, and estimate the price that would maximize profits. If each producer did this, it is likely that each would come out with a different figure for the "best price." Then, if each producer *knew* exactly what price would maximize profits and if there were no disadvantage in changing a price, once set, it could be expected that all these producers would come to the price set by the producer with the lowest profit-maximizing price. The situation is suggested in Figure 6.7.

The single domed-shaped curve would represent the revenue expected by each producer, assuming that each could expect to obtain just a third of the total. The curves A, B, and C represent the aggregate out-of-pocket costs for the three firms. In this case, the maximum profits for producer A would be obtained if the price for all three producers were set at the level corresponding to the quantity of sales for each producer of OA'. The maximum for B would be reached at the price corresponding to the quantity OB', and that for C at the price corresponding to OC'. If each producer knew his or her own maximizing price *and there were no impediments to price change,* the actual price set would likely be that corresponding to a quantity of sales for each of OC'. If a price were set below that level, all three would gain by revising their prices upward. If a price were set above that level, C would set a lower price, and the other producers would have to follow suit or accept less than a third of the total market.

In this case, a general drop in demand that reduced the prospective receipts at each possible volume of sales by 10 percent, and reduced costs by 10 percent, would leave the *quantity* at which each would maximize profits unchanged, but this quantity would correspond to a price 10 percent below the former level. In this case, if the dependently set price were perfectly sensitive to changes in demand or costs, the forces which would lead to the setting of the price at one level, with a given condition of demand and costs, would lead to a proportionately lower price if demand and costs dropped together.

The same general conclusion is indicated in the case where each producer is a dependent price-maker, but there is room for some price difference between them. If price were perfectly sensitive, then, whatever the pattern of prices reached in the industry with one level of demand and costs, if demand and out-of-pocket costs both fell 10 percent, the same forces could be expected to result in the same relative pattern of prices, but with each price 10 percent lower. Thus, according to sensitive-price theory, dependently made prices and perfectly competitive prices would tend to fall in proportion to any fall in general demand. The classical conception of a *general* fall in the price–wage level would thus make sense, if all categories of price were perfectly sensitive.[17]

In practice, however, dependently set prices are subject to the same pressures that tend to make independently set prices insensitive. For each producer, there is likely to be a range of prices within which the individual's aggregate profits would be substantially the same. And, instead of clearly defined curves of demand and cost, each producer must base his or her policy on more or less crude estimates. These two conditions combine to produce a range of indifference for each producer within which any price is about equally satisfactory, so far as aggregate profits are concerned. Also, there are the various advantages experienced by an independent price-maker in keeping to a price, once it has been established. If these were the only factors involved, it might be expected that dependently set prices would be as insensitive as independently set prices to short-run changes in demand and costs, with the range of indifference of the producer with the lowest range playing much the same role as that of the independent price-maker.

There is one important difference, however, for in the case of the dependent price-maker there is the possibility and danger of price wars. One producer may seek to enlarge his or her share in the total market by reducing prices below or further below that of other producers. They, in turn, may cut their prices to meet that producer's price, and he or she may cut again. Such a price war may seriously cut into the profits of all the producers in the industry, and is likely to be dreaded by most. If demand and costs both decline seriously, this is likely to engender price wars, and the price-cutter may be castigated as a "price chiseler." On the other hand, the fear of starting a price war may prevent downward revision of price to a somewhat lower level that would be more profitable to one or more producers. The net effect of the possibility and danger of price wars is probably to make some prices more sensitive and to make other prices less sensitive, depending on the particular conditions. In no case, however, is it likely to make prices as sensitive as prices made in the market are likely to be, though in the throes of a price war they may fall below the level that would be reached in a fully competitive industry with equal costs. This analysis would, therefore, lead one to expect that identical dependently made prices would be more or less insensitive to short-run changes in demand or in costs.[18]

Dependent Differentiated Price-Making

In other cases of dependent price-making, different competing producers may be able to set different prices for practically the same product, and yet each may have to consider carefully the effect of a price change which he or she might make on the price policy of his or her competitors. In such cases, the individual producer usually has some margin within which prices can be changed without producing a price reaction from his or her competitors. Perhaps a 5 percent change would not result in a price change by others, but a 10 percent change would result in a change of about the same magnitude by others. Thus, within limits, the individual producer could be expected to act like an independent price-maker, and beyond these limits like a dependent identical price-maker. This is a condition that seems likely to occur very frequently. Perhaps it is typical of a large part of modern industry. This mixed situation, like the simpler forms of price-making, can be expected to result in administered prices that are insensitive in the short run.

Long-Run Price Policy

There is one other factor that appears to contribute importantly to the insensitivity of prices where competition is imperfect. In the preceding analysis, it has been assumed that each producer would seek, so far as possible, to set a price that would maximize profits in the current period. But often this would not be "good business" from the longer-run point of view. Too high profits in the current period might induce new producers to come into the field and so reduce future profits. Too high profits might focus public attention, and lead to bad public relations and the possibility of antitrust action. For these and other reasons, it may be good business policy to set prices in good times lower than would bring in maximum current profits.

This "margin" would provide some slack, which would be taken up if prices were kept constant while a fall in demand and costs reduced the price that would maximize profits. A serious decline in demand would greatly reduce the danger of new producers coming into the field, while the smaller volume even at the initial price would mean less aggregate profits and so less danger from public reaction. Since the reasons for maintaining the price below the maximizing price would be dissipated by a general fall in demand and costs, there would be no pressure on the price-maker to reduce prices until the demand and costs had fallen so far as to bring the price that maximizes current profits below it. Thus, any difference between the "most profitable price" and the price that is regarded as "good business" acts as a buffer, which tends to make for less price sensitivity.

Rule-of-Thumb Pricing

There is one other type of price-making which needs to be considered. In a great many cases, prices are made on some rule-of-thumb basis, rather than on any nice calculation of the price likely to produce the maximum profit. Sometimes this has the effect of keeping prices as sensitive as raw material costs. For example, a retailer who administers prices on the basis of a standard percentage mark-up for different types of goods actually keeps his retail prices approximately as sensitive as the prices he or she pays. A 10 percent drop in the prices the retailer pays would shortly result in a 10 percent drop in his or her own retail prices. Thus, the retailer's prices would tend to be as sensitive as and no more sensitive than the prices he or she pays at wholesale. On the other hand, if the latter remained constant, and sales fell off, the retailer would not reduce prices unless he or she became overstocked and had to resort to clearance sales or similar special action to liquefy the inventory.

On the other hand, a manufacturer who set prices on the basis of costs, plus a standard percentage, and included depreciation in unit costs, would be introducing an item that would tend to make his or her prices insensitive to a general change in demand and in out-of-pocket costs. This would arise from the fact that depreciation costs are usually based on past prices, not current prices. They are, therefore, unaffected by a change in current prices. If the depreciation charge were a fixed amount *per unit of output,* regardless of the quantity produced or sold, then it would be an element of cost that was insensitive to changes in demand or in other costs. If a given amount of depreciation were spread over whatever quantity of goods it was expected would be produced or sold in a period, then, as sales and production fell, the cost per unit from this source would increase; thus, in part, offsetting reduction in operating costs. When this cost or other overhead costs are divided according to the volume that it is expected to produce or sell, the *total* costs per unit may even rise with a fall in volume in spite of a fall in all operating costs. Thus, where prices are set on a basis of total unit costs, plus a "reasonable" markup, a general fall in demand and in prices is not likely to provide as much pressure to reduce prices as if the prices were set in the market as the result of competition by price-acceptors, or set with the explicit purpose of maximizing current profits. Indeed, it may lead to no pressure for reduction, or even to some pressure for a price increase, if overhead costs constitute a large proportion of total costs.

Perhaps other factors contribute to price insensitivity. This analysis does not aim to be exhaustive. Its main purpose has been to show that in free markets, but in the absence of perfect competition, there are good reasons to expect that goods prices would be insensitive to short-run changes in demand and costs, even though demand and out-of-pocket costs fluctuated together; that this condition is likely to arise wherever competition is imperfect; and that it does not depend on the existence of monopoly.

Regulated Prices

The preceding analysis has been concerned only with price-making in a free market. It is obvious that regulated prices tend to be insensitive. The difficulties of changing a regulated price, once it has been set, are well known and stand in the way of quick adjustments. Railroad and public utility rates cannot be in a constant state of flux. Even more important, however, is the fact that when changes are made as a result of short-run changes in demand, they may be in the wrong direction or of only minor importance under the present semi-judicial technique of regulating prices. Under the technique of regulation that measures the reasonableness of a price by whether or not it will yield a "fair return on fair value," any fall in volume, due to a fall in demand, is likely to call for a higher, rather than a lower, price. This occurs for two major reasons. First, in measuring costs for this purpose, depreciation and other overhead charges are included in costs, so that, just as in the case of a cost-plus formula, any reduction in volume would spread the overhead costs over a smaller number of units, and increase the total unit costs, even though the out-of-pocket costs per unit remained the same. Second, when a given net return is to be realized from given property, a reduction in volume means that a higher net profit per unit must be realized to earn the "fair return." Under existing law, both of these are used to justify higher prices or rates when volume falls. To some extent, this may be offset by lower raw material costs and lower wage rates. But even if these fell in proportion to the fall in demand, the "fair" price or rate would not fall in proportion, and might even rise. Thus, regulated prices and rates tend to be insensitive, both in terms of magnitude of price change and in terms of frequency, so far as short-run changes in demand are concerned.

Collusive Prices

Where prices are set by collusive action, there is also reason to expect that prices will not be fully sensitive to changes in demand and cost conditions. Theoretically, it might be argued, as in the case of indepen-

dent price-making, that with a decline in demand and costs, the collusive price-makers would revise their prices downward in proportion.
But the difficulties of collusive pricing and price revision would be
added to the factors making independently made prices insensitive, and
thus tend to make collusive prices even more insensitive, while the
pressure to break away from a collusively set price would tend to work
in the opposite direction. It is likely that collusive prices would on the
whole be insensitive, but whether more or less sensitive than independently made prices would depend on circumstances.

The foregoing analysis has shown why prices tend to be insensitive
where competition is imperfect. It has been made clear that this insensitivity is not an outgrowth of monopoly. It could be expected to occur
in a competitive industry where there is sufficient differentiation in the
products of the separate producers to allow each to be an independent
price-maker. It could be expected where competition is active, but, as
in the automobile industry, there are not *and cannot be* a large enough
number of producers to force each producer into the position of a
price-acceptor with prices made in the market. If all industries were as
competitive as the automobile or steel industry, it could be expected
that prices would be insensitive. Monopoly, collusion, and regulation
undoubtedly add to the insensitivity of prices. *But so long as the bulk
of modern industry cannot be perfectly competitive, insensitive prices
would appear to be an inherent part of the modern economy, regardless of the extent of monopoly, collusion, and regulation.*

The Question of Lag

One further matter needs to be taken up before going on to the question
of insensitive wage rates. This is the question of whether or not the
insensitivity of prices is just a matter of short-run lag, and would tend
to be corrected by time. The answer would seem to be that, for many
of the same reasons that prices can be expected to be insensitive, they
are no more likely to adjust fully over a longer period of time than over
a shorter period. While, to a small extent, price insensitivity can be
regarded as a matter of delayed reaction, and be designated a matter of
lag, in the main it is not a matter of lag.

This can be seen easily in the case of the independent price-maker.
If there is a general fall in demand and in costs, which would theoretically call for a 10 percent cut in prices, it might induce the individual

to make that size cut. If he or she were customarily setting prices once every six months, and the fall in demand and costs took place in the middle of a period, the producer would be likely to hold the price change until the end of the period. In that case, the insensitivity of price would be simply a matter of lag. But it is much more likely that the producer's response to the 10 percent reduction in demand[19] and costs would be, say, a 5 percent reduction in price, and this would not be likely to be made until the end of his or her pricing period. In this case, the insensitivity would clearly be in part a matter of lag, that is, a delay before the adjustment was made. But the adjustment itself, when finally made, would be only partial.

The question therefore arises, if there were no *further* change in demand and in costs, would the producer be likely to reduce prices further and finally reach the full 10 percent reduction? At the end of the next price period, would he or she be likely to make another price reduction? So far as maximizing one's own profits are concerned, there is little reason to expect a further price reduction. If the producer's initial price was just right to maximize his or her profits at the initial demand, the individual is likely to want to keep prices on the high side of the "perfect" profit-maximizing price when demand in his or her own industry, or in all industry, is what he or she regards as abnormally low. By doing that, the producer will have to raise prices less when recovery comes, and the possible extra profits from a greater price reduction are not likely to be very significant. No matter how long the depression lasts, so long as recovery is "right around the corner," there will be no reason to make a cut in price below that which he or she made at the end of the first period, so long as demand and costs drop no further and the producer continues to hold his or her relative share of the market.

There is one theoretical possibility, however, namely, that a failure to reduce prices to the full extent indicated by the fall in demand and costs will lead some newcomer into the field. At first thought, this looks likely. The failure to reduce prices to the full 10 percent means an abnormal profit margin *per unit*. But this opportunity for new enterprise is more apparent than real. The fact that demand has fallen off and the individual's price has not fallen in accordance means that production falls with a resulting "overcapacity" for the industry. When the facilities in an industry are being only partially used, it is not the time to create additional capacity, unless some fairly revolutionary improvement in technique has become available.[20] Also, even though the profit margin per unit may be somewhat greater, the extra margin would be likely to disappear if additional competition were to develop in an over-capacity industry. Therefore, the larger profit margin is likely to be only a very mild and questionable inducement to newcomers, while the over-capacity is likely to be a serious deterrent. Indeed, there is likely to be more inducement to newcomers when demand is high than when demand is reduced. Therefore, except in the case of new technical developments, when demand drops there is not likely to be any more pressure to reduce prices from the possibility of the entrance of newcomers than from other demand and cost considerations. No matter how long the depressed demand continued, there would be no reason to expect the full 10 percent price drop.

This would be even more true if the price was initially set below the maximum-profit level, in order to prevent new entrance to the industry, or to prevent governmental action. If demand fell off, this would not be likely to bring any reduction in price unless the fall was very considerable. The lower demand would tend to reduce aggregate profits at the initial price and, therefore, reduce both the danger of newcomers and the danger of governmental action. Up to the point where the drop in demand was so great that the profit-maximizing price was significantly below the initial price, a drop in demand would not be likely to produce a drop in price, no matter how long the reduced demand continued.

The same would be true if the price were set on a cost-plus basis, with overhead costs playing an important role in total costs. The increased overhead costs per unit would continue so long as the lower volume of business was done, and simple continuation of the depressed demand would not alter the cost-plus calculus. It would reflect any reduction in operating costs per unit, due to lower raw material prices, wage rates, and so on, more or less offset by higher overhead costs per unit, but once these had been adjusted for, time alone would not call for further adjustments.

The problem is somewhat different in the case of dependent price-making. Here, most of the factors making for the continued insensitivity of independently made prices would be operating, but one factor, the likelihood of price wars, would work in the opposite direction. Where prices were dependently made, the longer a depression in demand continued and the greater the overcapacity in the industry, the more likely a price war would occur, which could lead to a general downward revision of prices in the industry. This would be a definite case of lag. But even with a price war, after prices had again come to adjustment, they are not likely to have made the full adjustment called for by the fall in demand and costs. The producer with the lowest "most profitable price" would not want to reduce prices in proportion to the reduction in demand and costs for the same reason that the independent price-maker would not want to do so. Therefore, while the price might temporarily be forced way down by a price war, price stability would be likely to be reestablished at a price above that indicated by the fall in demand and costs. Thus, in the case of dependent price-making, some price adjustment is likely to be a matter of a lag, but no continuance of the reduced demand and prices is likely to give complete adjustment.

Examination of other reasons for price insensitivity will disclose some reasons for attributing a part of the insensitivity to lag. But to an important extent, perhaps to a greater extent, it will be found necessary to ascribe it to other factors than lag, and to conclude that in large part it involves a lack of price adjustment, which will not be automatically corrected even though ample time were given for a full adjustment to be made.

Insensitive Wage Rates

So far, it has been assumed that wage rates were sufficiently sensitive so that they fell in proportion to a general fall in demand. In practice, however, wage rates are also likely to be insensitive to short-run changes in demand, quite as much as goods prices that are set under conditions of less than perfect competition. Indeed, the market for labor is almost invariably an imperfectly competitive market. In the absence of union organization, there are likely to be only a few "buyers" of labor in any particular locality for any particular type of skill, and the particular producers are able to set their wage rates either independently or in the light of the counteraction that other producers drawing from the same labor market may take. In the presence of labor unions, wage rates are likely to be the product of bargaining between producers and representatives of labor, with the resulting rates obligatory for a year or more at a time. In neither case are wage rates made in a competitive market, however much competition for jobs or workers may affect the rates set or agreed upon. Both cases need to be examined.

Producer-Administered Wage Rates

Before 1932, there was very little labor organization in the mass-production industries of the United States, and the bulk of wage and salary rates were set by the individual producer and changed from time to time in the light of such factors as the needs for labor, the wage rates being paid by others, the prices the individual could get for his or her product, and the available work force and skills. Whether the resulting wage rates were fair need not concern us here. What is important is whether or not wage rates determined in this fashion could be expected to be sensitive to short-run changes in demand. If a general drop in demand for goods occurred, could producers be expected to reduce their wage rates?

The answer to this question appears to turn very largely on whether or not the producer is able to control the prices of products. If the producer's prices are "made in the market," they will fall with the fall in demand. The producer is likely, in turn, to cut wage rates roughly in the same proportion. If some of the individual's other costs are insensitive, he or she may cut wage rates even more. On the other hand, if the producer does not reduce prices, but accepts the decline in demand in the form of a reduction in quantity of sales, he or she will have to reduce the working force, or employ it part time, and is, therefore, less likely to cut the wage rate as far as if he or she were selling the product in a perfectly competitive market.

There are two major reasons that contribute to this likelihood: first, the necessity of holding together the working force and, second, the relatively small proportion of total costs that are likely to be represented by labor. If a manufacturer cuts his or her labor force by 20 or 30 percent, this is almost certain to reduce the morale of the remainder. If, in addition, the manufacturer also cuts the wage rates of the latter, the reduction in wage costs may be bought at a heavy cost of further loss in morale and inefficient work. If, instead of reducing the working force, the manufacturer puts it on part-time, this cuts their earnings correspondingly, and a simultaneous cut in wage rates could again be an expensive form of cost reduction. In either case, a cut in wage rates without a cut in the price of the product would be hard to explain. Indeed, the producer might determine his or her price and wage policy as a single problem, planning to keep both prices and wage rates constant, or reducing both in somewhat the same proportion. Whether or not the manufacturer does this, he or she is not likely to cut wage rates as much if prices are reduced a little than if he or she is forced to reduce prices a great deal.

Such a decision on wage rates would be reinforced if labor made up only a small part of the producer's particular costs. For a producer who buys partly fabricated parts and completes their fabrication, labor may constitute as little as 10 percent of his total costs. For such a producer, a 50 percent cut in his or her wage rates would only reduce costs by 5 percent. Similarly, for a producer who buys raw material and only adds a little to its value in fabrication, a big cut in wage rates may reduce costs only a little. The disruption of production, resulting from a big cut in wage rates, might cost many times the saving in wage payments.

There are undoubtedly many other factors contributing to make wage rates relatively insensitive where they are set by producers whose product is sold under conditions of imperfect competition. Inertia, fear of disturbance, social considerations, and similar factors are likely to play a part. The exact factors leading to the insensitivity of producer-administered wage rates are not so important as the fact that there are good reasons why such wage rates tend to be insensitive.

Collectively Bargained Wage Rates

Wage rates that are arrived at by collective bargaining between representatives of labor and management are usually agreed on for a year or more at a time, and to that extent are rigid. Some measure of sensitivity may be introduced through a clause that adjusts wage rates within the period of agreement to changes in living costs. And if the change in economic conditions is sufficiently great, a collective agreement without such a clause may be renegotiated. But, in either case, the adjustment takes place only after a significant change in prices and living costs has occurred. In the bulk of cases, wage rates set by collective bargaining are rigid for the duration of the wage agreement.

When each particular wage agreement expires, the sensitivity of the adjustment in rates is likely to depend partly on the bargaining relations between labor and management and partly on the character of the industry. In situations like that of the construction industry in some communities where labor organization is strong and the separate producers or contractors are weak, a labor union may administer the rates much as management administers the rates in an unorganized industry.

In such a case, the rates are likely to be relatively insensitive to a general drop in demand, for much the same reasons that management-administered wage rates are likely to be insensitive. A union knows that in ordinary circumstances it iṣ easier for a union to accept a reduction in wage rates than to bring about an increase, so that it will hesitate to cut its rates when the fall in demand is regarded as temporary.[21] Even a very considerable fall in goods prices and living costs might occur with no reduction of wage rates in these circumstances. On the other hand, strong unions may revise their wage rates downward under the pressure to maintain jobs, as was the case with the clothing and coal industries in the recent depression.

Where the bargaining position of labor in an industry is weak as compared with that of management, the resulting collectively bargained wage rates could be expected to follow somewhat the same pattern as wage rates administered by management: fairly sensitive in some circumstances, fairly insensitive in others, but with this major difference, that within the period covered by a negotiated agreement, the rates would tend to be fixed.

In cases where the bargaining position of labor and management was about equally strong, there would also tend to be considerable insensitivity in wage rates, but again the degree would depend on circumstances. In a highly concentrated industry like steel, both labor and management would tend to accept insensitive wage rates, so that a general fall in demand would not result in a corresponding fall in rates. In a less concentrated industry, competitive pressures might be such that wage rates were somewhat more sensitive. But, in both cases, rates would tend on the whole to be insensitive to a general fall in demand that was regarded as temporary. One can, therefore, conclude that whether wage rates are administered by management, by labor, or collectively bargained, they are likely to be insensitive to a general decline in demand. For present purposes, the degree of insensitivity is of secondary importance. Nor does the above analysis attempt to be exhaustive of the factors making for insensitivity of wage rates. It is sufficient to have shown that there are reasons why wage rates, as well as goods prices, could be expected to be relatively insensitive to general changes in demand.

As in the case of goods prices, the insensitivity of wage rates can be regarded as only in part a matter of lag. Where there are union contracts, wage adjustments may be delayed by the contractual terms.

Where unemployment has continued over a longer time, there is more willingness on the part of workers to accept wage reductions and more pressure on employers to force a reduction. To this extent, insensitivity is a matter of lag. But where prices are made under conditions of imperfect competition and do not fall in proportion to demand and other costs, it is unlikely that wage rates will be reduced completely in proportion to the fall in general demand, regardless of whether they are administered by the employers or result from collective bargaining, and regardless of the length of time the unemployment continues. While specific exceptions are likely to arise, in the main it is not in the interests of either the specific employer or the specific union to force a complete reduction in wage rates in the absence of a more or less corresponding cut in the prices of the industry's products.

Other Insensitive Factors

In our actual economy, there are many other factors entering into production costs that make for insensitivity: for example, royalty rates set at a specified amount per unit; fixed rentals; certain types of taxes; and open contracts for the delivery of varying quantities of goods at agreed-upon prices. All such factors contribute to the insensitivity of prices, but need not be considered here in detail since the other causes of the insensitivity of prices and wage rates are so much more important.

The Diffusion of Insensitivity

So far, we have been considering price insensitivity primarily in terms of specific situations in an otherwise sensitive economy. In the case of goods, we have considered the price policies that would be adopted under various conditions of competition, if demand and costs both fell in the same proportion. In the case of wage rates, we have considered policies that would be adopted with a general fall in demand. And we have concluded that in each case insensitivity is likely to occur, regardless of sensitivity in other parts of the economy. But the insensitivity of goods prices is likely to be passed on into other prices and into wage rates, while the insensitivity of wage rates is likely to be passed on into goods prices.

The passing on of insensitivity in goods prices is obvious. If the price of a raw material is insensitive, products made from it are likely to be to some degree insensitive, because of the insensitivity of this element in their cost. If transportation rates are insensitive, nearly every product will have an element of insensitiveness. A given drop in the demand for apples will, for example, produce a greater proportionate drop in the price of apples as they leave the farm than the apples sold at wholesale in the distant city. The absolute drop in price may be the same, but the insensitive cost of transportation makes the proportionate drop different. Throughout the economic system, the insensitivity of some goods prices can thus be diffused to other goods prices.

The insensitivity of goods prices could also be expected to make wage rates less sensitive. If a general drop in demand did not lead to a proportionate drop in goods prices, wage policies would be made in the presence of a cost of living that did not fall in proportion to the general drop in demand. Both administered wage rates and collectively bargained rates would, therefore, be likely to be reduced less than if the cost of living fell in proportion to the fall in demand.

Finally, insensitivity of wage rates is likely to make goods prices insensitive by providing an additional insensitive element in costs. Thus, insensitivity can be expected to diffuse to a greater or lesser extent through the economy, whatever its source.

One cannot say how much the actual insensitiveness of goods prices and wage rates *initially* comes from a tendency of one or the other to be insensitive. Either *could* be the initiating factor, but actually they both result from essentially the same set of circumstances—the impossibility of perfect competition for either goods or labor in the bulk of modern industry. The two forms of insensitivity go together and reinforce each other. On the whole, where goods prices are most sensitive, it can be expected that wage rates will also be more sensitive and vice versa. But neither should be regarded as entirely the cause of the other.

The Varying Degrees of Insensitivity

It would also be reasonable to expect that goods prices would range in practice all the way from highly sensitive to highly insensitive. This would be due partly to the varying degrees of competition involved, ranging all the way from perfect competition to monopoly and regulation. It would also be due to the varying proportions in which sensitive and insensitive elements enter into costs. Wage rates also could be expected to vary in sensitivity, but since most types of labor are both fairly competitive and far from perfectly competitive, it can be expected that the range would be narrower.

Conclusion

The preceding theoretical analysis has indicated how unreasonable it is to apply the classical assumption of perfectly sensitive prices and wage rates to an economy in which competition is imperfect, and prices and wage rates are not set by purely market forces. This provides the first basic assumption underlying the monetary theory of employment— namely, *the assumption that the modern economy is, on the whole, an insensitive price economy in which prices and wage rates range all the way from highly sensitive to highly insensitive.*

Notes

1. Of course, the producer could presumably sell at less than the current price, but this possibility can be disregarded.

2. In technical terms, it may be said that a producer in the above situation faces a demand curve for his or her particular product so nearly horizontal within the range of the capacity to produce or supply, that, in deciding how much to produce or sell, the individual can entirely disregard the effect on price of his or her producing or selling more or less.

3. The particular producer would thus face a demand curve for his or her product that sloped down to the right to a significant degree within the range of the individual's capacity to produce.

4. Obviously, any seller is the *only* seller of the exact physical thing he or she is selling. Monopoly cannot be used in this sense, since it would then cover perfect competition.

5. If the term monopoly is so applied, practically every manufacturer and distributor is a monopolist, at least with respect to some part of his or her product.

6. Depreciation and similar non-out-of-pocket costs are not included, since in operating an *existing* plant, the operator is traditionally presumed to seek to maximize the difference between revenue and differential costs. That this rational objective is often obscured by modern accounting techniques does not invalidate this point.

7. More exactly, the tangents to the two curves must be parallel.

8. For short periods, a producer could, of course, protect him- or herself by having raw materials on hand or making forward contracts, but this is not done in a great many cases. Even if this is done, cost uncertainty due to joint costs would remain, as well as uncertainty with respect to demand.

9. It is notable that the traditional economic analysis takes *no* account of administered prices. The analysis is always made in terms of prices that are sensitive in the sense used throughout the text.

10. There are other possible pricing systems where competition is not perfect—for example, the auction, or the use of a price arbiter—but the fixed price and the bargained price are the two dominant forms so far as goods are concerned.

11. It should be noted that a buyer may adopt an administered-price system quite as well as a seller. A canner, for example, may set a buying price at which it will take all of the peaches of a specified grade that may be offered. But in the modern economy, such buyer-set administered prices are, on the whole, of secondary importance. The reverse is the case with respect to wage rates, as will presently be indicated.

12. The same can also occur in the case of short supply. A striking example is that of cranberries in a year of cranberry crop failure. The cooperative cranberry marketing association had advertised cranberries extensively and thus expanded their market. With a short crop, a much higher price could have been obtained in the particular year. Instead, in order to retain the good will they had established, the price was kept down and the whole crop sold to consumers in a few months. Thereafter, consumers found that "the season was over." The association believed that the smaller loss of good will, due to the inability to obtain cranberries in later months as compared with the loss if prices had been high enough to spread the stock through the year, more than compensated for the smaller profits in the particular year.

13. There are, however, certain special types of temporary change in demand that lead to a temporary price adjustment. An outstanding example is the seasonal revision of anthracite coal prices. These prices are of an administered character and are fairly insensitive when measured on an annual basis. But the demand for anthracite coal is so highly seasonal that prices are regularly reduced in the off season.

14. The curves of demand and marginal cost underlying the chart are those given in Panels A and B of Figure 6.2.

15. Exceptions to this occur in industries having *very* rapid technical improvement. The rayon industry from 1929 on is an example. The price of rayon dropped as much as sensitive farm prices from 1929 to 1932, but remained relatively stable in the recovery period.

16. It should be noted that, with each producer setting the same price, there can still be competition between them as each producer seeks to increase his or her share in the market by advertising, sales pressure, efforts to differentiate his or her product, and similar measures. This, of course, would not be price competition.

17. It should be noted that this conclusion implies that prices are sensitive when they adjust quickly to changes in demand or cost according to the dictates of demand and supply or demand and costs, and to the degree necessary to maximize profits in so far as the individual firm is able to control price.

18. The above analysis is made in terms of an equal change in demand and costs, and no effort has been made to show that the conclusion applies equally if demand alone or costs alone change, or if they change in different degrees. A little consideration, however, will show that it does apply.

19. Not a 10 percent reduction in volume at each possible price, but a 10 percent drop in price necessary to support each possible volume of sales.

20. As, for example, the improved rayon production, the continuous strip rolling mills, and methods for making paper pulp from Southern Pine, which were available during the early 1930s.

21. Sometimes an element of sensitivity arises when a union keeps the nominal wage rates rigid but, under stress of unemployment, unofficially condones the payment of less than union rates.

7

Aggregate Demand and Insensitive Prices

Once the assumption of price insensitivity is introduced into the analysis of general economic adjustments, it must be clear that a fall or rise in aggregate demand cannot be expected to cause a *general* change in the price level. Rather, a fall in aggregate demand that would produce a general price fall in a sensitive-price economy would, in an insensitive-price economy, produce very uneven results, with sensitive prices falling a great deal and insensitive prices falling less or not at all. The question arises, therefore, whether, in an insensitive-price economy, a fall in aggregate demand would lead to unemployment and if so whether price and wage adjustments could be expected to operate so as to reduce or eliminate unemployment as they could be expected to do in a sensitive-price economy. Could "a glut of commodities or dearth of money" be corrected through price adjustments? Would the only condition of equilibrium be one of optimum employment?

The price and production adjustments to be expected from a change in aggregate demand are much more complex in an insensitive-price economy than those to be expected in a sensitive-price economy. For this reason, it will be convenient to take up several simple situations and then combine them in such a way as to approximate the complexity of our actual economy. First, consideration will be given to what would happen if there were a drop in aggregate demand in an economy in which some prices were perfectly rigid and others perfectly sensitive; then, to the adjustment in an economy of intermediately sensitive prices; and finally, to the adjustment in an economy of all types of sensitivity and insensitivity.

In each case an initial condition of optimum employment and price balance will be assumed. This is taken to mean that practically every person able and desirous of working is employed except for a certain float of workers. This also means that the condition of optimum employment has existed for a long enough period so that prices have come into at least a rough and ready relationship to costs, so that in the absence of a change in aggregate demand there would not be significant price changes except as costs changed. This implies that with the initial prices and wage rates and the initial real stock of money, there is sufficient aggregate demand in the economy as a whole to keep the available workers fully employed.[1]

In considering the adjustment that could be expected, it is important to keep in mind the difference between the effect of price changes on demand in a specific industry and on demand for the total economy. When the price of a single commodity falls *and all other prices remain the same,* the demand for the particular commodity can be expected to increase. Demand will be shifted away from other commodities to it. Whether or not the net effect is an increase in the total demand for commodities is uncertain, depending on the particular circumstances. But when large numbers of prices fall together, the demand for each commodity cannot increase *at the expense of the demand for the others.* Prices and money income go down together without any direct effect on total demand. The net increase in demand arising from the fall in prices is brought about through an increase in the real stock of money that becomes redundant. It is this redundancy of money that stimulates a net addition to the *total* demand.

Adjustment with Sensitive and Rigid Prices

The first case to be considered can be simplified by assuming that half the prices in an economy are perfectly sensitive and the other half are perfect rigid, at least during the period of adjustment—a week, a month, a year. At first it will also be assumed that no rigid-priced goods enter into the cost of production of sensitive-price goods or vice versa. In such an economy, what effect could be expected from a drop in aggregate demand and would price and wage adjustments tend to eliminate any resulting unemployment?

The first effect of a drop in aggregate demand in such an economy would presumably be to force down wage rates and prices in the sensitive-price industries and reduce sales, production, and employment in the rigid-price industries. The fall in sensitive prices and wage rates could be expected to have two simultaneous effects. First, the lower prices in the sensitive-price industries relative to the fixed prices would tend to shift purchases from the latter to the former so that, with the real buying power of incomes unchanged,[2] physical sales, production, and employment in the sensitive-price industries would go up while those in the rigid-price industries would go down still further, with no significant effect on the fall in total employment. Second, the lower sensitive prices would increase the real value of the stock of money, and this would tend to make money redundant at the current level of income so that as far as this influence is concerned, the demand for both sensitive- and rigid-price goods would increase. This increase would presumably continue until the resulting increase in employment and real income was so great that money was no longer redundant. The net effect of these changes would be to reduce the fall in employment over what could have been expected directly from the fall in aggregate demand. The fall in sensitive prices would somewhat increase the real value of the stock of money and thus somewhat reduce the drop in aggregate demand. This would increase employment in the sensitive-price industries over the initial level, but leave a net reduction in employment in the rigid price industries.

At first thought, it might seem as though the fall in sensitive prices would go on until optimum employment was restored. However, if there were no significant shifting of workers from industry to industry, *maximum* employment in the sensitive-price industries would soon be reached and all further pressure downward on the sensitive prices would cease. Price equilibrium would thus be reached with the unemployment in the fixed-price industries not greatly affected, and with a great unbalance in the relation between sensitive and rigid prices.

Theoretically, an ultimate recovery in employment might be reached if the unemployed workers and capital in the rigid-price industries were to shift over to the sensitive-price industries, thereby forcing sensitive wage rates and prices down still further with a resultant increase in total demand and employment, but with a greater unbalance in price relationships. Actually, resources are not very mobile and the pressure to shift might not be great. Workers engaged in the industries with insensitive prices might be obtaining as high a total income from high wage-rates and part-time as workers in the sensitive-price industries with a full work week and low wage rates. This undoubtedly accounts in part for the relatively small movement of workers from industry to agriculture in the early 1930s. Similarly, capital in the high-price industries would be making much larger *unit* profits than the low-price industries, even though their volume of sales were small. As a result, the shift of resources would be very slow and might never be complete.

Assuming that the mobility of labor and capital is in part a function of time, one can conclude that, with prices partly sensitive and partly rigid and with an initial reduction in aggregate demand, an initial equilibrium could be reached at less than optimum employment, but that, as time progressed, the equilibrium would tend to be reached at successively lower levels of sensitive prices and higher levels of employment. If the adjustment period were sufficiently long and new influences did not intervene—as they surely would—a new equilibrium at optimum employment but unbalanced prices might ultimately be reached. But, in the meantime, unemployment would prevail with no quick-acting forces making for its elimination, and in the end resources would be insufficiently used in the rigid-price industries because prices were high in relation to sensitive prices.

The Effect of Rigid Prices as Costs

In the preceding analysis, it has been assumed that no rigid-price goods enter into the cost of production of sensitive-price goods or vice versa. If sensitive-price goods were included in the costs of production of rigid-price goods, it would not affect the above analysis significantly. But if rigid prices entered as costs in the production of sensitive-price goods, they would give an added influence preventing a quick adjustment toward optimum employment.

If, for example, railroad freight rates were perfectly rigid within the period of adjustment and constituted a significant element of costs in the production or distribution of each sensitive-price good as it reached the consumer or investor, equilibrium at less than optimum employment would be possible even though resources were perfectly mobile. If the initial price to the ultimate consumer of a sensitive-price good were $1.00 and this involved, say, 20 cents worth of freight haulage, its delivered price would not be likely to fall much below the 20 cent freight cost, no matter how much the demand for it might fall or however much other of its costs of production might fall. As the demand for it fell, its price would tend to become rigid as it approached 20 cents. However small the amount of the rigid costs involved in any sensitive-price good, its price would tend to become increasingly rigid as this amount was approached. As a result, in an economy with some rigid costs in the production of every good, prices would tend to become increasingly rigid as sensitive prices declined. At some point it would become a rigid-price economy, and all price adjustments tending to reduce unemployment would cease. Long before this point was reached, the insensitive element in costs would operate to slow up the adjustment. Thus, where some prices were sensitive and others rigid, insensitive costs would combine with immobility of resources to prevent a full correction of unemployment and make possible price equilibrium at less than optimum employment.

Adjustment with Intermediately Sensitive Prices

While in practice there are many prices, such as railroad and utility rates, which are perfectly rigid so far as short-run adjustments are concerned and many prices, such as those of most agricultural staples, which are highly sensitive, the great bulk of prices fall between these two extremes of sensitivity. A crucial question for the adjustment to a fall in aggregate demand in an insensitive-price economy is, therefore, what would happen if all prices were intermediately sensitive and there was a fall in aggregate demand? Would prices and wage rates adjust to the extent necessary to prevent or eliminate unemployment?

A first step toward answering this question can be taken by answering it for a greatly simplified economy. Assume an economy in which all prices are set by independent price-makers, and once set are regularly revised only once every three months; in which wage rates are set by producers and revised at the same time as their prices; and which the times of revision for different goods and wage rates are spread out so that not more than, say, 10 percent of the items are revised in any one week. In such a situation, what adjustments could be expected if there was a fall in aggregate demand?

The initial effect of a drop in aggregate demand under these conditions would be unemployment, just as in the case of an economy operated partly on sensitive prices and partly on rigid prices. Indeed, for those commodities whose price-revision date had not yet come, prices would be temporarily rigid. But after the initial period the two cases would differ, and the actual results to be expected would depend on special circumstances.

In Theory

Under one set of conditions, it could be expected that the unemployment resulting from the temporarily rigid prices would not long remain. If labor were the only cost involved in the production of each good, and if at each possible level of wage rates and total income there were a single price that would clearly maximize profits of each producer, then the pressure of the unemployed on wage rates and the efforts of producers to maximize profits could be expected to bring down the wage and price level fairly quickly, and increase employment so that the only condition of price equilibrium would be that of full employment. This can be seen by considering the policy problem faced by each producer as the time for price revision approached.

The first producer to revise prices after the fall in aggregate demand occurred would presumably be in a position to pay lower wage rates and still get all the workers required, but there would probably be a limit to the amount he or she would cut wage rates, at any one time, say, one-fifth. Assuming the producer's price was in adjustment with the demand for his or her product which existed before the general drop in demand, and that the drop in demand did not alter the producer's optimum price so long as wage rates remained at their initial level, a reduction of one-fifth in wage rates and therefore in costs would reduce the price for his or her product that would be expected to maximize the producer's profit.[3] This can be seen in Figure 7.1, assuming a one-fifth cut in wage rates.

With the same curve representing the aggregate revenue that the producer could expect at each possible price, and a one-fifth lower aggregate cost for each possible volume of output, the maximum aggregate profit would occur at a somewhat greater volume (B instead of A in Figure 7.1) and a somewhat lower price P' instead of P). The same kind of calculus would lead each producer to cut wage rates and prices.

Figure 7.1 **[Prices, Costs, and Revenues]**

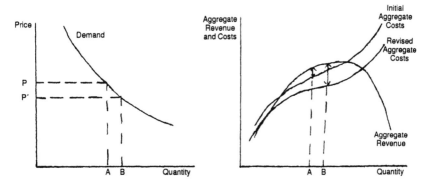

Source: These crude drawings are reproduced from Gardiner C. Means' original manuscript.

At first thought, it would seem as though the cuts in prices to gain an increase in volume would result directly in an increase in employment. However, the reduction of wage rates and prices would again mean a reduction in money income for any given volume of production. While the first producer to reduce prices might temporarily increase sales at the expense of other producers, as the latter reduced their wage rates and prices and total income fell, the demand for each product would fall insofar as the demand derived from income. At the end of the three-month cycle in which all producers had had an opportunity to cut their wage rates and prices, prices would be lower: but so also would be incomes, and it is problematic whether any significant increase in employment would have occurred directly from the lowering of prices and wage rates.

However, the fall in prices and wage rates would tend to make the money supply redundant, and this would create an additional demand that would increase both employment and income at the lower level of wage rates and prices. As long as unemployment provided further pressure downward on wage rates, the fall in the price–wage level could be expected to continue. As a result, a price–wage equilibrium would not be reached until unemployment had been virtually eliminated. Under the conditions outlined above, this might take more than one three-month cycle of price revisions, but should progress fairly rapidly and would not depend on the mobility of resources. Thus, under these assumed conditions, a fairly rapid automatic elimination of general unemployment would be theoretically possible with intermediately sensitive prices.

In Practice

It should be noted, however, that the above set of conditions are practically those of a perfectly sensitive price system. In an actual insensitive price economy, there are three conditions, any one of which would seriously postpone any such adjustment. First, most goods require other goods as raw material, so that labor is not the only cost. Second, the independent price-maker is not likely to reduce prices as much as is suggested above. And third, the administrative setting or collective bargaining of wage rates would prevent any such quick adjustment of wage rates. Each of these conditions is an essential part of modern industry, and any one of them alone would tend to spread the adjustment over an indefinite, perhaps an infinite, period.

The adjustment in the case where some goods enter into the costs of others involves a problem akin to that of infinite regression. The first producers to adjust prices would find costs other than labor fixed, since other producers had not yet adjusted their wage rates and prices to the new employment situation. They would presumably reduce part of their costs by reducing wage rates, and this would reduce somewhat the prices at which their maximum profits could be expected. But their reduction in prices would be definitely limited by costs that involved fixed prices. This same condition would apply to most other producers as they came to revise their prices for the first time. However, the second time prices were revised, each producer would find the prices of raw materials somewhat reduced, and this reduction in costs plus a further reduction in wage rates would call for a further reduction in prices. The adjustment in this case would tend to be very much slower than if labor were the only cost, and might continue in a more or less indefinite series as each producer adjusted prices to the price reductions made by his or her material and service suppliers during the preceding three months.[4] Whether the complete adjustment might be reached short of infinity is not important, but it is important that the process of adjustment would be greatly slowed up in its initial periods by the much slower fall in prices, so that a quick absorption of the bulk of the unemployed would not be likely.

Even more important in slowing up the adjustment would be the fact that insensitive prices, when revised, are not likely to be cut to the full extent indicated by the fall in costs or demand. As has already been pointed out, the zone of relative indifference and the uncertainty as to the most profitable price combine to make the price adjustment, when it comes, only a partial one. The price-maker would drop prices only to the top of the range of most profitable prices. As a result, the process of price adjustment would be slower. The indefinite regression would be longer.

Finally, if wage rates were set on a basis of collective bargaining with contracts covering a year at a time, a further cause of delay in adjustment would occur. Even if wage contracts allowed for adjustment as a result of changes in living costs, they would serve to slow up the adjustment process. To some extent, this would also be true if wage rates were administered by producers with an eye to long-run productive efficiency as well as maximum current profit.

These three factors—the importance to the individual producer of costs other than labor, the indeterminacy of *the* most profitable price, and the wage stabilizing effect of collective bargaining or wage administration—all contribute to slow up the adjustments to unemployment that could be expected if all prices were made by independent price-makers. The net result points to the same conclusion that was reached in the case of a fall in aggregate demand in an economy of sensitive and rigid prices, namely, that an initial equilibrium could be reached only at less than optimum employment but that as time progressed, the equilibrium would tend to be reached at successively lower levels of prices and higher levels of employment. And that if the adjustment period were sufficiently long and new influences did not intervene—as they surely would—a new equilibrium at optimum employment might ultimately be reached. However, in the meantime, unemployment would prevail, with no quick-acting forces making for its elimination.

Adjustment in an Insensitive-Price Economy

In actual practice, there are many other types of price or wage insensitivity besides those two discussed above. It will be found on examination that most if not all types help to postpone and to distort the economic adjustment that would result from an initial condition of general unemployment. However, it is not necessary to go into detail on each to present a generalized picture of the adjustment to a drop in aggregate demand, if all the various types of insensitivity existed and if prices ranged all the way from highly sensitive to highly insensitive with a corresponding range for wage rates.

Figure 7.2 **Price Adjustment to a Drop in Aggregate Demand** (Items ordered according to increased degree of price sensitivity)

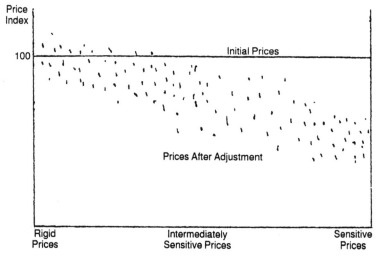

Source: These crude drawings are reproduced from Gardiner C. Means' original manuscript.

If there were a drop in aggregate demand in such a realistic economy, it could be expected that wage rates and prices would fall in the sensitive-price industries, that whether wage rates dropped or not in the rigid-price industries, prices would not drop, and that, in the intermediately sensitive industries, prices and wage rates would drop to an intermediate degree. Such a general shift in the price structure can be shown by the solid line and the scatter of dots in Figure 7.2, which represents the initial and the short-run equilibrium prices for different goods that are arranged from left to right according to increasing price sensitivity.

Items with highly sensitive prices, those at the right of the figure, would fall very considerably. The rigid prices represented at the left of the chart would not fall at all. Prices with varying degrees of intermediate sensitivity would fall in different degrees, as indicated in the center of the figure. In a very real sense, the price structure would rotate about the rigid prices. Of course, all prices of a given degree of sensitivity would not fall in exactly the same proportion because of the different characteristics of the demand and costs for different products. But the general character of the price rotation should be clear.

The effect of the fall in aggregate demand on employment would also vary more or less according to the degree of price sensitivity. At

Figure 7.3 **Employment Adjustment to a Drop in Aggregate Demand** (Items ordered according to increasing degree of price sensitivity)

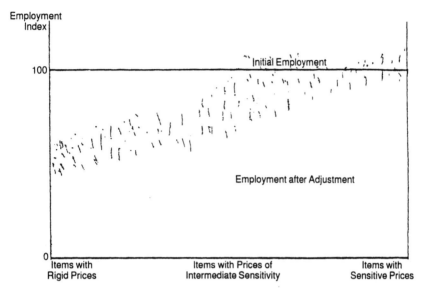

Source: These crude drawings are reproduced from Gardiner C. Means' original manuscript.

the sensitive end of the price scale, there would be no general reason to expect unemployment.[5] Demand for such products would be maintained, partly from a fall in prices that shifted demand from the items with less sensitive prices that had fallen little, to the more sensitive items which had fallen a great deal, and partly from the general increase in demand arising from the increase in the real buying power of the outstanding stock of money.

At the insensitive end of the price scale, the fall in aggregate demand could be expected to reduce sales, production, and employment. This effect would be somewhat mitigated by the stimulus to aggregate demand from the increased buying power of the stock of money resulting from lower sensitive prices. But it would also be aggravated by the shift in demand to the items whose prices had fallen. Which of these latter effects would dominate would depend very largely on the particular demand characteristics of the particular items. The aggregate effect on a representative group of insensitive-price items would probably be no very significant departure from the fall in sales, production, and employment arising from the initial drop in demand.

For intermediate items, it could be expected that the adjustment would be partly through a drop in price and partly through a drop in production and employment. For this central group, the loss in demand to the items with more sensitive prices would be offset to a greater or lesser degree by the gain in demand at the expense of the insensitive items. With a perfect offset, the increase in demand arising from the increased real value of money would provide the only net offset to the initial drop in demand. The closer the prices were to the insensitive end of the price scale, the more potent would be the loss of demand to more sensitive items. The overall effect on employment is suggested in Figure 7.3, which is similar in construction to the price chart except that the solid line represents the index of employment in the production of items of different degrees of sensitivity, and the dots represent the employment for each item after the adjustment to reduced aggregate demand has occurred.

Here again there is a rotation. But this time it is downward rotation of employment around that in the most sensitive-priced items.

In this adjustment, the decline in aggregate demand can be expected to produce a downward rotation of prices around insensitive prices, and a downward rotation in employment around that of items with the most sensitive prices. And this price and production adjustment could be expected to take place quite rapidly until employment at the sensitive end of the price scale had absorbed the workers available for producing such items. This could mean a significant reduction in general unemployment but not its elimination. So long as the unemployed were not so mobile that they could shift from industries with insensitive prices to those with sensitive prices—say, from amusements to agriculture—unemployment would continue at the insensitive end of the price scale. Thus, so far as any short-run equilibrium is concerned, it would be reached with complete recovery of employment at the sensitive end of the price scale, a partial recovery at the middle of the scale, and little reduction at the insensitive end. The result would be an equilibrium at less than optimum employment with no tendency for the unemployment to be eliminated except as workers and capital shifted to the more sensitive-priced industries. And since both the mobility of labor between high-wage part-time jobs and full-time low-wage jobs and the mobility of capital between high unit profit-small volume and low unit profit-high volume industries is likely to be low, there is no reason to expect a recovery of employment even over a very considerable period of time. And even if such a shift of resources did take place, it would be under a very unbalanced price structure.

Insensitive Prices and the Classical Theory of Employment

When the classical theory of employment is considered in the light of the preceding analysis, it must be clear that it cannot apply to an insensitive-price economy. A "glut of commodities or a dearth of money" cannot be wholly corrected by a fall in the price-wage level and the resultant increase in the real stock of money. A partial correction can be brought about through a fall in the more sensitive prices and wage rates. But the increase in the real buying power of the outstanding stock of money would be brought to an end so far as the short-run adjustment is concerned, when prices had fallen in the more sensitive-price industries to a point consistent with optimum employment in those industries. This would leave unemployment in the less sensitive-price industries, and there would be no quick-acting forces making for an increase in employment. The classical conclusion that equilibrium would be reached only at optimum employment would thus not apply to an insensitive-price economy.[6]

It is important to notice the significant departure from the classical assumption that accounts for equilibrium at less than optimum employment. It is not the Keynesian assumption that the rate of interest "is the price which equilibrates the desire to hold wealth in the form of cash with the available quantity of cash." We have already seen that this explanation of unemployment does not stand up in a sensitive-price economy. Rather it is the assumption of insensitive prices that leads to the possibility of equilibrium at less than optimum employment. It is this assumption that is the crucial departure from the classical assumptions. And it is this assumption that provides the basis for the monetary theory of employment outlined in this book.

The Effect of an Increase in Aggregate Demand

While the preceding analysis has been concerned with the effect of a fall in aggregate demand, it could be applied equally well, up to a point, to a rise in aggregate demand. Such a rise could be expected to increase sensitive prices; increase employment in providing items with insensitive prices; and increase both prices and employment to an intermediate degree for items whose prices are neither highly sensitive nor highly insensitive.

There is, however, one important exception to this general expectation. There is a limit to the volume of employment that is possible. As aggregate demand increases, this limit is approached and it seems reasonable to expect that, to an increasing extent, the adjustment to high demand will be in the form of price increases even for less sensitive price items. Whether insensitive prices are likely to become sensitive to increased demand before optimum employment is reached, or whether a considerable overemployment might be reached before insensitive prices became sensitive under the pressure of added demand is a matter of great importance for full employment policy and will be discussed in part V of this book. It is sufficient here to indicate this exception to the general proposition that an expansion in aggregate demand will tend to increase more sensitive prices and increase employment for less sensitive-priced items.

Conclusion

The preceding chapter has spelled out the first basic assumption underlying the monetary theory of employment, namely the assumption of an insensitive-price economy. This chapter has outlined the first main segment of the theory—that in an insensitive-price economy, a rise or fall in aggregate demand could, in general, be expected to work itself out partly in changes in sensitive prices, partly in changes in employment for insensitive priced items, and partly through a compound price and employment movement for intermediately sensitive items. This might be called an "Insensitive-Price Theory of Economic Adjustment."

Notes

1. For purposes of simplicity, changes in the labor force and in technology are excluded from immediate consideration.

2. If the same physical volume were produced the fall in sensitive prices would bring down money incomes, but because sensitive prices were lower the smaller money incomes could, in the aggregate, buy just the same physical volume of goods.

3. The assumption that the fall in demand had no effect on the optimum price

so long as costs remained the same, is, of course, an unlikely one, but is adopted to simplify the analysis. The limited character of this assumption has no effect on the actual analysis, however, since the fall in price–wage level would reestablish *real* demand at approximately its initial level, though at lower prices so that the optimum price after the adjustment would be at the same point on the real demand schedule.

4. Theoretically, the regression series could be infinite since some items are costs of each other—for example, steel as a cost of machinery to make steel.

5. There are, of course, exceptions to this. Employment could be expected to fall, for example, in an industry whose product was used only jointly with some other product whose price was rigid and dominated the cost to the user of the two products.

6. Ultimately, optimum employment might be reached if capital and workers shifted into the more sensitive-priced industries, but then the other basic branch of classical theory pointing to a tendency of prices to adjust so as to direct resources into the optimum uses would not hold.

Part III

A Monetary Theory of Aggregate Demand

8

The Demand for Money

In part II it has been shown that, on the assumption of an insensitive price economy, it could be expected that changes in aggregate demand would produce changes in employment as well as changes in prices and wage rates. This theoretical conclusion would hold true whatever the source of changes in aggregate demand. Part III will be concerned with the determinants of aggregate demand and will construct what might be called a "Monetary Theory of Aggregate Demand." A first step toward such a theory is an examination of the demand for money.

What Is Meant by the Demand for Money

There are several meanings that might be attached to the term "the demand for money," but there are only two that need to be considered here. The term might be used to refer to the demand for money *in exchange for other things*. Or it might be used to refer to the demand for money *as a store of buying power*.

The first meaning is employed when Mill says, "The demand for money consists of all the goods offered for sale."[1] Whether "goods" should be expanded to include securities, life insurance, and so on, is a matter of the particular problem in hand. The essential character of this usage is that the demand for money is made to turn on the offering of something in exchange for money. It can be referred to as "the demand for money in exchange."

The second meaning—the demand for money as a store of buying power—is employed when mention is made of the demand for cash balances. How much money does an individual, or an enterprise, or the community as a whole find it convenient, or expedient, or desirable to hold at a particular time? In this book, we are concerned with the demand for money only in this second sense. This will be the meaning implied when the term is used. To remind the reader that this is the meaning implied, the phrase will sometimes be expanded to read "the demand for money as a store of buying power."

Characteristics of the Demand for Money

The demand for money as a store of buying power should be one of the most basic concepts in economic literature. Yet, it has often been neglected in theoretical discussions and, until recently, little effort has been made to measure the demand statistically. In the traditional literature, the concept of the demand for money in exchange was often introduced as an alternative way of speaking of the aggregate offering of goods. But prior to the appearance of the saving–investment theory, the whole matter of the demand for money as a store of buying power was apt to be discussed simply in terms of the need for money to carry on transactions and the hoarding of money.

It is sometimes suggested that money renders satisfaction only through the things that it can buy and that, therefore, the demand for money can only be discussed in terms of these purchases. But actually, money that is not spent can render its owner a service. It carries over the owner's power to buy from one transaction or one period to another and holds it in a highly liquid form. It would be as wrong to say that money rendered its possessor no service except when spent as to say that a fire insurance policy brought no service unless the house burned down. It is true that the value of fire insurance derives from the things that can be bought with the insurance money if the home burns down. But even if there is no fire, the insurance has reduced the risks of the owner and given him a feeling of greater financial security. Few house owners will say that their insurance payments were wasted because their houses failed to catch fire. In somewhat the same way, money on hand can give its owner a feeling of financial security and flexibility even though it is not spent. In any period in which it is not spent, it renders a service simply as a liquid store of buying power. In this sense, the demand for money is not a demand for the things money can buy. It is simply a demand for a liquid asset.

For this reason, it is just as appropriate to discuss the demand for cash balances as it is to discuss, say, the demand for inventories. The businessperson usually has to have some inventories in order to do business. He or she also usually has to have some cash on hand, at least to make change. A larger than the minimum possible inventory is desirable because it helps to reduce bottlenecking, gives customers a larger choice, allows the filling of orders with a minimum of delay, and in other ways helps the conduct of the business. In a similar way, a large cash balance helps the conduct of the business. It is a protection against getting caught short if receipts don't live up to expectations, gives suppliers of raw material, credit, and so forth, a sense of the firm's stability, allows unexpected opportunities to be seized, and generally gives the management of the firm a sense of security and flexibility since they are not having to pay too much attention to a close matching of the flow of money into and out of the enterprise.

But just as too large inventories can be a waste of capital funds, so too large cash balances can be a waste of capital funds. Except when speculating in inventories, a firm is not likely to increase its inventory to the point where there is *no* operating advantage in having more inventory. Investment in inventory must "pay its way" just like other investment. The most economical inventory is likely to be smaller than that which is most convenient physically. Some risk of bottleneck or delay or lost sale is better than too much inventory. Similarly, cash balances can be too high for the most economical use of capital. Such large cash holdings that the management *never* has to concern itself with balancing the flow of money in and out of the enterprise, never has to sell securities or borrow to finance some unexpected opportunity would usually be uneconomical. Both with inventory and with money holdings, the management has to balance off the different opportunities to use its resources.

A similar conclusion seems justified with respect to the money holdings of individuals. There are advantages in having a large cash balance—less danger of running short or overdrawing on account, readiness to take advantage of unexpected opportunities or meet unexpected obligations, prestige in the community from having large balances, a general feeling of flexibility, and similar considerations. On the other hand, the individual with access to the security markets or other investment opportunities is not likely to hold such large cash balances that *all* the advantages of being liquid are realized. The advantages of a return on investment will compete with the advantages of greater liquidity. Thus, both in the case of the enterprise and that of the individual, it seems reasonable to assume that money balances as such render a very real service as buying power quite apart from that which is rendered by the things they buy; and that, in most if not all cases, lack of resources prevents this service from being pushed to satiety.

It is also important to notice that money is always performing this service of a store of buying power, regardless of how long or short a time it is held. A distinction is sometimes drawn between "money in circulation" or "needed in business transactions" and money that is "hoarded." Such a distinction would seem to have no *real* significance. The trader who receives money from a sale and spends it five minutes later, is using that money as a store of buying power during those five minutes, just as much as the miser who buries a pot of money before a hearth. In both cases and for all the cases intermediate between these extremes, the possessor of money is using money while he or she possesses it as a store of buying power. Whether the money is held for five minutes or five days or five years, it is hoarded and out of circulation for that period.[2] The basic question of this chapter is, therefore, what factors determine the demand for money as a more or less temporary store of buying power.

Major Determinants of the Demand for Money

Probably the two most basic determinants of an individual's demand for money are assets and income.

In the case of assets, it seems reasonable to suppose that a representative group of wealthy individuals are likely to hold more money on hand than a comparable group with little wealth but the same level of income. The greater wealth gives more elbow room. It provides a basis for satisfying to a greater degree both the desire for liquidity and the desire for other assets. Money is not the only store of value. It has to share the storage function with stocks and bonds, real estate, loans, productive equipment, and other types of assets. But it seems likely that with other factors given, the greater the wealth to be stored, the larger the amount of money that will represent the optimum balance between money holdings and other types of assets.[3] It is not suggested that the same *proportion* of total assets would be kept in the form of money, but only that the absolute amount would tend to be greater. Presumably, the proportion would depend on other factors.

In the case of income, also, it seems reasonable to suppose that a representative group with large incomes are likely to hold more money than a comparable group with smaller incomes but an equal amount of assets. The larger money holdings would arise partly from the almost mechanical effects of a larger money income. If the recipient of a large income were to dispose of this income either in consumption or in the acquisition of other types of asset just as fast as an individual with a small income, his or her *average* money holdings would have to be larger since the amount to be disposed of was larger. In addition, the person with more income, like the person with more assets, would have more elbow room. Satisfying his or her desire for liquidity to a greater extent would likely be one of the ways in which the individual enjoyed this greater income.[4]

In practice, the decisions that determine the amount of money an individual holds may be considered in quite different terms. As a rule, a person's actual money balance is the net resultant of a series of decisions that are usually couched in terms of whatever is being given or received in exchange for money. Will the person take on additional work? Sell some asset? Buy more of this or that? Except where these decisions just offset each other, their net effect is to increase or deplete the individual's money balance. From time to time, a person may have occasion to consider a particular expenditure in relation to its effects on his or her money balance. In contemplating the purchase of an auto, an individual may have to decide between a serious depletion of his or her money holdings, the disposal of some other asset, borrowing to finance the purchase, or a combination of all three. The person is likely to choose the second or third if the first would reduce his or her money holdings to an inconvenient point. More generally, if an individual has the necessary leeway, he or she is likely to control the rate of current expenditure and holdings of earning assets in the light of money holdings, curtailing expenditures or converting earning assets into money if his or her balance gets too low, and either increasing expenditures or transferring the money into some earning asset when the level gets too high.

At the lowest levels of income and assets, money holdings are likely to be almost a mechanical function of income. Current income or credit must support the individual from one pay period to the next. Not much, if any, money can be carried over. And the exigencies of living do not usually allow much room for significant accumulation of money.

When income and assets are higher, the individual has the problem of determining the desirable range within which to keep the money balance in the light of assets and income. In practice, a person is likely to arrive at the general magnitude of the money balance that seems appropriate in the light of his or her income and assets. The actual money balance would then tend to fluctuate around this magnitude as a result of day-to-day activities and decisions, most of which are not made with specific attention on their effect on an individual's money holdings.

The general magnitude that a person adopts as his or her general level of money holdings would presumably represent a balance between several factors. It would reflect the balance between more income and less income-producing effort. It would reflect the balance between holding more assets in each of the other possible forms in which savings can be stored. In perfect balance, the individual would have so arranged matters that there would be no gain in spending more or spending less on consumption, or in making a net shift of any part of his or her money balance into other types of assets or converting other assets into money.[5]

Of course, such a balance is not likely to be achieved by an individual, but for a representative group of individuals such a balance may be fairly closely approximated. The unexpected development that leads one individual to hold more money than best fits his or her requirements is likely to be more or less matched by an unexpected development that leads another person to hold less. For a large enough group, such special influences would tend to offset each other, and something like a continuous balance might be maintained between aggregates of assets, incomes, and money holdings.

Likewise, in the case of business enterprises, a rough balance is likely to be kept between assets, income, and money holdings. A group of companies with a given volume of assets, but doing more business than another group with the same volume of assets, is likely to hold larger money balances. So also companies doing the same volume of business but having a larger volume of assets are likely to hold larger money balances. Thus, for the community as a whole, business and nonbusiness together, it seems reasonable to take assets and net income as two important determinants of the demand for money.

It also seems reasonable to assume that basically the relation between assets, income, and money is a matter of real, not nominal, buying power. An increase in prices, with real incomes and assets the same, might not immediately increase the demand for money in exactly the same proportion, but over a period there is no reason to think that it would not increase in about the same proportion. On the other hand, an increase in real income without any increase in money income would almost certainly bring about an increase in real money holding as a part of the higher standard of living it allowed. Thus, in equilibrium analysis, the focus should be on the real demand for money and its relation to real income and the real value of assets, even though in practice there may be a considerable lag in the actual adjustment.

These basic factors of real income and assets are not, however, the only factors determining the total demand for money. Seasonal factors, degrees of uncertainty, the risks and returns to be expected from assets other than money, and the dynamic factor of expected changes in income and in the value of assets all play a part in determining the total demand for money. Each of these factors will be considered in turn.

Seasonal Factors and the Demand for Money

Seasonal factors in the demand for money have long been recognized. Monthly and quarterly settlement periods are well known as periods in which the demand for money as a store of buying power goes up. The individual or enterprise with heavy bills to pay at the end of the month is likely to allow money holdings to build up toward the end of the month. The individual then pays the bills and the money holdings of recipients increase in turn and are likely to be excessive for a few days. Thus, for the few days at month's end the total demand for money to have on hand is abnormally high. To some extent this extra demand for money is accompanied by an extra demand for credit, as particular individuals or enterprises borrow to pay their month's end bills and repay the borrowings when others in turn make payments to them. If this credit is supplied by creating additional bank money, as is so often the case, the added demand for money to hold is met in part by an added stock. In either case, the monthly rise in the demand for money and the comparable rise at the time of quarterly payments are well recognized in banking circles, at least in their credit accompaniment, and their effects are in large part offset by appropriate banking action.

A similar shift in the seasonal demand for money as a store of buying power comes in the fall, when farm crops are being moved to market. Many farmers receive the bulk of their income in the fall through selling the season's crop. In this period, farmers' total holdings of money go up markedly. Some of their money is quickly used to pay up accounts with local merchants and to buy supplies and equipment. But an appreciable part continues to be held for a time. And even that paid to local merchants serves for a time to swell the money holdings of the farm regions. If the total demand for money outside farm areas remained constant, the combined farm and nonfarm demand would mount at the crop-moving season.[6] As in the case of the monthly bill period, this demand may also be in part a demand for credit, and may result in a temporary expansion in the stock of money. But the demand for money is separate from the demand for credit.

These seasonal demands for "cash on hand"—monthly and quarterly payment periods, crop moving demand, and others, such as the Christmas demand—all contribute to a regular seasonal fluctuation in the demand for money. As such they are more or less predictable.

Changes in Uncertainty and the Demand for Money

The effect of changes in uncertainty are less well understood. Individuals and enterprises are constantly having to make decisions and take action when the outcome is uncertain. Also, the degree of uncertainty may be greater or lesser according to the current conditions. In some periods the "business visibility" may be high. Trends of development are freely projected into the future, and a high degree of confidence may exist as to "what is going to happen next." At other times, the clouds of uncertainty may close in so that business visibility is low and actions are taken more nearly on a day-to-day basis.

A change in the degree of uncertainty tends to alter the total demand for money. Business decisions might be made in one period on the assumptions that business activity is likely to stay relatively constant and that there is no greater likelihood of its falling slightly than of its rising slightly or the reverse. But a serious threat of war abroad would increase the uncertainty as to what would happen next. It would then become unlikely that business activity would remain relatively constant. A serious boom or a serious depression would be more likely than stable activity. And the likelihood of a boom might be just equal to the likelihood of a depression. Thus, the *average* of the probabilities could be the same as before but the dispersion would be greater. This increased uncertainty would mean that enterprises would tend to postpone important decisions of all sorts until it was clearer "how the cards were going to fall." The signing of contracts for the construction of new plants would frequently be postponed, and the money that it was expected to use for this purpose might be allowed to accumulate. In many industries, the inventory loss from a fall in prices would be greater than the gain from an equivalent rise, so that in these industries the increased uncertainty would lead to a preference for money rather than inventory in excess of minimum requirements and efforts to convert at least part of inventory into money. Considerations of this sort could be expected to alter the demand for money.

Individuals also could be expected to respond to increased uncertainty by increasing their demand for money. For many individuals and families, there is the necessity of playing safe when uncertainty increases. The war episode above might bring an equal promise of greatly increased and greatly reduced income. But for many families, the danger of less income must outweigh the equal possibility of more income and the decision is quite likely to be made to reduce expenditures, particularly on semi-durable and durable goods, until it is clear whether the family income is going up or down. The old car will be made to run another season, clothes will be worn a little longer, and the more dispensable items of current consumption will be dropped. If the threat of war is dissipated so that the extra uncertainty disappears, and if income is maintained, the durable and semi-durable goods can be bought and the living standard can be quickly raised to its former level. During the period of uncertainty, however, the family's money holdings are likely to accumulate. This constitutes an increased desire to hold money in place of the things it can buy.

A sudden threat of war would provide an unusual cause of a change in uncertainty. But in ordinary times, uncertainty is by no means a stable factor. It can be expected that uncertainty will increase and decrease from a variety of causes, some random and some growing directly out of economic developments, and thus lead to fluctuations in the demand for money.[7]

Risk-taking, Returns, and the Demand for Money

A third group of factors affecting the demand for money are those concerned with the taking of risks and the prospect of returns. Whatever the conditions as to uncertainty, an individual or enterprise can hold assets in more or less risky form. And the proportion of assets that are held in more or less risky form will depend in large part on the prospect of return.[8] As a result, the risks and prospects of return on other assets can affect the demand for money.

That this is so in the case of loans is clear. As Keynes has pointed out, the demand for money as a store of buying power is a function of interest rates. If interest rates were high, there would be a tendency to "put money to work" through loans rather than to hold cash. If interest rates were very low there would be a tendency to allow cash balances to accumulate rather than make loans. This would apply particularly to those individuals and enterprises with sufficient resources to make for easy access to the loan market. If call loan rates were 8 percent, individuals and enterprises with large resources would "economize their bank balances," keeping more of their liquid funds on loan. But with a call loan rate of 1 or 2 percent they could be expected to keep a much larger proportion in the form of money. Similarly, with government and corporate bonds and with other loans, the higher the prospect of return with a given set of risks, the greater the inducement to loan funds rather than to hold them in the very liquid form of money.

The same reasoning would apply to equity capital.[9] If the prospects of return were high, individuals and enterprises would tend to put their funds to work in things rather than hold them in the form of cash. Interest rates might be so low that large blocks of funds were held as cash rather than loaned. Yet if opportunities developed to invest in productive enterprises that were quite risky, but promised high rewards, funds would be used in this way and the demand for money to hold would fall even though interest rates remained the same. This would apply both to an individual's investment in his own business and to his investment in the equity securities of enterprises he does not control. It would also apply to the investment decisions of corporate management.

Dynamic Factors

A fourth and vitally important group of factors affecting the demand for money are those growing out of change and the expectation of change. The expectation of a fall in goods prices will presumably increase the demand for money, as individuals and enterprises prefer to hold their resources to a greater extent in the form of money until the expected fall has taken place. In such periods, inventory in excess of that needed for current operations is a less desirable form of asset as compared with money than when no price decline is expected. And similarly, durable goods, both consumption and capital, whose purchase can easily be delayed, are less desirable than money with which they can subsequently be bought. Likewise, an expected fall in security prices would presumably lead to a postponement of purchase and also a selling of securities already on hand. Both of these would involve an increased demand for money.

Conversely, an expected rise in goods prices or in security prices is likely to decrease the demand for money as a store of value. This may take the mild form of a forehanded inventory accumulation and advance buying of durable and semidurable goods or rarely, in case of runaway inflation, it may take the form of "a flight from money" as it did in Germany after the first World War. In the first case it would involve only the specific action of buying ahead because of expected higher prices. For the individual, this might be financed either by saving less or by reducing current money holdings. In the second case it would be primarily an effort to get rid of money. These and similar dynamic swings in the demand for money are of vital importance for an understanding of business fluctuations.

The Demand for Money

The demand for money as a store of buying power can be expected to reflect the effect of all these factors—the basic factors of income and assets, the seasonal factors, those arising from the degree of uncertainty, those arising from the will to take risks, and those arising from change and the expectation of change. In no sense can the total demand for money be regarded as a static thing. It is something that can be expected to move up or down under a complex variety of factors, some predictable, others quite random so far as economic conditions are concerned.

Not only can we expect that individuals and enterprises will adjust their money holdings to their incomes, assets, and so on, but it is also reasonable to expect that, for the economy as a whole, the amount of money outstanding will influence the propensities to consume and to invest. That this is a necessary corollary can be seen by considering the behavior of individuals and enterprises having too much or too little money and then the implications of this action for the whole economy.

Obviously, if individuals with a given income and assets find themselves with too much money, they can easily reduce their holdings. They may increase their rate of expenditure on consumption for a period; they may spend more on investment goods; or they may invest the extra money in loans or other securities. In the first case, there is a temporary increase in the propensity to consume. In the second case, the propensity to invest goes up temporarily. Only where they invest in loans or other securities is there no change in their propensities to consume or to invest in goods. Similarly, a business enterprise can easily dispose of a surplus of cash. It may invest more in goods; it may acquire loans as other securities, or it may pay out more in dividends. The first of these would represent a temporary increase in the propensity to invest. Thus, for individuals and enterprises taken separately, a surplus of money can lead to a temporary increase in the propensity to spend on goods.

Not only *can* a surplus of money lead to a temporary shift in the propensity to spend, but in the aggregate of a representative group of individuals and enterprises it is almost certain to do so. Some individuals are likely to spend a part of the extra money on goods; some enterprises are likely to use a part of the extra cash on investment goods. Thus, it seems reasonable to expect that, in practice, for large groups of individuals and enterprises or for the economy as a whole, a surplus of money will lead to extra spending on goods.

When the individuals or enterprises are considered separately or in small groups, it is obvious that the extra spending is temporary. As soon as the surplus money has been spent, the extra spending comes to a stop and the propensities to consume and invest fall to the level they would have occupied originally if the money holdings had not been excessive. Indeed, when individuals or enterprises are taken separately, the extra spending arising from the surplus of money is likely to be so temporary that it tends to be disregarded in general economic analysis.

For the economy as a whole, however, the increased propensity to spend arising from a surplus of money is not likely to be temporary. In the case of a single individual, the surplus money can be disposed of. It can be passed on to someone else. But, for the economy as a whole, surplus money does not disappear by being spent. What constitutes surplus for one person simply becomes surplus for someone else. For the community as a whole, the extra money remains and can be expected to cause a more or less permanent increase in the propensities to consume and invest. As a result, it can be expected that the propensities to consume and invest will be higher with a large than with a small real stock of money.

Conclusion

This chapter has shown that the demand for money is a demand separate from the things money can buy, and that its satisfaction must compete with the satisfaction of other wants, as other wants compete with it for the available limited funds. The holding of larger cash balances can contribute to the standard of living or to business efficiency, just as having more of other things can do. Individuals and enterprises can be expected to adjust their money holdings to their income, assets, and other factors just as they adjust the use of their resources in other directions. Also, when individuals have large cash balances, it can be expected that they will spend a larger proportion of their income on consumption than if their income and other factors were the same and their cash balances were smaller. Similarly, enterprises can be expected to invest more freely when their cash balances are large than when they are small, provided other conditions are the same. It is this last that provides the first basic assumption underlying the monetary theory of aggregate demand, namely *the assumption that the propensities to consume and invest are higher with a large real stock of money than with a small real stock.*

Notes

1. John Stuart Mill, *Principles of Political Economy,* ed. W.J. Ashley. New York: Kelley, 1961, p. 490.
2. The artificiality of the distinction is emphasized by two facts. One is the arbitrariness of the assumptions that have to be made in order to measure either money in circulation or money hoarded. The usual procedure is to *assume* that the volume of money necessary to carry a given volume of business is constant and that money in excess is hoarded. But this procedure arbitrarily assumes the point at issue. The second fact is that in the modern banking system, deposits are fungible, so that when part of the money in a bank account is withdrawn, it is not possible to say how long it has been held except where only one deposit has been made. Thus, for the typical bank account, it would be impossible to say what part was "in circulation" and what part was hoarded.

3. This is likely to be true if only because the management of a large block of assets is likely to require larger money transactions. But other considerations are also likely to contribute.

4. By foregoing the extra income the individual might obtain, through holding a larger part of his or her assets in earning form rather than in the form of money.

5. In technical terms, the marginal utility of money as a store of value would be just equal to the marginal utility of each other type of asset, and the marginal utility of consumption would be just equal to the marginal utility of holding more money.

6. Of course, if the stock of money were constant, the farm area could not increase its money holdings unless the rest of the community were willing to hold less. How others are induced to hold less is discussed in a subsequent chapter.

7. It is important to note that the changes in the total demand for money due to changes in uncertainty are not the same as changes due to expected changes in price level. The two are often associated, but they have separable effects.

8. Other factors such as retention of stock control over a business can also enter in.

9. At some points Keynes appears to treat interest rates as actually *including* rates of return on equity capital. This might be a justifiable procedure for some purposes, but in a discussion of buying power and saving, loans and equity securities play importantly different roles. This will be brought out in a subsequent chapter.

9

Assets and Economic Management

The second basic assumption underlying the monetary theory of aggregate demand has to do with the effect of asset values on economic management. In most discussions of the saving–investment theory, it is assumed that asset values have little, if any, effect on either the propensity to consume or the propensity to invest. Yet in the challenge to Keynes's saving–investment theory, it has already been shown that the real value of the outstanding money stock could have a very profound effect on both saving and investment. Here it will be suggested that the real value of other assets could also have a significant effect and for much the same reasons. Asset values as well as income have to be taken into account in economic management.

The importance of assets in economic management is obvious. In the case of any economic unit, whether individual, family, or enterprise, the management problem is not simply to acquire and dispose of income. Assets are likely to be carried over from one period to another so that for any given period, a management has for disposal the assets carried into the period as well as the income received during the period. An individual might have assets worth $15,000 at the beginning of a year and receive $5,000 in income. The total resources that the individual must manage would then consist of $20,000, not $5,000. In the absence of any changes in asset values, the total of his or her consumption, plus the assets he carried into the subsequent period, would equal $20,000. It is this total of assets and income that are the subject of economic management.

The problem of economic management can be simply stated as that of making the most effective use of the resources available. For the individual or family, this includes the use of resources of labor and skill and assets to bring in income; the disposal of income on the wide variety of consumption goods or its retention in one or more different types of assets; and the retention of assets carried into the period or their disposal to finance consumption or to acquire other assets. For a business enterprise a somewhat similar combination of factors is involved—the retention or disposal of assets initially carried into a period, the acquiring and handling of revenue during the period, and the carrying of assets into the next period. In each case, it is the combined assets and income that are managed to the advantage of the economic unit concerned.

For present purposes, the discussion of economic management can be limited to very broad categories. Assets can be grouped into consumption goods, capital goods including land, securities, and money.

Theoretically, it is possible to spell out the conditions for perfect economic management by an individual or family. An individual would have to maintain a balance between leisure and more income-producing effort. The person would have to balance the advantages of current consumption with the advantages of adding to or the disadvantages of reducing assets; he or she would have to maintain a balance between each type of consumption; and, of most importance here, would have to maintain a balance between each type of asset so that there would be no advantage to be gained from converting one type of asset into another. Stated in money terms, the individual equilibrium condition would involve both an equilibrium between holding money and spending money for consumption, and between holding money and the possession of each other type of asset.

In practice, no individual or family is likely to operate with such care that anything like perfect management is attained. Rather, there is likely to be a rough and ready adjustment. An individual or a family is likely to develop a pattern of living and to make changes in this pattern from time to time so as to bring its income, its expenditure on consumption, and its holdings of different types of assets into better balance in the light of current developments. For large groups of individuals the effect of this management should be apparent in the aggregate pattern of behavior covering both income and assets.

In the case of the business enterprise also, the problem of economic management is not simply one of dealing with income. A balance must likewise be kept between income and assets and between different forms of assets.

The inclusion of assets in the calculus of economic management has significance in two ways. First, the assets held at the beginning of a period can be expected to affect the disposal of income during the period and, second, any change in the value of assets during the period can be expected to affect both the disposal of income and the form in which assets are held. These two effects can be discussed separately.

Initial Assets and the Disposal of Income

How the initial possession of assets will affect the disposal of income can be expected to depend very largely on the motives that lead to saving. The two most widely recognized motives for saving are to use the savings as a means to future expenditure and to use the savings as a means to income.[1] In the first case, the assets are important primarily because they represent buying power, in the second because they represent a source of revenue. Often these objectives are combined, but the effect of assets on saving is different depending on the motive, and the effects can be examined separately.

To the extent that saving is undertaken for the purpose of security it can be expected that, in general, the larger the initial buying power held by a particular individual or family, the smaller the proportion of its income that it will save to provide additional buying power.[2] The family with large assets and a given income could be expected to save less than the same family with the same income but much smaller assets. Usually the possession of more buying power would reduce the relative advantages of further addition to buying power, as compared with the advantages of additional consumption. There may be exceptional cases in which the buying power held is so small that saving to protect the future seems fruitless, but where a real nest egg of assets would induce saving. In such cases, up to a point, more assets would induce more saving. But in general, where saving is primarily to protect the future, it seems reasonable to assume that the greater the buying power at the beginning of a period, the smaller the tendency to save.[3]

Where saving is primarily for the purpose of deriving income from the use of savings, the effect of initial assets on saving would appear to be of quite secondary importance and the direction of the net effect is not certain. In some cases, the possession of large earning assets might reduce the pressure to add further to earning assets and thereby reduce the saving that would be made from a given income. In other cases, greater earning assets might create even greater pressure to save so as to expand the assets. The prospect of return, not the amount of assets already held, is likely to dominate the decision to save.

So far as total savings of individuals and families are concerned and regardless of the purpose of saving, it seems likely that the greater the initial assets, the smaller the proportion of a given income that is likely to be saved. This can be expected partly because it would almost certainly be true if the only reason for saving were security, partly because saving for income is not likely to be affected very much one way or the other by initial assets, and partly because other reasons for saving are of secondary importance.

In the case of business enterprises, it is not so much the size of assets as the form in which they are held that influences saving and investment. A large corporation does not save more or less simply because it is large. But if two corporations have equal *physical* assets and opportunities to invest, the one with the largest amount of cash and salable securities is, of course, more easily able to and therefore is likely to invest more and save less, than the one without so much uncommitted capital. The company with a large volume of assets in the form of money or salable securities can expand its plant without the necessity of floating an issue of its own securities, and without withholding an abnormally large proportion of its current earnings from its stockholders. Thus, in general, a greater amount of uncommitted capital in the hands of business can be expected to stimulate investment and reduce business saving.

In practice, the effect of assets on economic management would be most evident in comparing the saving and investment propensities for periods in which a large change in assets has occurred. In a peacetime prosperous period, the annual change in assets might not be sufficient to have a marked effect in successive years. But the accumulation of assets over a longer period could be significant. It might, for example, account for a tendency for the propensity to save to decline through time, which some students of the subject believe exists.[4]

On the other hand, a major change in asset holdings of individuals and enterprises, such as occurs during a war, might have a sufficient effect to be measurable in increasing both the propensity to consume and that to invest. There is some evidence to suggest that the propensity to consume was higher after World War I than before.[5] This could be explained by the increase in liquid assets of individuals and enterprises resulting from the increase in government debt. For a similar reason, the great increase in liquid assets arising from government financing of World War II can be expected to increase both the propensity to consume and that to invest, provided, of course, that the increase in liquid buying power is not dissipated by a major price rise. The more than $200 billion increase in government debt held directly or indirectly[6] by individuals and enterprises serves both to make the individual holders more secure and under less pressure to save in the future, and to provide enterprises with highly liquid funds with which to take advantage of any investment opportunities that arise. Thus, the propensity to save can be expected to be significantly lower and the propensity to invest significantly higher than if this debt had not been created.[7]

Changes in Asset Values and the Disposal of Income

It is not only the value of assets at the beginning of a period that affects the disposal of income, but also the value of assets during the period. A change in the real value of a particular set of assets can have two quite different effects.

One effect is entirely dynamic. As Keynes has pointed out, a rise in the value of assets can create "windfall gains," which are likely to be treated by many recipients as a sort of quasi-income with the result that they save less out of their true income. This is a dynamic effect that comes to a halt once the value of the assets has ceased to rise.

There is also a continuing effect. The greater real value of the assets means that the holder's apparent power to buy in the future is increased. Because of this greater real buying power, an individual would be under less pressure to save and a business would be freer to invest, provided, of course, that the assets were not physically needed in its activities. For example, if an individual is saving with the major objective of putting his or her children through college, and with no change in goods prices or income, finds that his or her securities are worth $10,000 rather than $5,000, the individual is that much nearer his or her goal and can reduce his or her current rate of saving. Similarly, an enterprise that finds its salable securities worth $2 million rather than $1 million is in a better position to obtain additional funds for expansion. Thus, even if we completely disregard the dynamic effect of a rise in the real value of assets, such a rise could have a continuing tendency to increase both the propensity to consume and the propensity to invest. The reverse effect could be expected from a decline in asset values. For simplicity, this nondynamic effect of a change in asset values will be referred to hereafter as the equilibrium effect.

It should be recognized that this equilibrium effect of a change in asset values arises primarily from a change in the real buying power of assets measured in terms of the current or expected cost of living. A doubling in the dollar value of securities relative to the dollar value of items going directly into the cost of living, or a similar doubling of land values or the value of capital goods, could be expected to have a significant effect on the saving and investment propensities. The bulk of assets held by individuals and enterprises consists of assets that do not go directly into consumption, and are therefore subject to changes in real value that can produce this equilibrium effect. The magnitude of changes in asset values, particularly in the case of securities and land values, is such that it seems reasonable to ascribe to this equilibrium effect the power to alter significantly the propensities to save and invest, even within relatively short periods of time.

Changes in Asset Values and the Proportioning of Assets

Changes in asset values can also have an important effect on the proportioning of total assets among assets of different types. If a certain proportioning of assets among capital goods, securities, and money seemed appropriate to individuals, at one set of asset values, presumably a readjustment would be necessary if a significant rise in security prices might change the proportions. Individuals would then seek to convert some of their securities into cash balances or into capital goods of one sort or another. A similar equilibrium reshuffling of assets could be expected from a reduction in security prices or from a change in the value of other types of assets.

In the case of business enterprise, a significant change in the value of any particular type of asset, other than assets physically used in business, could also be expected to lead to a reshuffling of assets. For example, a significant rise in the value of its marketable securities would presumably lead an enterprise to hold more of its assets in capital goods and in cash balances once a new equilibrium was reached.

This effect of asset values on the propensities to save and to invest takes on major importance when it is recognized that the real buying power of a given aggregate of assets can vary within very wide limits. A piece of land or a security that promised a more or less permanent stream of income of $100 a year would have a current real buying power of $5,000 if the future income were discounted at the rate of 2 percent, but only $2,000 if the income were discounted at the rate of 5 percent. A very much wider range in the real buying power of such an asset would be possible. This means that within a very considerable range, a difference in the real buying power of assets could significantly affect both the propensity to consume and the propensity to invest. Quite apart from the dynamic effects, a rise in asset values could be expected to reduce the propensity to save and increase both the propensity to consume and the propensity to invest.

This conclusion provides the second basic assumption underlying the monetary theory of aggregate demand—*the assumption that the propensities to consume and to invest are higher with a high real value of assets than with a low real value of assets.*

Notes

1. Other reasons for saving, such as, for instance, the inability of the very rich to spend the whole of their income on consumption, or the desire to display a large bank account, are of wholly secondary importance for the present study.

2. The above proposition is given in the mathematical sense in which saving might be negative.

3. It should be noted that the above is dealing only with an identical group of individuals under two different sets of conditions. It does not mean that persons with large assets are likely to save less from a given income than *other* persons with smaller assets. All the above means is that a given group of individuals or families would save less from given income if their initial assets were large than if they were small.

4. It should be noted that the effect of assets on the propensity to save would be very difficult to disentangle in the analysis of time series using data for a single peacetime period. The gradual growth of assets would be absorbed in a time trend and important short-run or cyclical changes in asset values would correspond to changes in income.

5. [Editor's Note: Unable to identify.] Cite Louis Paradiso's Survey article. The evidence in this article is by no means conclusive. The change in relationship coincides with the point at which two time series were spliced, and could be due

to an imperfect splice. Also it has not yet been definitely established that a regression of saving on income gives a function representing the propensity to save.

6. In part, the government debt is held by banks and insurance companies, and so on, but individuals and enterprises possess claims corresponding to this part of its debt and thus have an indirect interest in it.

7. It should be noticed that the decreased propensity to save or the increased propensity to invest does not arise primarily from the *spending* of war savings, but from the fact that war savings will tend to reduce the necessity for further saving. As a result, it could be expected that a smaller amount would be saved out of any given income.

10

The Determinants of Aggregate Demand

Once it is assumed that the propensities to consume and invest are higher with a large real stock of money than with a small real stock, and that they are higher with a high real value of assets than with a low real value, it will be found that the stock of money outstanding and the demand for money are the central determinants of aggregate demand.[1] This conclusion is in contrast to that of the saving and investment theory, which makes saving and investment the central determinants. According to that theory, the level of aggregate demand is determined by the relation between the propensities to save and to invest. A change in one relative to the other would change the level of aggregate demand; and with the two propensities given, the level of aggregate demand would be determinate. The dominant position of money can be seen by considering whether it is saving in relation to investment which determines aggregate demand, or only saving in the form of money.

Saving versus Additions to Money Balances

Current discussions of saving and investment have made it abundantly clear that, in any period, the total volume of saving and the total volume of investment in goods must be equal, and that any tendency away from equality will force economic adjustments such as will maintain them in equality.[2] But, because the current discussion seldom goes into the detail of total saving and total investment, it misses certain important characteristics of the problem of adjustment, and the crucial role played by saving in the form of money.

Goods versus Token Saving

The first step in clarifying the role of saving and investment in determining aggregate demand is to draw a distinction between two different forms of saving. It is not possible to save without having the proceeds of saving in some form. The proceeds of saving may take the direct form of goods. This would be the case where an individual used part of his or her current income in building an addition to the house or where an enterprise invested part of its current income in plant, equipment, or inventory. Or the proceeds of saving may take the form of tokens that represent some kind of future claim. This would be the case where current income was invested in stocks or bonds, or loaned. It would also be the case where income was simply kept as a net addition to money holdings. By definition, all saving not in the form of goods must be in the form of tokens.

The distinction between these two types of saving is important because saving in the form of goods does not give rise to a problem of aggregate demand. The individual who saves by putting part of his or her current income directly into capital goods is both saving and investing in goods as a single operation. If the only possible form of saving were saving in goods, there could be no problem of economic adjustment to make saving and investment equal. They would be equal without any economic adjustment. A decision that resulted in saving would also be a decision to invest in goods. A change in the propensity to save would have no effect on aggregate demand because it would also be a change in the propensity to invest. In these circumstances a tendency to oversave would be impossible.

The relation between saving and investment can influence aggregate demand, therefore, only where saving is in the form of tokens. Then some individuals or enterprises save by adding to their holding of tokens—money, loans, securities, and the like, while others finance investment in goods by disposing of or issuing tokens. The decision to save and the decision to invest in goods are separated by tokens. Yet in any given period the saving in tokens and the token-financed investment in goods must be just equal. If there is a tendency for one to be greater than the other, some economic adjustment is necessary to bring them together. Thus, the real saving–investment problem must center not on total saving and total investment in goods, but on the narrower field of token saving and token-financed investment. Saving in goods can be deducted from both sides of the equation.

The Main Problem: Saving in Money

The saving–investment problem can be still further narrowed down by the fact that quite simple adjustments can be expected to eliminate tendencies to oversave in any form of tokens other than money. This can be seen if we examine each type of token-saving in turn.

The simple corrective in the case of loans is obviously an adjustment in the level of interest rates. If there were initially a tendency to save in the form of loans, more than could be absorbed by the demand for loans, a fall in interest rates could bring the two into balance. Even if lower interest rates did not stimulate borrowing and did not reduce saving, they could force saving to take some other form than loans. Most particularly, as Keynes has pointed out, interest rates could be expected to fall to a point where savers would prefer to hold their savings in the form of money rather than make further loans. Whatever the demand for loans might be, an adjustment in interest rates could always bring the desire to save in the form of loans into equality with the demand for loans. The lowering of interest rates might to some extent reduce saving or stimulate investment, and thus serve in part to correct the initial tendency to oversave. But to the extent that it induced savers to prefer to hold their savings in the form of money or stocks or some other token form rather than in the form of loans, it would not eliminate the tendency to oversave but simply change its form.

The same line of reasoning would apply to a tendency to oversave in the form of securities, except that in this case it would be the rise in the price of securities rather than a fall of interest rates that acted as the corrective. For example, a net effort to save and invest more in common stocks than could be absorbed by the net current issue of common stocks would force up stock prices. To some extent, the rise in stock prices might stimulate consumption or stimulate investment in goods, thus serving in part to correct the initial tendency to oversave. But in part, perhaps in large part, the rise in security prices would change the tendency to oversave in the form of securities into a tendency to oversave in some other form.

The situation is somewhat different in the case of saving in the form of savings bank accounts or insurance. Here, the funds saved are in fact handed over to an institution for holding or disposal. An initial tendency to oversave in these forms is not likely to be corrected by a change in interest rates or the price of insurance. Within wide limits, both types of institutions usually accept whatever funds are placed with them. What form the tendency to oversave takes then depends on how the savings banks or insurance companies attempt to use the funds. As long as they hold the funds as a net addition to their money holdings, the saving in the form of savings deposits or insurance by individuals has been, in essence, converted into saving in the form of money by the savings banks or insurance companies. If the latter invest in loans or securities, they transfer the oversaving into an overdemand for loans or securities and this in turn would be corrected or converted into other forms by a fall in interest rates or a rise in security prices.

Further analysis will show that a tendency to oversave in any other type of token except money would likewise be corrected by an expansion of consumption and investment, or converted into a tendency to oversave in some other form of token. In some cases, the particular type of token saving would mean the handing over of decision to some other agency as in the case of savings deposits and insurance. In other cases, the excessive demand for the particular type of token would lead to some form of price adjustment, as in the case of loans or securities, which would serve either to correct the tendency to oversave or convert it into a tendency to oversave in some other type of tokens, or a combination of the two.

Since a tendency to oversave in any form of token except money would be converted into a tendency to oversave in some other form of token, except, of course, to the extent that it was corrected, the only form of oversaving that could survive adjustments in interest rates and security prices would be a tendency to oversave in the form of money. A tendency to oversave in other forms would automatically be either corrected or converted into a tendency to oversave in the form of money. The heart of the saving–investment problem is, therefore, not a general tendency to oversave or even a general tendency to oversave in the form of tokens, but a tendency to oversave in the specific form of money—a tendency to save *and build up money balances*. Only as a tendency to oversave involves or leads to an effort to build up money balances will it present a problem of adjustment, which is likely to involve a change in aggregate demand. It is not just a tendency to oversave but a tendency to oversave *in the form of money* which is significant.

Increased Demand for Money as an
Initiating Factor

The foregoing analysis would seem to imply that, while an effort to oversave must be accompanied by an effort to build up money balances in order to affect the level of aggregate demand, the initiating factor is the effort to oversave. Actually, this would not seem to be necessarily the case. An effort to increase money balances *without any initial tendency to oversave* could be expected to be just as effective in bringing about a reduction in aggregate demand. With no initial alteration in either the propensity to save or the propensity to invest, a simple effort to shift assets from other forms of token into money could be expected to affect the level of aggregate demand. For example, if the community in the aggregate made the effort to convert security holdings into money, this effort to build up money balances could be expected to result in reduced aggregate demand. It would bring down the value of securities without significantly altering the total securities outstanding or the stock of money outstanding. As has been seen in chapter 9, a fall in the value of securities could be expected to have the equilibrium effect of reducing both the propensity to invest and the propensity to consume, and would thus reduce aggregate demand. This initial desire to shift the form of token assets would create a tendency to oversave. And an effort to shift from money assets into other types of token assets could be expected to result in a higher level of aggregate demand. Thus, not only must a tendency to oversave involve an effort to build up money balances if it is to affect the level of aggregate demand, but an effort to build up money balances that does not involve an initial effort to oversave can have the same effect. In each case the demand for money is crucial.

Money as the Determinant of
Aggregate Demand

The preceding analysis leads to the conclusion that the crucial determinant of aggregate demand is the relation between the demand for money and the outstanding stock of money. If the outstanding stock of money is greater than the community chooses to hold at the initial level of prices (including wage and interest rates) and the initial level of incomes, that is, if money is redundant, the effort to dispose of it can be expected to reduce interest rates, raise security prices, and increase the demand for both consumption and investment goods. The rise in the value of securities (and perhaps also real estate and other goods assets) can also be expected to stimulate expenditure on both consumption and investment goods. Equilibrium could be expected only when interest rates had so risen that individuals and enterprises in the aggregate would rather hold the total stock of money outstanding rather than add further to their making of loans; when security prices had risen to the point that they would rather hold the stock of money than add further to their purchase of securities; and when incomes had so increased that they would rather hold the outstanding stock of money than add further to their expenditure on goods for consumption and investment. Redundant money could thus be expected to bring about an expansion in aggregate demand.

In similar fashion, a deficiency in the stock of money relative to the demand for money at the initial price and income levels could be expected to result in a contraction in aggregate demand.

Equilibrium could be reached only when aggregate demand was sufficient and just sufficient to induce the community to hold the outstanding stock of money rather than attempt to spend more or less than its current income on goods. In this situation, the community in the aggregate would want to spend just the amount of its current income on goods, and there would be no tendency for aggregate demand to change except as the demand for money or the stock of money was altered. This theory might be called a "Monetary Theory of Aggregate Demand."

Notes

1. It is worth noting that, in an equilibrium situation, no single factor can be referred to as *the* determinant in any absolute sense. In an equilibrium, the factors would presumably be so adjusted that a change in *any* factor would cause a change in the equilibrium, and thus would deserve the title of determinant equally with any other factor.

In the above analysis, money is referred to as the central determinant in a relative sense only. The problem of focus is analogous to that involved in making the sun rather than the earth the center of the solar system. Relativity has taught us that the sun goes around the earth just as much as the earth goes around the sun, and that either the sun or the earth could properly be used as the point of reference in describing the movement of the planets. But obviously the use of the sun as center gives a clearer picture of what goes on. Similarly the author believes that using money as the central determinant results in a clearer economic picture.

2. As saving and investment are defined by Keynes.

Part IV
A Monetary Theory of Employment

11

A Monetary Theory
of Employment

The preceding chapters have laid the basis, and in some measure forecast, the theory of employment being presented here by outlining an insensitive-price theory of economic adjustment and a monetary theory of aggregate demand. The first theory explains why changes in aggregate demand could be expected to work themselves out through changes in both prices and employment. The second theory explains the level of aggregate demand in terms of the relation between the demand for money and the stock of money outstanding. In combination these theories can explain the level of employment in terms of the demand for and the stock of money outstanding, and thereby provide for what might be called a *monetary theory of employment.*

According to an extreme application of this theory, the level of employment in a perfectly rigid-price economy would be determined by the level of production and *real* income at which the demand for money was just equal to the stock of money outstanding. If for some reasons the individuals and enterprises of the community in the aggregate sought to add to their money holdings while the stock of money remained constant, the level of employment would fall. If the community in the aggregate wanted to reduce its money holdings while the stock of money remained constant, the level of employment would, if possible, rise. Similarly, if the stock of money were altered without correspondingly altering the demand for money, the level of employment would change.

Such a theory is in direct contrast to the classical position that, in a perfectly sensitive-price economy, the level of prices would be determined by the level of money income at which the demand for money was just equal to the stock of money outstanding, with the price level moving up or down according to changes in the relation between the demand and the supply of money.

The general statement of the monetary theory compounds these two extreme positions, making both employment and prices contribute to the adjustment of the demand for money to the actual supply. According to this theory, *a deficiency of money in relation to the demand for money could be expected to cause both prices and employment to fall, with employment falling most where prices were insensitive and prices falling most where sensitive; and a surplus of money in relation to the demand could be expected to cause a reverse movement, except that as full employment was reached or surpassed, more of the adjustment could be expected to take place through price increases.* A demand for money in excess of the supply could be expected to result in a fall in both employment and prices. A redundant money supply could be expected to produce higher employment and higher prices. The relative role of employment and prices in the adjustment can be expected to depend on a variety of factors, such as the relative insensitivity of prices, the extent to which resources are already employed, and other conditions surrounding the excess or deficiency in the demand for money. Furthermore, an excess or deficiency would be expected to have a differential effect, tending to affect prices more where they are sensitive and tending to affect employment more where prices are insensitive.

The Basic Propositions

Underlying this theory are three simple propositions:

1. In any equilibrium situation, the amount of money outstanding must be sufficient and only just sufficient to satisfy the community's desire to hold buying power in the form of money, rather than spend more or less on consumption and investment goods.

2. A change in the relation between the total demand for money and the outstanding stock of money would alter the level of real income and employment at which equilibrium would be reached.

3. Any development that produced a change in the aggregate level

of real income and employment must operate through changing the total demand for money as a store of buying power at the initial level of income, or by changing the stock of money outstanding.

These three propositions, if accepted, would provide a monetary explanation of equilibrium at less (or more) than full employment. This chapter will be concerned with developing and justifying these propositions and indicating their limitations.

Equilibrium and Monetary Balance

The first proposition, already indicated in the theory of aggregate demand, is fairly obvious—that under equilibrium conditions the total demand for money as a store of buying power and the outstanding stock of money must be just equal. If individuals or enterprises have more cash on hand than they find it convenient or desirable to hold, they can readily dispose of it, swapping it for other assets or spending it on consumption. So long as they have ready access to markets, the possessors of money who continue to hold it must be assumed to prefer to hold money, at least for the time being, instead of exchanging it for any of the things they could buy. As a result, individual equilibrium would not exist if an individual had money on hand, wanted to spend it, and had easy access to markets for things they wanted to purchase.

For the economy as a whole, equilibrium would not exist if, on balance, the community wanted to build up or deplete its money holdings. If some individuals or enterprises wanted to add to their money holdings while others sought to reduce theirs, the two groups might just offset each other. But if either group overbalanced the other, it would mean that existing market relationships were not in equilibrium. A net effort to build up money balances would mean a reduced demand for things—goods or securities (including loans). A net effort to reduce money balances would mean an expansion in the demand for goods or securities or both. So long as either imbalanced condition existed, the current price and production relationship would not be in equilibrium and some economic adjustment would be set in motion.

Certain characteristics of equilibrium should be noticed. Equilibrium would involve both the distribution of assets as between goods, securities, loans, money, and other possible assets; and the balance between income, consumption, and additions to assets. In an equilibrium condition, there would be no general tendency for the community, on balance, to shift from goods into money or the reverse; from securities into money or the reverse; or in any other way to convert one type of asset into another. Part of the community might be shifting from one type of asset to another while a second part was making the reverse shift, but there would be no *net* effort to make such a shift. The community, on balance, would be just content to hold each type of asset in the amount currently outstanding. Likewise, equilibrium would exist only if there were a balance between the holding of assets in different forms and the rates of income and consumption. This would mean more than simply that income was at the point at which the propensity to save and the propensity to invest in goods were equal. It would mean that the desire to save in *each form* of asset was just equal to the secretion [sic] of assets in that form. It would also mean that total consumption and total assets were in balance.[1] It is the combination of this complex balance between assets, income, and consumption with the economics of insensitive prices that gives the present theory its particular character. And at the heart of this complex balance is the necessity that the demand for money as a store of buying power and the outstanding stock of money should be just equal.

A Change in the Demand for Money

Not only would an equilibrium exist only if the demand for money and the stock of money were equal, but a change in this relation would alter the level of real income and employment at which equilibrium would be reached. In a subsequent chapter, we will consider the effect of a change in the stock of money outstanding. Here, we will be concerned only with the effect of a change in the demand for money. How would an increase or decrease in the demand for money as a store of buying power affect the level of incomes and employment if there were no corresponding change in the stock of money?

To answer this question, three different cases need to be considered: (1) an effort to build up money balances out of current income; (2) an effort to build up money balances by shifting from goods assets into money, and (3) an effort to build up money balances by shifting from securities or other token assets into money.

The Effort to Increase Money Balances
Out of Income

The first case—an effort to build up money holdings out of income—might involve an increase in saving or might simply reflect a shift in the *form* of saving. The community might be spending the whole of its income on consumption and investment goods, and then for some reason it might seek to consume less and hold the extra savings in the form of money. Or the community might make no initial change in its disposal of income between saving and consumption, but might choose to hold a larger part of its current savings in the form of money and less in the form of investments. In either case, it would be attempting to add to its money holdings out of income.

Whether the effort to build up money balances out of income involved an increase in saving or simply a shift in the form of saving, it would result in a fall in the demand for goods, provided, of course, that there was not an equal or greater increase in the stock of money. An effort to increase in saving with no effort to invest the proceeds would obviously involve a direct reduction in the total demand for goods. A shift in the form of saving would have the same effect though the line of causation may be less obvious. If the individuals or enterprises that attempted to shift from other forms of saving into saving in the form of money were initially saving in the form of goods, then it is clear that the effort to shift into saving in the form of money would also mean a direct reduction in the total demand for goods. But if they were initially saving in the form of loans or securities, the effect would be indirect. Their failure to make loans or buy securities at the old rate would reduce the buying power flowing into the hands of those who were in a position to spend the savings of others on goods for investment or consumption. With no change in the levels of interest rates and security prices, there would be a decline in the demand for goods from borrowers and security issuers as a result of a dearth of funds to spend. Actually, some rise in interest rates and a fall in security prices might be expected because of the dearth of funds.[2] The better terms offered to savers would increase the desirability of saving in the form of loans or securities, and thereby reduce the tendency to add to money holdings. But the tendency would not be entirely eliminated since the terms for borrowing or issuing securities would be worse, and so there would be less inducement to "take the savings of others and put them to work." Thus, even though the demand for goods financed directly out of income remained the same, the demand for goods financed by borrowing and security issue could be expected to fall.[3] It must therefore be clear that a net effort to build up money balances out of income would result in a decline in the total demand for goods regardless of whether the effort involved a reduction in consumption or a shift in the form of saving.[4]

It has already been pointed out that with a perfectly sensitive price–wage system, such a general fall in the demand for goods would not necessarily lead to a fall in the level of employment. The reduced demand for goods would lead to a fall in the price–wage level. As money incomes fell, the desire to hold savings in the form of money would be reduced or—saying it another way—the real buying power of the stock of money would increase, until the existing stock of money was capable of satisfying the current desire to hold savings in the form of money. Thus, the buying power of the outstanding stock of money could adjust through changes in the price level to whatever volume the community chose to hold. In equilibrium, the level of price–wage rates and *money* incomes would be that at which the desire to hold real buying power in the form of money and the real buying power of the stock of money were equal, and if prices and wage rates were assumed to be perfectly sensitive, a decline in total demand would not lead to a decline in employment.[5] This gives support to the extreme position of classical economics insofar as it applied to an economy of perfectly sensitive prices.

But in an insensitive-price economy, a general decline in the demand for goods could not lead to a general fall in prices. If prices were perfectly fixed, at least during the period of adjustment, a fall in demand would lead to a fall in sales. This in turn would lead to a fall in production and employment.[6] If some prices were fixed while others were sensitive, the fall in demand would, as we have already seen, produce a combination of falling prices for some items, falling production for others and a combined price and production fall for still others. To the extent of the price fall, the real buying power of money would be increased and operate to partially correct the tendency to build up money balances. But this corrective effect would be accompanied by the fall in employment. And the latter would also help to correct the tendency to build up money balances by reducing real incomes. A new equilibrium would be reached only at a lower level of both prices and real income and employment. The conclusion seems inescapable that, in an insensitive-price economy, a net effort to build up money balances out of income must lead to a lower level of employment.[7]

The Effort to Convert
Real Investments into Money

The same conclusion would also follow where there was a net effort to build up money balances by converting goods assets already on hand into money. This would occur, for example, if business sought to convert a part of its inventories into cash. The current demand for goods by customers could be satisfied out of inventory. Thus, buying power could be taken out of the hands of consumers without putting in an equivalent amount through replacing the inventory. And because of the failure to replace inventory, the total demand for goods, investments as well as consumption, would be less. As in the earlier case, this would lead to a fall in the level of employment to the extent that prices were insensitive. The same line of reasoning would apply if business sought to convert a part of its investment in fixed assets into cash by not reinvesting the recovery of capital represented by allocations to depreciation. In either case, the effort to build up money balances at the expense of either inventory or fixed assets would lead to a lower level of employment, provided, of course, that prices were insensitive and the stock of money was not altered.[8]

The Effort to Shift from Other
Token Assets into Money

In the third case—that involving an effort to shift from loans or securities into money—the conclusions are the same but the line of reasoning is again somewhat more complex. A net effort of the community to shift the form of assets held from loans and securities into money would presumably not involve any initial change in the demands of borrowers and security issuers for funds to invest in goods, nor in the demand for loans and securities arising from the disposal of current income. But the effort to shift the *form* in which token assets are held would force security prices down and interest rates up. This would tend to increase the advantage of holding loans and securities rather than money and so tend to limit the effort to shift from other token assets into money. If this were the *only* effect of the higher interest rates and lower security prices, the effort to shift the form of token assets would tend to be self-correcting as far as the levels of income and employment were concerned.

But the rise in interest rates and the fall in security prices would also tend to discourage borrowers and security issuers from obtaining funds for investment in goods. As a result, a decline in investment in goods would result. Even though expenditure on consumption was maintained, the aggregate demand for goods would decline and lead to unemployment where prices were insensitive.

In addition to the effect of the change in rates of return, the lower security prices could also be expected to increase the propensity to save, since because of their smaller real buying power, the securities would represent a smaller bulwark against the future.[9] This would increase the importance of saving and tend to reduce the propensity to consume. Insofar as extra saving took the direct form of goods, the total demand for goods would remain unchanged. To the extent it took the form of efforts to save in loans or securities, it would tend to offset or correct the initial change that led to lower security prices. But to the extent that it led to an effort to save more in the form of money, it would mean a further deficit in the total demand for goods and additional unemployment. Thus a net effort to shift from loan and security assets into money would tend to reduce the total demand for goods, both through a change in the rate of return on such token assets and through the reduced buying power of securities.

While the preceding analysis has not covered all the possible ways in which the community might attempt to build up its money balances, it has examined the main possibilities. And in each case it has been shown that the effort to increase money balances as a result of an increased demand for money would involve, or could be expected to bring about, a fall in the total demand for goods with a resultant decline in money incomes. The same line of reasoning would indicate that, if the demand for money fell while the outstanding stock of money remained constant, the total demand for goods would increase, and if prices or wage rates were insensitive, real national income and employment would rise. The conclusion, therefore, seems warranted that a change in the aggregate demand for money relative to the stock of money would alter the level of income at which equilibrium would be reached.

The effect of changes in the supply of money is more complicated and will be discussed in detail in a subsequent chapter. It is sufficient here to indicate, first, that under modern conditions, the amount of money outstanding is not a result of economic forces but of monetary and fiscal policies that may or may not be closely related to monetary needs; and second, that changing the stock of money outstanding may also change the demand for money, so that the effect of such a change will depend to a considerable extent on the method by which the money is introduced or removed. These matters will be considered in discussing possible measures for attaining full employment. It will be apparent there that a change in the *relation* between the demand for money and the outstanding stock of money originating on the money side can be just as effective in altering the level of employment as one originating on the side of money demand.

A Change in Employment Requires a Monetary Change

The third basic proposition underlying the monetary theory of employment is that any development that produces a change in the level of real income and employment must operate through changing the demand for money in relation to income or by changing the stock of money outstanding.

It must be apparent that this proposition is limited to employment in producing for sale. Obviously, individuals could produce more goods for their *own* consumption and thus increase total hours worked without any change in monetary relationships. Also, there could be an increase in goods produced and bartered for other goods without any monetary change. The employment that is necessarily dependent on a monetary relationship is only that which arises through the medium of money.

The proposition is also limited to conditions in which the relation between real income and employment is stable. Obviously if productivity were to increase it would be possible to have a decline in employment even though total real income remained constant. If changes in productivity were to be taken into account, the proposition would have to be limited to real income. It would then read that any development that produced a change in the real income must operate through changing the demand for money in relation to income, or by changing the stock of money outstanding. Employment would then depend on real income *and* productivity.

Even when this third proposition is clearly limited to employment arising through money transactions and to conditions of stable productivity, the logic justifying it is somewhat complex because of the many factors that have to be taken into account. At first thought, there would seem to be many cases where it would not appear to be true. If an auto company closed down to retool or a coal mine became exhausted, people would be thrown out of work and their incomes would decline. This would seem to mean a decline in employment and incomes without any change in the demand for money or the outstanding stock of money, except that resulting from the decline in incomes itself. But careful tracing through of the effects of this change will show that it would result in a *net* decrease in employment only if it increased the demand for money or reduced the stock of money outstanding.

This can be seen by following through the effects of the closing down of an auto company. If the auto company had continued in operation, the money incomes of the workers would have come either from the sale of cars to ultimate purchasers or from the willingness of the manufacturer or the dealers to build up inventories. Consideration of what happens to the money that was *not* spent on the autos of the closed company will show that, under at least one set of circumstances, the closing would involve no decline in *total* income and employment. Suppose that the "trade" stopped selling the cars from the closed company at the same time that the plant closed down. This would mean that the consumers who would otherwise have bought cars from the closed company would have to turn elsewhere. If they spent *exactly* as much on other makes of cars and no change in the inventory of the "trade" took place, incomes derived from the production of other cars would have to increase by just the amount that incomes declined from the stoppage of the closed company, and employment would increase in the production of other cars by as much as it declined in the closed company.[10] In this case, there would be no change in the demand for money as a store of buying power and no change in total employment.

In this situation, a change in total employment would take place, however, under various circumstances, but in each case it would involve a change in the demand for money or a change in the stock outstanding. If consumers chose not to buy the cars of other makers but to hold the money they would have spent until the closed company reopened, employment would fall. If the trade handling other cars chose to meet the new demand by converting its inventory into cash, employment would decline. If the trade handling the car that was out of production chose to convert its inventory into cash, consumers could still buy the make, and so would not generate employment through the purchase of other makes. But in each case the demand for money would go up. In the first case, the closing of the plant would have caused the demand for money on the part of consumers to increase because they couldn't get the make they wanted; in the second case, the trade handling the cars would have an increased demand for money to the extent it turned its inventory into cash; in the third, it would be the closed-down company or its dealers that had the increased demand for money in place of inventory.

There are many other possibilities: consumers might spend the extra money on other goods with no effect on the total demand for goods; or consumers might have planned to buy on bank credit so that they had no extra money, but rather the outstanding stock of money was smaller than it otherwise would have been; or the companies reducing inventories might use the proceeds to reduce their debt to banks and so reduce the stock of money; or they might use the funds to buy other goods and so maintain demand, or to retire securities and so set up a longer train of causation. But in each case, if it is followed through to the end it will be found that the closing of the plant would reduce employment only if somewhere in the system it led to an increased demand for money or to a reduced stock of money.

The same conclusion must be reached when the problem is considered in more general terms. Suppose that under one set of conditions, the community is willing and just willing to spend the whole of its current money income on goods for consumption or investment. Unless something occurred to cause a change in the rate of spending, the level of incomes would be stable and in the absence of a change in productivity or price level, employment would be stable. Under these conditions, a decline in income and employment could occur only if, at the current level of money incomes, the community wanted to spend *less than the whole of its current income* on goods.[11] If the stock of money were fixed, and all transactions were for money, the reduced demand for goods could arise only because the community sought to pay out for goods less than it was currently receiving, that is, it wanted to increase its money holdings at the current level of incomes. It is this effort to increase money holdings—to spend less than its current income—that would result in reduced income and employment, and these would decline until the community's income was so much lower that it was again content to hold only the outstanding stock of money and spend the whole of its current income. Similarly, an increase in income would mean a desire to spend on consumption and investment more than the total of current incomes and a desire at the current level of incomes to reduce money balances.

The same conclusion would apply when account is taken of the possibility of price changes, provided the conclusion is stated in real terms. A rise in prices with the stock of money constant could lead to reduced employment, but only because the higher prices have the effect of reducing the real stock of money and perhaps altering the demand for money. The shrinkage in the real stock of money would mean that the stock of money was insufficient to satisfy the demand for money at the initial level of real income, unless the shrinkage was offset by a decline in the demand for money. Except in the latter case, the effort to build up money balances would mean that the community would seek to spend on consumption and investment less than its current income. Sales, production, and employment would therefore fall. But in this case, as in the others, the change in employment would be a result of a change in the relation between the real stock of money and the demand for money in relation to income.

The only serious exception to the proposition occurs in the case of changes in productivity.[12] The proposition would still hold that a change in real income could occur only if there was a change in the relation of the demand and the stock of money, but employment could alter as a result of changed productivity without any change in the level of real incomes. However, for the purposes of this analysis it is the short-run equilibrium that is important. And the proposition stands that changes in real income, and changes in employment in so far as the latter is a constant function of real income, can occur only if there is a change in the relation between the real stock of money and the demand for money in relation to income.[13]

Conclusion

The conclusion that money is crucial to the level of employment is not surprising, if one considers that the whole process of production and income creation is carried out through the medium of money, and that any change in economic behavior is likely to be expressed in the holding or use of money balances. For example, at an initial equilibrium, stability can occur only if the community in the aggregate is just willing, at that level of income, to spend the whole of its income on goods for consumption and investment. An increase can come only because individuals and enterprises want to spend in the aggregate *more* than the whole of current income. This means that at the current level of incomes they wish to reduce their money holdings. Since money holdings cannot be reduced simply by spending them, incomes must increase until the community is just willing to hold the outstanding stock of money rather than spend more on goods, just as the interest rate must adjust so that the community is willing to hold the whole of the money stock rather than make additional loans. For this reason, a change in the relation between the total demand for money and the outstanding stock of money would necessitate a change in the level of income, and a change in the level of income would be possible only if there were a change in the relation between the demand for money and the stock of money. Since, according to the insensitive-price theory of economic adjustment, changes in income and employment are intimately tied together, this means that, *in an insensitive-price economy the level of employment is dependent on the relation between the demand for money as a store of buying power and the outstanding stock of money.* This, in its basic essentials, is the monetary theory of employment.

If this theory is valid, it can give an important guide in appraising policies that are proposed for attaining and maintaining the optimum level of employment in an insensitive-price economy. To do this, each proposal would have to be valued in terms of how it affected the demand for money as a store of buying power, and how it affected the stock of money outstanding. Action that decreased the demand for money without altering the outstanding stock could be expected to increase employment. Action that increased the stock of money without altering the demand for money could be expected to increase employment. But action that increased the stock of money and at the same time increased the demand for money to an exactly equal extent could be expected to have no effect on the level of employment. Since in many cases a given action is likely to affect both the demand for and the stock of money, the more general statement would be that action which decreases the demand for money more than it decreases the stock outstanding or increases the stock of money more than it increases the demand for money, could be expected to increase employment while the reverse changes would decrease employment. But before these implications of the theory are discussed, the importance of testing the theory must be emphasized.

Notes

1. In abstract theoretical terms, perfect equilibrium would require that for each individual and enterprise, the marginal utility of each possible type of asset was just equal to the marginal utility of every other type, and the marginal utility of each type of consumption was just equal to the marginal utility of each type of asset. In practice, it would be sufficient that the advantage of more or less consumption, or more or less of this asset, or that was not sufficient to induce a change in the pattern of consumption or assets.

2. If interest rates and security prices were fixed, the dearth of funds would account directly for a fall in the demand for goods from those who use the savings of others.

3. It is worth noticing that the resultant decline in the total demand for goods would take place with *no* change either in the total propensity to save or in the investment opportunities at each possible level of interest rates and security prices. It would result solely from a shift in the *form* in which savers chose to hold their token savings, and the effect of this on interest rates and security prices.

4. It should be noted that in case of a shift from saving in the form of securities to saving in the form of money, a fall in security prices could have the effect of stimulating saving in all forms and, to the extent of greater saving in forms other than goods, would still further reduce the total demand for goods. This possibility will be discussed in the following two sections.

5. Of course, equilibrium would never be reached if the stock of money were to contract as rapidly as the price level fell.

6. The *immediate* effect of a fall in sales is likely to be an unintentional accumulation of inventory, which would offset the effect on employment of the fall in sales. But this would be temporary and represents an unstable condition. It would be included by recognizing the accumulation as a temporary, perhaps involuntary, increase in the demand for investment goods, which for a time partially offsets the effect of a decline in the demand for goods in other directions.

7. It is recognized, of course, that in the above case, the effort to build up money balances by spending less of current incomes on consumption reflects, in the language of the saving–investment theory, a decline in the propensity to consume, while the effort to shift from saving in goods to saving in money reflects a change in investment opportunities. But the effort to save more in the form of money and less in the form of other tokens involves a change in neither the propensity to consume nor the investment opportunities.

8. It is recognized, of course, that in the above case the net effort to shift from goods assets into money would reflect, in the language of the saving-investment

Figure 11.1 **[Income and Money Demand]**

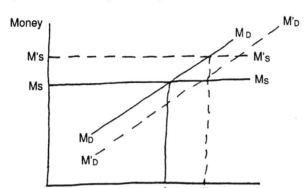

Source: These crude drawings are reproduced from Gardiner C. Means' original manuscript.

theory, a reduction in the opportunities to invest. This does not, however, appear to be a very appropriate way to describe this situation—particularly in the case of inventories.

9. This would be in addition to the *dynamic* effect of the change in security prices. We are not concerned in this equilibrium analysis with windfall gains or losses, that is, with the quasi-income or negative income represented by a *change* in the value of assets, but only with the different effect of different values of assets.

10. This assumes exactly the same amount of employment was provided per unit of value in the other companies as in the closed company.

11. This includes, of course, the goods that are obtained by having additional workers.

12. A minor exception would arise from the usual lag between purchase and sales transaction and the actual payment of money as a result of the transaction.

13. The justification for this conclusion can be shown more clearly by means of graphic analysis. In Figure 11.1 let the solid line M_DM_D represent the demand for money which would exist at each possible level of income, other factors being already given. If the line M_sM_s represented the stock of money outstanding, the demand for money and the stock would be equal at an income represented by the distance OI. If this is the initial level of income, and then income increases to that represented by the distance OI', this must have been brought about by factors that caused a decrease in the demand for money at the significant levels of income such as is represented by the dash line $M'_DM'_D$, by an increase in stock of money represented by the line $M'_sM'_s$, or by a compound movement of these two factors. If neither the stock of money nor the demand for money in relation to income changed, the stock of money and the demand for money would be equal only at the initial level of income, that represented by the distance OI.[2]

12

The Necessity of Testing the Monetary Theory

The first part of this book has been entirely theoretical. Assumptions have been made—some less, some more realistic—and the implications of these assumptions have been worked out. The process has been entirely in the realm of logic. Like problems in arithmetic or geometry, the conclusions reached, if logically correct, are implicit in the assumptions explicitly stated or inferred. Nothing new has been added by the analysis except a clarification of what is implicit in the combined assumptions. Any theory, however logical, must therefore be tested by the appeal to fact if it is to be a practical guide to policy. This chapter aims to open up the problem of making such an appeal.

There is one peculiar characteristic of the testing of a general theory that needs to be kept constantly in mind: a general theory can for practical purposes be *disproved* by a single fact; it cannot be *proved* by any number of facts.[1] The theory that the moon is made entirely of green cheese, if wrong, could be disproved by a single sample that was not green cheese. If right, it could not be proved by any number of samples. Each successive sample that turned out to be green cheese would increase the likelihood that the theory was correct but could not clinch it. Thus, a general theory can be definitely disproved, but proof can be only relative.[2] If the theory is consistent with all the available facts it becomes plausible. If it continues to be consistent with new facts as they become known, it may become an increasingly reliable basis for making policy, indeed may become so generally accepted as to be regarded as "proved." But all that can properly be said of it is that no fact has yet been found inconsistent with it.

Finally, it should be recognized that the problems of testing an economic theory are in many ways comparable to the problems involved in those physical sciences that cannot carry on laboratory experiments. The astronomer is no more able to move stars around in order to test a theory than is the economist able to manipulate a national economy for theory testing purposes. Yet, the testing and acceptance of some of our most basic scientific knowledge has resulted simply from observation of the heavens.[3]

The main testing problem in economics, as in astrophysics, is to develop hypotheses that are capable of being tested, to use the hypotheses in making predictions as to what can be expected under observable conditions if the hypotheses are valid, and to check the prediction against events. Hypotheses that lead to correct prediction are not themselves *necessarily* valid. Their success would, however, increase the likelihood of their validity. Likewise, hypotheses that lead to false prediction are not necessarily invalid. There may be extenuating circumstances,[4] but unless the extenuating circumstances are reasonably obvious and acceptable, false predictions are likely to discredit a theory. By this predicting (whether it be the timing of the eclipses, the bending of light as it passes the sun, or the magnitude of employment), and the subsequent check-up, the more dependable theories can be winnowed from the less.

In addition to the test by projection, any theory must meet two preliminary factual tests. First, are the assumptions of the theory consistent with known facts, and, second, have events in the past followed a pattern consistent with the theory?

In actual practice, the testing of a theory of the sort set forth here must be a matter of years and should engage the activity of opponents to the theory as well as proponents. All that will be attempted here is to indicate the validity of certain assumptions underlying the present theory, show how actual developments have been consistent with certain of the expectations implicit in the theory, and make a single major prediction which, if it proved to be correct, would go a small way in supporting the validity of the monetary theory of employment.

Assumptions Underlying the Monetary Theory

The three most important assumptions underlying the monetary theory of employment have already been indicated and can be listed as follows:

1. A significant body of prices are relatively insensitive to changes in aggregate demand.
2. The aggregate demand for goods is, in part, a function of the real stock of money outstanding.
3. The aggregate demand for goods is, in part, a function of the real value of nonmonetary assets.

The first two of these assumptions are essential to the monetary theory as an explanation of the level of employment; the third is an integral part of the theory as it has been presented here, but is not essential. These assumptions are important, not because they are the only assumptions underlying the theory, but because they involve a significant departure from the assumptions usually made in theories of employment.

The Insensitivity of Goods Prices

The first of these assumptions has become so generally accepted in recent years that it needs little substantiation. The insensitivity in the prices of government services and those of regulated utilities is common knowledge, as well as the fact that such services play a larger proportionate role in our economy now than they did in the days when employment theories for a sensitive-price economy were developed. The insensitivity of unregulated industrial prices has received much attention.[5] Only in the field of agriculture is there a large proportion of prices that behave in the classical sensitive fashion.

The insensitivity of unregulated industrial prices can be graphically brought out in two figures. The first, Figure 12.1, shows the relative frequency of price change in the items making up the wholesale price index of the Bureau of Labor Statistics.[6] The items at the left of Figure 12.1 changed price infrequently and consist, for the most part, of industrial products; those at the right of Figure 12.1 changed frequently and consist, for the most part, of agricultural products and goods made directly from them.[7] That nearly a third of all the items showed fewer than twelve price changes in eight years is striking evidence of insensitivity.

Figure 12.2 shows the relation between infrequency of price change and the magnitude of the price drop in the great decline of prices from 1929 to 1932.[8] As in Figure 12.1, the infrequently changing prices are at the left and those that change more frequently are at the right. The

Figure 12.1 **Administered and Market Prices** (617 items from B.L.S. wholesale price index distributed according to frequency of price change)

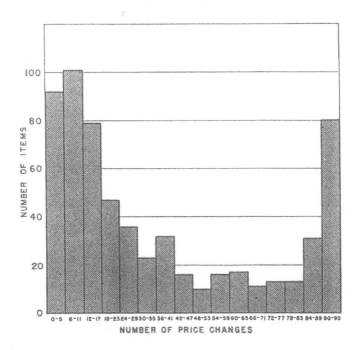

Source: Based on data given in Appendix 2, table I of *The Structure of the American Economy: Part I, Basic Characteristics.* June 1939, National Resources Committee.

individual dots represent the indexes of the prices of the different items in 1932 with the 1929 prices as 100 (the solid line). It is clear from Figure 12.3 that the more highly administered prices, those tending to change infrequently, also tended to drop least in the three-year period, and those with the greatest frequency of change tended to drop most. Of course, *within* each group there was a considerable dispersion of behavior, as is indicated by the scatter of dots. But for the price structure as a whole, it can be said that there was a downward rotation of prices as aggregate demand declined.

These two figures would be pretty conclusive proof of the insensitivity of a large body of prices to changes in aggregate demand if it were not for one fact. It might be that the difference in the relative fall

Figure 12.2 **Rigid and Flexible Prices**

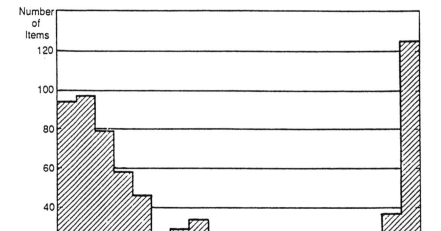

Number of Price Changes, 1926–1933

in prices was due to differences in the income elasticity of demand and not to insensitivity of prices. Presumably the depression drop in demand for some commodities was greater than for others. If all prices were perfectly sensitive it might be expected that some prices would drop more than others. Theoretically, this *could* explain the difference in the drop in prices at the right and the left sides of Figure 12.2. But if this were the explanation, we should expect that where prices dropped little it would be because the demand dropped little, and the greatest drop in prices would reflect the greatest drop in demand. Actually, the

Table 12.1

Price and Production Drop for Certain Major Industries

1929–32

	Price drop (in percent)	Production drop (in percent)
Motor vehicles	12	74
Agricultural implements	14	84
Cement	16	55
Iron and steel	16	76
Auto tires	25	42
Leather products	33	18
Petroleum products	36	17
Textile products	39	28
Food products	39	10
Agricultural commodities	54	1

Source: *The Structure of the American Economy*, p. 386.

reverse is the case. As can be seen in Table 12.1, there was a tendency for production to fall greatly in the industries with the smallest drop in prices. Clearly, the small drop in prices was not in general due to the absence of a significant fall in demand. The statistical evidence thus clearly points to prices that are relatively insensitive to changes in demand in a short-run period.[9]

Whether or not the insensitivity of prices that these data show was due to insensitivity of costs is immaterial to the validity of the monetary theory of employment. There is ample evidence that some of the insensitivity was due to insensitivity of wage rates and other costs, and that some was not due to insensitivity in costs.[10] But we are not here concerned with the cause of the insensitivity of goods prices, only with the statistical evidence indicating the fact of insensitivity. This fact of insensitivity of goods prices means that in a part of the economy, prices cannot adjust easily and quickly to fairly general changes in demand. It justifies the first basic assumption underlying the monetary theory of employment.

Money and the Aggregate Demand for Goods

The second assumption underlying the theory, namely, that the demand for goods is, in part, a function of the real stock of money outstanding, is more difficult to establish statistically. Essentially, this assumption says that the higher the real stock of money outstanding, the more the community will spend on goods.[11] If this were a simple and constant relation, it should not be difficult to establish statistically, but it is reasonable to expect that the demand for money, like the demand for any particular good, can vary from time to time for reasons other than changes in income. Individuals or enterprises may want to speculate in inventories and thus reduce the demand for money. Interest rates may fall and increase the demand for money. Or a variety of other factors can change the demand. This means that, over a period of years, a high correlation between the amount of money outstanding in different years and the volume of goods purchases for consumption and investment is not to be expected.

Actual figures for money holdings and aggregate expenditure do show a rough correspondence in the short-run shifts as can be seen from the figure. (A figure will be inserted here showing, from 1913 to 1942, the real stock of money outside the Treasury and Commercial Banks and real Gross National Product.) [Editors' note: This figure was not found in the Means manuscript.] Except for the two war periods when conditions were abnormal, the two curves tend to rise and fall together. The short depression in 1921–22 and the long depression of the 1930s are both mirrored in the stock of money outstanding.

There is not, however, a constant relation between the two. The real money stock has tended to increase relative to the real expenditure on goods. This can be explained partly in terms of trend—an increasing demand for money relative to income and expenditure through time, perhaps in part due to the accumulation of assets—and partly in terms of interest rates, with the demand for money increasing with lower interest rates. However, if these two factors do not explain the whole of the variation in the relationship, this could be explained by variations in the demand for money arising from other sources. Thus the data given above *are consistent with* the assumption that the demand for goods is in part a function of the volume of money outstanding, though other factors also appear to affect demand.

However, these data cannot be said to give very conclusive support to the assumption that the demand for goods is a function of the real stock of money. There are other possible assumptions with which the data are also consistent. Most particularly, it might be argued that an increase in real economic activity generates an increase in the real stock of money. Perhaps definitive testing of this second assumption can come only through sampling studies that seek to discover what factors influence the amount of money individuals and enterprises choose to hold and what causes them to change their holdings. Such sampling surveys might determine the validity of this assumption, and also indicate the magnitude of the effect of different factors in determining the demand for money and the effect of the supply of money on the demand for goods.

Nonmonetary Assets and the Aggregate Demand for Goods

The third assumption—that the aggregate demand for goods is, in part, a function of the real value of nonmonetary assets—is almost impossible to test with the statistics now available since there is no adequate series representing the value of assets. Efforts to test this assumption should include both the development of adequate estimates of the value of nonmonetary assets, which can then be related to real income and sampling studies that seek to discover the role of asset values in economic management. For the present, all that can be said on these three basic assumptions underlying the monetary theory is that:

1. The insensitivity of prices is pretty clearly established.
2. The assumption as to the relation between money and aggregate demand is consistent with the evidence for recent years but not proved.
3. The assumption as to the relation between nonmonetary assets and aggregate demand cannot yet be tested.

Consistency with Developments in Recent Years

A second step in the procedure for testing the monetary theory is to examine the actual developments of recent years to see if they are consistent with the theory. This is a huge undertaking that cannot be carried out in this volume. All that can be done here is to consider certain of the more important developments from this point of view. If the theory of employment is valid, the effect of changes in aggregate demand on prices and production must be those indicated by the insensitive-price theory of economic adjustment, and the changes in aggregate demand must be consistent with the monetary theory of aggregate demand.

The Effect of Differences in
Aggregate Demand

Data are available for the depression and recovery of the 1930s to check the first of these requirements, the effect of differences in aggregate demand on prices and production. Between 1929 and 1937 aggregate real demand dropped approximately 40 percent and recovered to approximately its initial level.[12] According to the insensitive-price theory of economic adjustment, a decline in aggregate demand should be expected to produce (1) a downward rotation of prices with the insensitive prices dropping little and the sensitive prices dropping more; and (2) a downward rotation of production with production at the insensitive end of the price scale dropping most. Likewise, a recovery in aggregate demand should result in corresponding upward rotations. That this is exactly what happened is borne out by Figure 12.3, which shows the price and production behavior for the least frequently and the most frequently changing prices in the Bureau of Labor Statistics wholesale price index, with about 15 percent of all items of the index in each group.

It is clear from Figure 12.3 that in this particular period of great differences in the level of aggregate demand, the differences worked themselves out primarily in a major change in production for the most insensitive prices, and primarily in price changes for the most sensitive priced items. For the latter group, government crop control reduced production somewhat in 1933 and the following years, but before that, production had been relatively stable in spite of a 50 percent drop in prices, while the insensitive price group showed more than a 50 percent drop in production, but less than a 10 percent drop in prices.[13] Thus, price and production behavior from 1929 to 1937 was approximately that which could be expected on the basis of the insensitive-price theory of economic adjustment.[14]

Money and the Level of Aggregate Demand

The second test by past experience, that of the monetary theory of aggregate demand, can only be explored briefly here. The theory would lead one to expect that changes in aggregate demand would occur only when there was a change in the relation between the demand for money and the stock of money. Figures for the stock of money are given in the figure [Editorial note: This figure was not

Figure 12.3 **Production and Prices of Administered and Market Price Commodities**

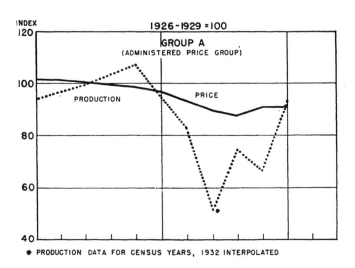

* PRODUCTION DATA FOR CENSUS YEARS, 1932 INTERPOLATED

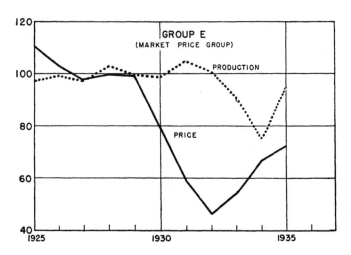

Source: See Appendix 18, Section 24 of *The Structure of the American Economy: Part I. Basic Characteristics*, June 1939, National Resources Committee.

found in the Means manuscript], and figures for aggregate demand can be deduced from aggregate expenditure, but no basis has yet been developed for measuring changes in the demand for money. Sampling studies and analysis of the behavior of individual companies may someday lead to the creation of an independently derived index of changes in the demand for money, which could serve to test the theory. With available statistics, the most that can be done is to derive from the figures of money outstanding and of aggregate demand a rough index of changes in the demand for money that would have to have taken place if the monetary theory of aggregate demand is valid. If other considerations make such changes in the demand for money seem likely, this would suggest that the actual data is at least consistent with the monetary theory of aggregate demand.

Such an index of hypothetical changes in the propensity to hold money is given in the figure [Editors' note: No chart exists in the manuscript] for the years 1919 to 1941. The index has been derived simply by dividing an index of the real stock of money outstanding in each year by an index of the real volume of expenditure on goods and services as represented by a deflated national income series. The resulting index is necessarily crude. It rests on the assumption that a line representing the demand for money at different possible levels of income at a given point in time would not only be straight but would pass through the origin. While it seems quite possible that the propensity to hold money can be closely approximated by a straight line, it seems almost certain that such a line would pass above the origin, since there is a clear tendency to hold more money per unit of income in depression than in prosperity.

The conclusions from this analysis might be called mildly favorable to the monetary theory. The events covered are reasonably consistent with the monetary theory of aggregate demand. That is, no important change in aggregate demand took place that could not be explained by an actual change in the stock of money or by a change in demand that might reasonably have taken place. But, because there is not *independent* information available on changes in the demand for money, the only definitive conclusion that can be reached is that examination of the data did not disprove the theory. However, the data do tend to give some slight support to the theory, in that they show a pattern of behavior that is not only consistent with it, but would not be expected in the absence of some such theory. The data is thus somewhat encouraging to the monetary theory, but in no way conclusive.

A Forecast for Testing

The next few years may, however, give an important opportunity to test the weakest link in the monetary theory, the relation between money and aggregate demand. War financing has greatly increased the real stock of money and other liquid assets in the hands of the public. If the monetary theory is valid and the real stock of money remains permanently higher than before the war, there should be a more or less permanent increase in the propensities to consume and invest, and so a permanent increase in the level about which aggregate demand fluctuates. This effect should be reinforced by the increase in the real value of the nonmoney assets. If these shifts actually take place, it means that schedules representing the propensities to consume and invest after the war should be higher than the corresponding schedules before the war. If statistical measurements show such a shift, it will be a significant vindication of the theory.

Three difficulties arise in making such a test: (1) A general rise in prices may eliminate the increase in the real value of the stock of money so that no shift in propensities survives; (2) the abnormal character of the demand and supply of goods in the immediate post-war years may distort the relationship; and (3) the actual propensities to spend may not be known.

A Price Rise

The first of these difficulties does not seem to be too serious, since it is unlikely that the whole of the increase in the real stock of money and other assets will be eliminated by price increases.

The Transition to Peace

The second difficulty, the abnormal character of demand as a result of the war, is also not too serious. It means that the first two or possibly three years after the war cannot be used as satisfactory tests of the theory. This is unfortunate because the longer the lapse of time after the big increase in money stocks occurred, the more likely that other new factors will come into play and submerge its effects. It seems likely, however, that this difficulty can be minimized by analysis of expenditures for separate categories, such as nondurable goods in relation to disposable income.

Can the Propensities Be Determined?

The third difficulty in testing seems likely to be more serious, since it is not clear that the propensities to consume and invest can be accurately measured. It is often assumed that, by plotting a time series of consumer expenditures against the corresponding series of consumer disposable income, a relationship can be discovered that represents the propensity to spend on consumption. If this is the case, then the monetary theory would require a higher expenditure on consumption in relation to disposable income after the war than before.

However, it has never been established that the regression of consumer expenditure against disposable income represented the propensity to consume. If, as the monetary theory suggests, there is some factor, in this case money, which increases the propensity to consume or the propensity to invest, or both, in a regular fashion, then to the extent that this factor causes changes in activity, there will be a smooth regression of consumption (or investment) on disposable income, yet the regression would *not* represent the propensity to consume (or invest).[15]

If the regression of consumer expenditure on disposable income does not represent the propensity to consume, then it would be possible for the postwar consumer expenditure to lie on the prewar regression and yet represent an increased propensity to consume. Indeed, if the fluctuation in activity before the war had been *solely* due to changes in the stock of money, which caused regular shifts in the propensities to consume and invest, the war-increased stock of money would be expected to increase the propensities to consume and invest, and thus support a higher level of activity; but consumer expenditure would fall on the prewar regression line unless some extraneous factor caused a change in the propensity to consume or to invest.

If this conclusion is accepted, the simple analysis of time series does not appear able to provide a definitive test of the monetary as compared with the saving–investment theory, and one must resort to sampling studies or to more complicated analyses of time series. On the basis of the monetary theory, one can predict that both the propensity to consume and the propensity to invest will be considerably higher than before the war, unless a major price rise reduces the real value of the money stock to something like prewar levels. Insofar as the regression of consumer expenditure does represent the propensity to consume, this prediction means that the postwar consumer expenditure should lie above the prewar regression.

Recent Events

It is too soon to test the theory by the postwar data, partly because of the abnormal catching up demand and partly because so many goods, particularly durable goods and services, are not yet freely available at current prices.[16] However, statistics for consumer expenditure during the last year are suggestive. In the figures below, prewar data for consumer expenditure in toto and for the major divisions of expenditure—nondurable goods, durable goods, and services—are plotted against disposable income and the prewar regressions drawn in.[17] To this have been added the corresponding data for the war years and, most important, for the four quarters of 1946. [Editors' note: Means intended to insert figures here, but none were found in the manuscript.]

Expenditures on durable goods and on services continue to be low in relation to the prewar regressions, though durable goods sales are rapidly approaching the prewar relation. Nondurable goods sales, on the other hand, are [Means did not specify a number] percent above the prewar relation. To some extent this high relation can be attributed to catching up demand. It has been suggested that an important part of this high demand was the result of spending on nondurables because durable goods were not available, *and would disappear when expenditures on durables reached the postwar relation to disposable income.* However, the rapid expansion in durable goods sales during 1946 has not prevented an expansion in nondurable goods sales. Durable goods sales have risen almost to the prewar relation to disposable income, but nondurable goods sales, instead of falling, have risen even further above the prewar relation. As a result, total consumer expenditure has begun to climb above the prewar relation, even though many services and durable goods are still undersupplied. If this climb continues and total consumer sales remain consistently above the prewar relation to disposable income, even after the bulk of the catching up demand has been satisfied and durable goods and services are freely available, this would seem to lend considerable support to the monetary theory of employment.

Conclusion

The preceding analysis has not attempted to give an adequate test of the monetary theory. Its purpose has been, first, to emphasize the need for testing the theory, second, to show that the theory is consistent with certain readily available facts, and third, to open up the problem of testing so that a more intensive testing can be undertaken both as to consistency with past events and as to forecasts of future events. The remaining chapters will be written on the assumption that the theory is not only logically sound but is proved by events to be valid.

Notes

1. The reality of "a fact" is often questioned. The meticulous reader may want to substitute the term "event" for the term "fact" in the above. An event would then be that part of the space-time continuum upon which the instruments of perception were focused for the purpose at hand. The "fact" would then be the abstraction that summarized those elements in the event that were regarded as significant for the purpose in hand.

2. It should be noted that the reverse may be true of a specific theory. Thus, the theory that there is green cheese on the moon, if correct, could be proved with a single sample, but if incorrect could not be disproved by any number of samples.

3. The creation of elaborate apparatus for observing the heavens should not be confused with the conducting of laboratory experiments, that is, with the manipulation of the factors being observed.

4. The forecast that mixing hydrochloric acid and sodium hydroxide will produce salt and water is not basically disproved if, at the moment of mixture, a stroke of lightning ionizes the ingredients. The forecast is wrong, but the extenuating circumstances may require only a more careful wording of the theory.

5. See particularly Gardner C. Means, *Industrial Prices and Their Relative Inflexibility,* Senate Document 13, 74th Congress, 1st Session; Gardiner C. Means and Associates, *The Structure of the American Economy,* National Resources Committee, 1939, chapter VIII.

6. It is frequently suggested that, because of the methods of reporting to the Bureau of Labor Statistics, the actual *weekly* statistics of the bureau probably somewhat exaggerate the infrequency of price changes. However, the monthly data (average of weekly data), which were used in the Table 13.1, exaggerate the frequency of the changes reflected in the weekly data. This arises from the fact that a price change in the middle weeks of a month will cause the *average* for the month to lie intermediate between the price at the beginning and at the end of the month, so that in a three month period, if the only price change was of this sort, the monthly averages would show two steps of change and the single price change would be reported as two changes in the above figure. This is likely to be most important for the least sensitive prices. These two effects are roughly offsetting.

7. The 194 items represented by the two left-hand bars, which changed less than twelve times in eight years, include only fourteen items that are agricultural or closely related products: cornflakes; wheat cereal; bread (two items); crackers (three items); powdered cocoa; grape juice; tobacco products (three items); opium; California redwood. The 123 items represented by the two right-hand bars, whose price changed seventy-eight or more times in eight years, include only twelve items not agricultural in character or directly derived from agricul-

tural products: fuel oil (two items); gasoline (three items); kerosene; paraffin; steel scrap; antimony; silver; tin; zinc.

8. From Gardner C. Means, *Industrial Prices and their Relative Inflexibility*, Senate Document 13, 74th Congress, 1st Session, p. 3.

9. It is not being suggested here that the price-makers should have dropped their prices, only that prices should have come down *if the classical assumption of price sensitivity was to have been met.* The failure to come down is a reflection on the validity of the classical assumption, not on the behavior of the price-makers.

10. Indeed, insensitivity of wage rates may sometimes be a result of insensitive prices rather than the reverse, as a producer decides to hold a price and also to hold wage rates.

11. In saving–investment terms, this assumption is that the propensities to consume and to invest will both be higher with a large real stock of money outstanding than with a small real stock.

12. See Chart I, page 2, *The Structure of the American Economy,* see note 5. The changes in real income shown in the chart are presumed to reflect equivalent changes in aggregate demand.

13. It may be argued that the primary difference in behavior for the different groups is explained by the fact that one group is dominated by capital, and durable, goods, while the other is largely made up of agricultural products. This may explain why there is a tendency for some items to become insensitive and others not. But if capital and durable goods prices were actually "made in the market" and were therefore sensitive, they could have been expected to fall as much as or more than agricultural prices.

14. It should be noted that the theory itself was developed to generalize the behavior of prices from 1929 to the end of 1935. Thus, the consistency between theory and practice in this period is to be expected. However, the theory insofar as it relates to the differential effect of changes in aggregate demand on prices and production was fully worked out by the author before the end of 1935, as is indicated in "Notes on Inflexible Prices," *American Economic Review Supplement,* Vol. XXVI, No. 1, March, 1936, p. 23. This means that the consistency of events with the theory *after* 1935 is in some degree a support of the theory.

15. This possibility can be brought out clearly in a diagram. Let the solid lines in Figure 12.4 represent an initial condition with line PC representing the initial propensity to consume, and PS representing the initial propensity to spend on both consumption and investment goods (the difference between PC and PS would represent the initial propensity to invest). The intersection of PS with OD would then represent the point at which total expenditure just equaled disposable income, thus establishing the level of activity at a disposable income OA. Then, if an increase in the stock of money caused an increase in the propensity to consume to the level represented by $P'C'$, with a resulting higher propensity to spend in total represented by $P'S'$, the new level of activity would be represented by a disposable income of OB. However, if the actual figures for expenditure on consumption were plotted against actual disposable income, the regression line obtained would be the dotted line passing through X and Y. This is clearly not a regression representing a propensity to consume at either the initial or the second point in time, or to any intermediate point. In the case above, the regression line is steeper than either assumed propensity to consume.

16. The low supply of services is in large part a lack of rental housing, but also a lack of telephone, electric power, and similar utility services and various retail functions, domestic servants, and so on.

17. Cite Department of Commerce. [Means provided no specific citation.]

Figure 12.4 [Income, Consumption, and Stock of Money]

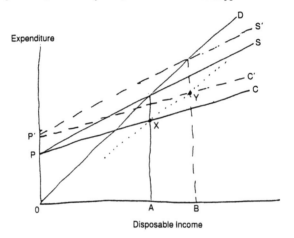

Source: These crude drawings are reproduced from Gardiner C. Means' original manuscript.

Part V

Problems of
Corrective Action

13

The Problem of Maintaining
Full Employment

The present chapter is concerned with the theoretical problem of *maintaining* full employment, once a condition of equilibrium at full employment has been established. Such a condition of equilibrium will first be sketched for a somewhat simplified economy. Then, attention will give given to the major changes, other than changes in goods prices, which, according to the monetary theory of employment, could lead to insufficient or excessive employment. And finally, corrective action of various sorts will be considered, some of a more and some of a less desirable character. In carrying out this analysis, no effort will be made to take account of dynamic factors or the fact that, in a dynamic economy, a condition of equilibrium may never occur—may indeed be impossible. The purpose here is to explore certain of the implications of the monetary theory, not to lay an immediate basis for policy.

An Equilibrium at Full Employment

A condition of full employment could be said to exist if the only unemployment were voluntary or due directly to the lack of perfect mobility of resources. It would presumably exist if the effective demand for goods were adequate to absorb all the goods that could be produced by those willing and able to work, except as output was limited by the current techniques of production and the relative immobility of resources. For the immediate purpose, it is not necessary to go deeper into the meaning of full employment. In any concrete situation, the determination of full employment is likely to be a problem of practical politics rather than a technical problem.[1] Of more immediate importance is the question of what is meant by equilibrium.

Equilibrium at full employment could be said to exist if there was full employment, and if there were no forces inherent in the economic situation itself that would force a departure from full employment in either direction. There would not be such an equilibrium, for example, if the condition of full employment were reached so rapidly that the process engendered speculative activity that would lead to over-employment, or if it were reached by speculative activity that would presently collapse and lead to underemployment. At a full employment equilibrium, the total demand for goods in each successive period would be sufficient and just sufficient to absorb the goods that could be produced at full employment in that period, and the rates of produc-tion, consumption, and investment would be such that there was no initial tendency to depart from this condition. Such a condition would exist if the outstanding stock of money was just equal to the demand for money at the level of income corresponding to full employment, and if there was no tendency for either the demand for or the stock of money to change. Under these hypothetical conditions, the economy could be expected to run along on an even keel. The question to be considered in this chapter is what sort of developments could throw the economy off this even keel, and what measures could be taken to prevent or offset these developments.

Changes Making for Under-
or Overemployment

It is not difficult to list the major types of changes that could lead to under- or overemployment, so long as it is recognized that the change *must* involve a change in either the demand for or in the outstanding stock of money. This conclusion of the monetary theory means that the whole problem can be covered by investigating the different types of changes in the demand for money and in the stock of money outstanding.

The investigation can be simplified by limiting it to the action of five essentially different types of economic or accounting units: indi-viduals, business enterprises, investment companies, banks, and gov-ernment. It will be assumed that business enterprises carry on all the production of goods (commodities and services), while individuals act only in their capacity of obtaining and disposing of money incomes, consumption goods, and token assets. This accounting separation of individual and business activity actually exists for most of the American economy.[2] The activity of investment companies—investment trusts, saving banks, insurance companies, and so forth, and the banking system—will be assumed to be limited to transactions involving only token assets.[3] It will be assumed that money can enter or leave the economic system through the action of either the banking system or government but not otherwise. And also, government action will be assumed to include only the handling of token assets and the production of services financed out of taxes or through borrowing (including the issue of money). Any government production of goods for sale will be excluded from consideration.[4] Finally, all problems of international trade and finance will be excluded so that the analysis will be dealing only with a closed economy. Such a simplified economy will allow consideration of the major types of changes leading to under- or overemployment. Minor changes such as might arise in conjunction with government production for sale, the nontoken transactions of banks and investment companies, and the activities of eleemosynary institutions can be worked out by the reader after the major types have been covered in the simplified economy outlined above.

In this simplified economy, any change that throws the economy off its even keel must come from a change in the pattern of behavior of one or more of the five groups of economic units. In what follows, the major possible changes in pattern on the part of each group that could lead to under- or overemployment will be considered separately. Changes in the pattern of behavior of the aggregate of individuals will be considered first, followed by that of business investment companies, banks, and finally government. It must be understood, of course, that any concrete departure from a full employment equilibrium might arise from a simultaneous change in pattern on the part of more than one group, while an action by one group that by itself would cause a departure from such an equilibrium might be offset by action of other groups tending in the opposite direction.

Changes Initiated by Individuals

Individuals could throw the simplified economy off its even keel and threaten unemployment if, in the aggregate, they sought to build up their money holdings and there was no offsetting change in the desire of other groups to hold money balances, and no change in the amount of money outstanding. Such an effort of individuals to build up money balances might take any one of four major forms.[5] Individuals might seek to add to their money balances

1. by spending a smaller part of their incomes on goods;
2. by increasing their incomes through greater productive activity;[6]
3. by investing a smaller part of their incomes in loans and securities; or
4. by reducing their holdings of other token assets.

Each of these types of action would lead to unemployment unless there was counteraction elsewhere in the system. The first type, smaller spending on goods, would involve a direct reduction in the aggregate demand for goods (assuming the demand for goods from other sources remained the same); the second, greater offering of labor, would mean additional involuntary unemployment if not used, or, if used, would mean an increase in the aggregate of goods available without an increase in the aggregate demand for goods. The other two changes, buying fewer securities out of income or converting securities already held into cash, if not offset would lead to reduction in the level of security prices with resultant employment-reducing repercussions on the economic management of both individuals and enterprises. In whichever way individuals, in the aggregate, sought to build up their money holdings, unless an exactly offsetting change took place on the part of one or more of the other five groups, a new equilibrium could be expected only at less than full employment.

It is likely that historical examples of each of the types of change in individual demand could be found. A "buyers' strike," such as is purported to have occurred in 1920, would exemplify the first. The secular growth in the demand for money that results from the normal secular growth in the labor force and production is an example of expanding income to add to money balances. A flight from loans and securities into gold was traditionally an essential ingredient of a gold panic, and a flight from securities into money was certainly a part of the 1929–32 debacle. Undoubtedly, examples could be found of an aggregate effort of individuals to add to their money holdings by investing a smaller proportion of their current saving in loans and securities. Here are four major types of action that could lead to underemployment. The reverse actions—efforts to bring down money balances in any of the four ways—could lead to overemployment and inflation.

Changes Initiated by Business Enterprise

A comparable series of actions by business enterprises could also lead to under- or overemployment. Efforts on the part of businesses to increase their aggregate money holdings, unless offset by a reduced demand by other groups or an increase in the money stock outstanding, would lead directly or indirectly to unemployment. In the case of business, there would be four major ways in which money balances could be increased:

1. by converting inventories into "cash";
2. by converting fixed assets into "cash"[7] (through not reinvesting in goods the recovered capital represented by allocations to depreciation);
3. by converting tokens other than money into "cash" (this would include newly issued securities and new loans as well as securities already held); and
4. by adding to "cash" out of earnings.

As in the case of individuals, each of these efforts to build up money balances would lead to unemployment unless offset elsewhere in the system. Converting inventories into "cash" would mean satisfying current demand out of inventories without fully replacing them. This would cause a direct reduction in aggregate demand. Converting fixed assets into "cash" by not investing funds allocated to depreciation would mean the using up of the "inventory of capital equipment" without replacing it, and lead to unemployment in much the same way as a conversion of ordinary inventory into "cash."[8] The effort to build up money balances by selling securities, by borrowing, or by other purely token transactions would mean that other groups in the system were placed under pressure to reduce their money holdings while security prices would be reduced. For reasons already indicated, this would result in unemployment unless offset by other action in the system. A building up of money balances out of earnings would mean that enterprises were not disposing of the whole of their income dividends or investment, and were thus a depressing influence unless their action(s) were offset. Thus, in each case, the effort on the part of business to build up money balances would lead to unemployment if not corrected.

Historical examples of efforts to convert inventories and fixed assets into cash are not difficult to find. Nearly every depression has involved an effort of particular enterprises to become more liquid by converting inventories into cash, by holding the proceeds of depreciation as cash rather than acquiring new equipment, by converting securities into cash, or by reducing dividends. Often the efforts to become more liquid have been thwarted by the lack of more money to hold, and so may not show up in statistics, but that the effort is a usual concomitant of depression is common business knowledge.

Changes Initiated by Investment Companies

The case of change initiated by investment companies is simple under the assumptions of the simplified economy. The only way they could increase their money holdings would be (1) by converting a part of their portfolios of loans and securities into "cash," or (2) by issuing additional obligations and holding the proceeds in cash. In either case, the action would force a reduction in the money holdings of other groups with the resultant effects on employment.

Changes Initiated by the Banking System

Banking action leading to unemployment would not take the form of building up of money balances, but of reducing the stock of money outstanding. Under the American banking system, operating banks can reduce the stock of money outstanding in two main ways: (1) by selling securities from their portfolios, and (2) by contracting their outstanding volume of loans.[9] Also, the Reserve banks can decrease the money outstanding through selling securities in the open market. In each case, the effect on employment would be essentially the same as that of an effort of individuals or enterprises to build money balances by reducing their holdings of securities or loans, but with this difference. The individual or business action would involve an increase in the demand for money and a decreased demand for securities or loans. The bank action would also involve a decrease in the demand for securities or loans, but it would involve a decrease in the outstanding stock of money rather than an increase in the demand for money. Also the bank action might, under particular circumstances, be forced by borrowers who repaid loans and were unwilling or unable to borrow further. Thus, the money stock might contract, not because banks wanted to reduce loans but because they were unable to make new loans in sufficient amounts.

Changes Initiated by Government

Government action is probably the most complex because it can affect the monetary balances on both the demand and the supply side. It can draw money away from other units in the system and thereby increase its money holdings or retire money from circulation in three major ways:

1. by increasing its tax revenue;
2. by decreasing its expenditures; and
3. by borrowing (or retiring its debt at a slower rate).

Each of these actions, whether it is employed to increase the money holdings of government or to retire money outstanding, would tend to reduce employment. Tax collections held continuously as cash on hand would take buying power out of people's hands without simultaneously putting an equivalent amount back through expenditures, and thus reduce the demand for goods and employment. Decreased expenditure would have a direct effect on employment. Borrowing for the purpose of holding larger money balances or for retiring outstanding money would tend to force down security prices and thus tend to reduce employment. Thus, an effort of government to build up its money holdings or to retire outstanding money would be likely to bring a reduction in employment, unless a counterbalancing change took place elsewhere in the economy.

The Net Effect of Changes

In practice, it can be expected that in any given period there would be many offsetting changes, some tending to bring about a reduction in employment, others tending to increase employment. Thus, if individuals sought to buy less for consumption and add to their money holdings while business, in the aggregate, sought to add to inventory and reduce its money holdings, the two could be exactly offsetting and there would be no effect on total employment. Or, government might seek to sell bonds and add to its money holdings while individuals sought to shift a part of their assets from money into bonds.

There may even be three- or four-way offsets. Individuals might seek to spend less on consumption and hold more money, while banks were seeking to expand the money stock through buying securities, and business enterprises were seeking to expand their fixed assets, selling securities to finance the expansion. These three actions could be in amounts just sufficient to offset each other with no change in the total demand for goods and employment.

But in practice there are likely to be changes that are not offsetting, and the net effect is likely to be under- or overemployment unless appropriate action is taken.

Corrective Action

In exploring corrective action to maintain full employment, no effort will be made to suggest what kind of measures should be adopted. In some cases, a certain amount of under- or overemployment might be preferable to the corrective measures that might be taken. The purpose in this chapter is to explore the kind of measures that could be effective, not to evaluate or recommend such measures.

Corrective action can be divided into three main types. It may be preventive, as where measures are taken to keep fluctuations in business inventories to a minimum. It may be specifically offsetting, as would be the case if the banking system offset a flight from securities into money by buying securities and expanding the outstanding stock of money. And it may be generally offsetting, as where expansionist action is taken to increase employment without specific attention to the changes that have initiated the unemployment. Since the generally offsetting action involves certain complex problems that will be discussed in the next chapter, these will not be discussed here. Attention will be focused in this chapter only on preventive action and specifically offsetting action.

One other distinction needs to be drawn before considering corrective measures. The action that requires correction may be temporary, requiring only a temporary corrective, or may call for a permanent corrective. Some measures may serve in either case, while some would be more appropriate for a temporary and others for a continuing change.

Preventive measures will be concerned with minimizing disruptive actions on the part of individuals, business enterprises, and investment companies. For the purposes of this analysis, offsetting actions will be limited to those which can be taken by government and by the banking system.

Preventive Measures

Preventive measures would aim to limit the extent to which individuals, business enterprises, and investment companies seek, *in the aggregate,* to build up or deplete their money holdings by either shifting out of or into other assets, or by the way in which they dispose of their income. If each group in the community were willing, at full employment, to maintain its money holdings constant, or if any change in the desire of one group to hold money were just offset by an opposite change in the other groups, and if the money stock remained constant, the economy would remain on an even keel. This would mean no general effort to shift from inventories into money or the reverse; no general effort to convert securities and loans into money or the reverse; and no general effort to save or dissave in the form of money.

Actually, it would be most undesirable to attempt to put a straitjacket on the holding of money balances. Within considerable limits, it would be better to offset shifts in the demand for money by changes in the volume of money outstanding. But to some extent the short-term shifts in the demand for money could be reduced. How far such measures should go can only be considered after considering the problem of offsets. Here they are introduced only for discussion.

Minimizing General Shifts between Inventories and Money

Various measures could be taken to prevent major shifts from business inventories into cash or the reverse. First, more accurate information on actual inventories is needed with an indication of the ways in which changes in inventory are being financed. Second, it should be possible to make estimates as to what volume of inventory is needed, industry by industry, to carry on the volume of production that could be expected at full employment. These estimates might be arrived at both on the basis of historical experience and on the basis of estimates by individual industries or businesses as to what their industries or companies are likely to require. Such estimates would presumably not be very precise, but should provide a rough guide to measure abnormally high or low inventories and to appraise inventory changes. These two types of information should serve to warn the business units in an industry when inventories are becoming excessive and, up to a point, could be expected to lead to greater stability. Beyond a point, however, information that competitors were shifting from cash into inventory or the reverse might lead to greater speculation and less stability of inventory. However, since the information on inventories is needed for other purposes, this is a risk that would have to be taken.

A second type of action to stabilize inventories is that taken by individual business or industries. The automobile industry is outstanding in this respect, with a close control of production and inventory so that the only significant variations in inventory are due to the normal seasonal variation in demand for cars and the level of production itself. How far individual industries can go in this direction is not clear, but undoubtedly much more can be done than is now customary.

A third area of measures to encourage stability of inventories lies in the field of credit. In some industries a significant volume of inventory is carried on bank credit. If the banking system were in a position to raise interest rates and even limit credit extension where inventories were excessive or increasing too rapidly, and to extend credit more liberally when they were low in relation to production or falling too rapidly, this might contribute somewhat to stability. It must be recognized, however, that the effort to shift between cash and inventories is not a matter of borrowing from the bank but of using cash on hand, and as such is only indirectly affected by bank action on the terms of credit. Banking policy as a method of controlling the total stock of money outstanding will be discussed later.

A fourth possible type of measure aimed at minimizing the shifts between inventory and money would be penalties for *excessive* inventory accumulation or depletion. Whether such action would be desirable would depend on the ease of carrying it out, both from the point of view of government and of business, and how effective it would be in adding to stability. It is not being recommended here, but certainly the possibilities should be explored.

Other methods for minimizing general shifts between inventories and money may be developed, but there is the likelihood that preventive measures alone will not be sufficient. Offsetting measures on the part of the banking system and government will be discussed after measures have been considered for minimizing other types of monetary shifts.

Minimizing General Shifts between Fixed Capital and Money

The appropriate relation between the total amount of fixed capital and total production is much less determinate than that between inventory and production. While the inventory necessary to a given volume of production cannot be reduced below some figure without interfering with production, and cannot rise above some figure without being unnecessarily large, the fixed capital can very widely. To get out a given volume of production, an enterprise may use old or new machinery and more or less valuable equipment. The timing of change from old to new or more complex can usually be varied within a wide interval without too serious interference with efficiency. Also through depreciation financing, fixed capital can be converted into cash almost as fast as capital is recovered in the form of allocations to depreciation. Thus, fixed capital can, within limits, be converted into cash or cash into fixed assets without great delay.

To some extent, better information on fixed capital outlay might reduce the swings, particularly as national estimates of need and information on business intentions as to fixed capital outlay and financing are obtained.[10] Particular businesses and industries could go some distance in the direction of regularizing their expenditures on fixed capital and the method of financing it. Government might find ways of encouraging stability, though how much could be done in this direction is far from clear. Possibly, some kinds of adjustment in depreciation rates for income tax purposes might be worked out, which would help somewhat. But on the whole, shifts from money balances into fixed capital, and the reverse, seem likely to be a significant source of possible under- or overemployment in spite of preventive measures.

Minimizing Shifts between Securities and Money

Because of the highly organized character of the security markets, a shift between securities and money is one of the easiest things for an individual or enterprise to make, yet it is impossible for a community as a whole to do so except as new securities are issued or old ones retired. Someone must hold the outstanding securities. And it is not enough to say, if the community as a whole wants to shift from securities into money, let security prices fall until they are low enough to discourage the net effort to shift into money. That way lies depression and unemployment, while the reverse effort to shift from money into securities can generate boom and overemployment.

Some measures are possible to minimize shifts into and out of securities, but their aggregate effect is likely to be small. It is doubtful if added information would reduce the effort to shift significantly, though better information is needed as to what groups hold securities at any given time—individuals, enterprises, investment companies, and banks—and how changes in their aggregate holdings are being financed. Interest rates on security loans and particularly large margin requirements could be used to some extent, but as in the case of inventories, loan limitations are more important on the side of controlling the amount of money outstanding than on the side of limiting the shift between money outstanding and other assets. Investment companies might be penalized for too great swings between money and security portfolios.[11] The same might be applied to producing enterprises, at least so far as the flotation of new securities is concerned,[12] but both the difficulties and the rigidifying effects would be greater. Penalties to keep individuals in the aggregate from shifting from securities into money or the reverse are likely to be hard to devise and administer, and promise to have relatively little effect.

Minimizing Shifts in the Disposal of Income

The problem of minimizing shifts in the disposal of income is not one of reducing the shifts between spending on consumption goods and spending on investment goods, or even the shifts between consumption and saving, but only the shifts that involve an aggregate effort to build up money holdings out of income or to reduce money holdings by spending in excess of incomes.

Individuals could throw the economy off its even keel if, in the aggregate, they attempted to build up their money balances out of income. In the late 1930s in the United States, an effort by consumers to add only 5 percent to their money holdings out of income during a single month, could mean a direct reduction in aggregate demand something like 10 or 15 percent for that month and indirect repercussions of far greater magnitude. However, it is difficult to see how reasonable freedom of choice on the part of individuals could be maintained at the same time that measures were taken to keep their demand for cash balances stable. Suggestions have been made for taxing money holdings or for taxing money holdings that didn't turn over fast enough. Such measures would, theoretically, serve to reduce the accumulation of money holdings out of income and might serve to reduce the shifts. As such they deserve to be investigated but their administrative difficulties, inflexibility, and far from certain effectiveness weigh against them. And anyway, their effectiveness in reducing changes in the demand for money would come, not from the existence of the tax, but in changes in rate, a much more difficult matter to administer.

If business enterprises, in the aggregate, use their profits simply to build up large money holdings, the effect on employment can be as great as if they shifted out of inventory or fixed capital. To the extent that net earnings are not distributed as dividends or invested in goods or securities (including credit extension), they must result in increased money balances. Whether such an accumulation of money holdings out of earnings could be distinguished and penalized is doubtful, but each business could legitimately be urged to distribute in dividends all the earnings it does not use in its own activity, or invest in securities, or need to expand its cash holdings with growth in its activity, and thus keep its money holdings from fluctuating more than is necessary for the conduct of business.

Undoubtedly there are other preventive measures that deserve consideration. In each case, the problem is to stabilize the desire to hold money on the part of each group. But it must always be remembered that the more drastic preventive measures are aimed to limit the freedom of action of the individual or enterprise, and that, short of the more drastic action, shifts in the demand for money as a store of buying power are likely to throw an economy off its even keel. This raises the question of how far it would be possible to maintain the freedom of action for individuals and enterprises, and yet maintain an even keel through banking and government action that would *offset* and thus neutralize the effects on employment of those actions that would otherwise lead to under- or overemployment.

Experience with Offsetting Actions

The use of specific offsetting actions is not new. The United States has developed three types of actions that are regularly used to offset certain types of free actions that otherwise would lead to boom or depression. But in each case the action is concerned with bank reserves, what might be thought of as "bankers' money." It seeks to prevent certain changes in the demand or supply of bankers' money from affecting the volume of money in the hands of the public.

Offsetting Changes in the Demand for Bank Reserves

In setting up the Federal Reserve System, the United States changed the character of bank reserves. It established a flexible reserve in place of gold. Before the reserve system was adopted, each bank had to have a reserve of gold and was forced to regulate its creation of deposits according to its gold holdings, so that in normal times the volume of deposits would be closely related to the stock of gold within the country. But in times of business uncertainty, banks would want to hold more gold in relation to their deposits than in more normal times. This would mean an increase in the total demand for gold without a change in the stock of gold. Bank liquidation would develop. The stronger banks would draw gold away from the weaker banks, and the scramble for the limited stock of gold could develop into a gold panic. The bank liquidation and gold panic would reduce the money supply, disorganize production, and contribute to depression. But under the Federal Reserve System, deposits with a Federal Reserve Bank took the place of gold as the basic reserve of the operating member banks, while gold became a reserve behind the deposits of the Reserve Banks. This meant that when, in time of stress, the operating banks wanted to increase their reserves in relation to deposits, the increase in demand for reserves was not a demand for gold but for deposits with the Reserve Banks, and these could be temporarily expanded to satisfy this demand.[13] Thus, it became possible to remove one important source of depression. The depressive effect of an excessive demand for "bankers' money" could be offset by increasing the supply.

Offsetting the Effect of Changes in the Form of Money

A second major type of offset has developed in the practical operation of the Reserve System. For a long time, our banking system has made money in the form of currency virtually interchangeable with money in the form of demand deposits so far as individual bank customers are concerned. But because of the way the banking system is set up, any shift from deposits to currency would reduce bank reserves, and any shift from currency into deposits would increase bank reserves. As a result, even though the total demand for money on the part of individuals and enterprises remained constant, the *form* in which money was held would affect bank reserves. An increased desire to hold money in the form of currency would reduce bank reserves and, in the absence of offsetting action, would lead to bank liquidation, a contraction in the total stock of money, and depression. In practice, the Federal Reserve System has tended to offset the effect of the shift from deposits into currency or the reverse. When deposits have been shifted into currency, thus reducing bank reserves, the reserves have been replenished by rediscounting or through open market operations. When currency returned to the banking system, the extra reserves have been withdrawn. Thus, changes in the *form* in which the community wanted to hold its money could be neutralized. Individuals and enterprises were free to hold their money in whatever form they chose, but the banking system could be so operated that a change in form had no effect on the total money stock outstanding, and no effect on the level of employment.

Offsetting the Effect of Gold Flows

The third type of offsetting action has to do with neutralizing a flow of gold into or out of the country as a result of an unbalance of international payments. An outflow of gold would reduce the reserves of operating banks while an inflow would increase their reserves. In the absence of offsetting action, an outflow would tend to bring bank contraction and a reduction in employment while an inflow would produce an expansion. But in recent years the central authorities have in large part offset these movements of gold through open market operations and reserve requirements.

Offsetting Changes in the Demand for Money

In each of the three types of offsetting action discussed above, central banking has been used to prevent changes in the demand for, or the stock of bank reserves, from having adverse effects on employment. Thus, changes in the demand for or stock of "bankers' money" can be neutralized. Could similarly offsetting actions be taken with respect to ordinary money?

Shifts between Money and Other Tokens

Technically, the simplest type of offsetting action that the banking system could undertake would be involved in shifts between money and securities. If the banks were to buy securities when individuals and enterprises in the aggregate sought to shift from securities into money, and to reverse this process when the public wanted to reduce its money holdings and add to its securities, the disorganizing effects of these shifts would be neutralized at the same time that the relative values of particular securities were allowed to seek their own level. This would go far to make the *form* in which token assets were held relatively unimportant, just as current Reserve policy makes the *form* in which money is held relatively unimportant.

Three major problems would have to be faced if such a policy were adopted: Who should be responsible for token offsetting action? Who should incur the profits and losses involved? And how to determine when and what action is needed?

The question of responsibility naturally focuses on the banking system. Before the war, the central authorities in our system, as now organized, could act in such a way as to force member banks to contract their portfolios—to sell securities or reduce their loans and thus reduce the stock of money outstanding, but it could not force an expansion in portfolios. It could only make certain conditions, but not all conditions, favorable for expansion. Furthermore, even in the case of the need for contraction in bank portfolios, the central authorities would hesitate to force contraction if it meant serious losses to member banks. As a result, there were definite limits to the power of the central banking authorities to bring about an offsetting exchange of money for securities, or the reverse when it was needed. The war has somewhat altered these limitations, but they still exist.

If this type of offsetting action were to be undertaken, serious consideration should be given as to whether the present powers of the Federal Reserve Board are sufficient. What other powers should be created? To what extent should the offset be carried out through open market operations of the Reserve Banks, to what extent through member banks, and to what extent, if at all, by a new agency?

A second but closely related problem is that of who should suffer any losses that may be involved in offsetting money–security shifts on the part of the public. It is clear that offsetting action cannot be taken only when it promises a profit. It must be taken when it is needed. This means that, in some situations, actions would have to be taken that were expected to result in loss. While, over a period of years, profits and losses might even out, the organization for performing this function should not be built on the assumption that only action will be taken that promises no losses. This means that the job cannot be handled on a private profit-seeking basis. It is essentially one to be financed through government, and then paid for by the community as a whole.

The third and more difficult problem is to determine when action is necessary to offset an aggregate shift between money and securities. It would not be the purpose of the offset to maintain a constant level of security prices. If the earnings of enterprises increased it would be natural for security prices to rise. It would also be natural for security prices to fall if capital became scarce. But with no change in the desire to save, in investment opportunities, or in earnings, an effort to shift from securities into money or the reverse would call for corrections. It seems likely that, in practice, ways could be found for determining when offsetting action was needed, while the amount of offsetting action could be judged increasingly well with experience.

Shifts between Money and Inventory

A second type of shift that could be fairly easily offset would be that involving inventories, though there is no existing agency equipped to perform this function. The proposal has often been made that the money of the country should be based on a "market basket" of commodities, or to be more exact, on warehouse receipts for selected com-modities. If this were done, the banking system could offset aggregate shifts between money and inventories. Or a special government agency, somewhat like the Commodity Credit Corporation, could be created, not to stabilize inventories or commodity prices, but simply to offset aggregate shifts between money and inventories.

As in the case of offsetting money–security shifts, if this function were to be performed, it would clearly be a responsibility of govern-ment or the banking system and any losses should properly be financed by the community as a whole through government. The problem of determining when action was called for would be serious. Neither a change in commodity prices, as such, nor changes in aggregate inven-tories would justify action. Seasonal inventory changes, changes in costs of production, and a host of other factors would have to be taken into account. But where the changes in inventories appeared to repre-sent a desire to shift between aggregate inventories and aggregate holdings of money, offsetting action would presumably be called for.

Shifts between Money and Fixed Capital

It is difficult to see how the banking system could be used directly to offset the third major type of shift, that between money and capital goods. It is not the function of the banking system to own capital goods except for direct banking use. However, it would be possible for government to offset shifts between money and capital goods through public works, provided the public works were financed through a re-duction in government holdings of money, through government issue of new money, or through borrowing from banks in such a way as to increase the total stock of money outstanding. But there are limits to such an offset, both because of the time necessary to put into effect a significant change in the volume of public works and because, if the correction called for were very large, there might not be sufficient opportunities for useful public works to provide a complete offset. Technically, however, changes in the volume of public works financed in such a way as to increase the outstanding stock of money could be used to offset the effects of efforts to shift from fixed capital into money or the reverse.

In this type of offset, however, the government action would not be a reversible action, as would be the case if government or the banks were to accumulate inventories or securities in exchange for money, where the rest of the community was seeking to shift from inventories or securities into money, and then reverse the process as the more normal demand for inventories or securities was re-established. It could serve, at least in part, to stabilize fixed capital outlay, but the public works themselves could not properly be sold to private individuals when the latter wanted to reduce their money holdings and increase their holdings of capital goods.

Shifts in the Disposal of Income

The offsetting of efforts to build up money balances out of income involves a greater variety of possible offsets. If individuals sought to add to their money holdings by saving less in securities and more in money form, the banking system could provide an offset by creating additional money through the purchase of securities or increasing their loans. If individuals sought to build up their money holdings out of income by consuming less, government could offset this by reducing its taxes on individuals or increasing its expenditures and financing the resulting deficit by adding to the total stock of money.[14] If business enterprises sought to build up their money holdings out of earnings, government could again offset the effect through reduced taxes or increased expenditure.

Conclusion

In all of these cases of specific offset, the action of the banking system or government would aim to increase or decrease the stock of money outstanding by a method closely parallel to the method by which individuals or enterprises were seeking to increase or decrease their money holdings. Equilibrium would be maintained by satisfying the urge to alter money holdings, and this would be done through specific measures that lead to no other general repercussions. Offsetting a shift from securities into money by removing some of the securities from the market would prevent a fall in security prices *that would otherwise take place,* but would not institute any major impulse to change the equilibrium condition.[15] The same would be true with a shift between money and inventories or a money-financed public works offset to an effort to build up money holdings out of fixed capital. Tax reduction to offset the building up of money balances out of income might have more ramifications since money incomes would be altered, but under some conditions it might have only the simple offsetting effect, while government spending to provide increased consumption or public works could provide a direct offset of the accumulation of money out of income either by curtailment of consumption or the curtailment of goods investment.

It should be remembered that the foregoing specific offsets would have as their objective the *maintenance* of full employment. They would constitute measures to be taken when an initial condition of full employment was threatened by a change in the demand for money as a store of buying power. It would also be possible to adopt generally offsetting measures that would tend to offset the effect of changes that would otherwise lead to under- or overemployment, without specific attention to the particular character of the change. But the effects are likely to be more complex and are more easily analyzed as measures to attain full employment from an initial condition of over- or underemployment—the subject of the next chapter.

Notes

1. In the above, important issues with respect to the condition of full employment are purposely avoided. Not only is the determination of statistical figures to represent full employment likely to be difficult, but the appropriate figures would depend partly on the measures that were taken to reduce the need for mobility of resources and to increase their mobility.

2. Only in the case of farming, distribution, and the professions is a significant part of production not incorporated or otherwise legally separated from the individuals conducting it. In the case of an important part of unincorporated enterprise, separate accounts are kept for the business activity so that the individual and the enterprise are two separate accounting entities. It simplifies the analysis to regard all enterprises in this fashion, including farming.

3. For convenience, the "business operations" of investment companies and banks, such as the purchase of office space, the hiring of workers, and so on, will be left out of account and attention will be given only to their portfolios of loans and investments, plus their money holdings and the corresponding liabilities.

4. Any government production for sale can be lumped with business production insofar as the present purposes are concerned.

5. A fifth major possibility would exist if individuals were assumed to have an inventory of consumer goods on hand that they *could* convert into cash if they desired to do so. This would increase the aggregate offering of goods without an increase in aggregate demand, and so lead to unemployment.

6. This possibility is important primarily in connection with the secular

growth in the lab and production, and results in a secular increase in the demand for money.

7. It should be noticed that business in the *aggregate* cannot convert its fixed assets into cash through the sale of fixed assets by one business to another. Sale to nonbusiness units is being excluded by assumption.

8. In both cases there would be what, in the language of the saving–investment theory, is called disinvestment.

9. Foreign withdrawal of gold is excluded above partly because international actions are being postponed to chapter 17, but primarily because the Federal Reserve Banks customarily offset such action. Similarly, the Reserve offsets the contractionist pressure on operating banks that would arise if individuals and enterprises shifted their holdings of money from the form of deposits into the form of currency.

10. In Sweden, regular reports are obtained from each business as to its plans for outlay on fixed capital for the coming year by quarters. These have been found to be fairly dependable indications of what is actually expended. In the United States, reports from the largest companies and a sample of medium and small companies would probably be sufficient.

11. On the ground that it is the function of investment companies to invest, not only to hold idle money balances whose fluctuations aggravate business fluctuations.

12. Some rough relation might be required between the issue of new securities and the plans for using the proceeds, so as to guard against grossly excessive building up of cash balances, but such a procedure is not likely to be too effective.

13. In some circumstances, the power to rediscount at the Reserve Banks serves as an *automatic* corrective. In other circumstances, the action has to be through open market operations that require positive decision on the part of the management of the Reserve System. The most outstanding example of the latter type of offsetting action is the open market operations of 1931. If the objective of these operations was to stop the violent bank liquidation and "reserve panic" of 1930–31, it must be regarded as brilliantly successful though seriously tardy. Those who criticize the operation as a failure usually expected it to produce economic recovery, a quite different objective. Such offsetting action could neutralize the excessive demand for reserves and prevent it from forcing greater depression. With the banking system as it was operating in 1930–32, it is very doubtful if open market operations of any legal magnitude could have produced recovery.

14. Either through the issue of additional money or through borrowing from banks in such a way as to increase the total stock of money outstanding.

15. Presumably the *relative* prices of securities would shift, as the effort to shift into money involved one set of securities and bank purchases affected a somewhat different set, but the level of security prices as a whole would not be greatly modified.

14

The Problem of Achieving Full Employment

This chapter, like the preceding one, is concerned with a theoretical problem, in this case the problem of getting from an equilibrium at less than full employment to an equilibrium at full employment. This problem differs from that of maintaining full employment in three major respects:

1. Action to increase employment is not a simple offset to some otherwise depressing development in the economy, but aims to set up a new set of relationships that will support a higher level of employment, and therefore the action can be expected to involve more complex repercussions.
2. Action can be expected to have two quite different effects, one that will be called the "process" effect and lasts only while the action is being taken—as, for example, while the stock of money is being increased—and another that will be called the "continuing" effect, and lasts after the action has been taken and results from the changes brought about by the action—as, for example, the larger stock of money outstanding as a result of monetary expansion.
3. Action to increase employment is likely to result in significant increases in prices and wage rates. Where the problem was only one of maintaining employment, it was reasonable to assume a stable price–wage level (since no increase in aggregate demand was involved). But to increase employment an increase in de-

mand must be brought about, and this means added pressure on prices and wage rates.

In the analysis of this problem, the conditions to be expected in an equilibrium at less than full employment will first be outlined. Then the problem of increasing employment will be considered on the assumption that prices and wage rates are fixed. Price changes and the possibility that they can defeat any efforts to increase employment will be reserved for discussion in the next chapter. As in the preceding chapter, the main purpose is to explore further implications of the monetary theory, not to lay an immediate basis for policy.

An Equilibrium at Less than Full Employment

In contrast to an equilibrium at full employment, stable equilibrium at less than full employment could be said to exist if there were involuntary unemployment in excess of that due to the lack of perfect mobility of resources, and if there were no automatic forces tending to increase employment. This condition would presumably mean that the effective demand for goods was not adequate to absorb all the goods that could be produced at full employment. It would also mean there were no forces inherent in the situation that would change the level of employment. Most particularly it would mean that, even though there were extensive resources unemployed, there were no *net* incentives to reduce prices or to shift resources to the production of the more sensitive-priced goods.[1] With this equilibrium, the aggregate demand for goods in each successive period would be sufficient and just sufficient to absorb the goods that could be produced by the number of persons initially employed, and the rates of production, consumption, and investment would be such that there would be no initial tendency to depart from this condition.

Such a condition of equilibrium would also mean that the outstanding stock of money was sufficient and just sufficient to satisfy the demand for money at the current level of income, and that there was no tendency for either the demand for money or the stock of money to change. Any increase in income as a result of increased employment and production would make the demand for money exceed the outstanding stock. The resulting effort to build up money balances would make the aggregate supply of goods exceed the aggregate demand, and force down production and employment. Similarly, a reduction in incomes would make the money supply redundant and force up production and employment. Under these hypothetical conditions, the economy could be expected to run along on an even keel at less than full employment. The question to be considered in this chapter is what measures could be taken to increase employment to a satisfactory level.

Increasing Employment in a Rigid-Price Economy

In a rigid-price economy, the problem of increasing employment to a satisfactory level would be primarily one of increasing aggregate demand, provided the rigid prices and wage rates were in reasonable relation to each other. Any measures that would increase the aggregate demand for goods could be expected to lead to an increase in sales, production, and employment. If the rigid prices and wage rates happened to be those that would be consistent with optimum use of resources, a sufficient expansion in demand could be expected to result in optimum use of resources as well as full employment. If the rigid price and wage structure was not consistent with optimum use, full employment could be reached, but with some distortion in the use of resources as the production and use of some goods was pushed to extremes and other goods were insufficiently produced and used. Only with an extreme distortion of the price–wage structure would an expansion in aggregate demand not result in an increase in employment.[2] In the present analysis, it will be assumed that prices and wage rates, though rigid, are in reasonable relationship to each other, so that a sufficient increase in aggregate demand would result in full employment.

As has already been indicated, the problem of increasing aggregate demand is essentially one of increasing the stock of money relative to the demand for money, or of reducing the demand for money relative to the stock outstanding. In what follows, fiscal and monetary measures for altering this relation will first be considered, and then other possible measures.

Fiscal Measures

So much attention has been given, in recent discussion, to fiscal measures as a method of lifting employment that elaborate analysis is not required here. A federal deficit, whether as a result of reduced taxes or of increased expenditures, could be expected to stimulate employment. It is important, however, to show just how the deficit would alter the relative demand for money and show that it could be expected to have both a process effect while the deficit was being incurred and a continuing effect in subsequent periods. In order to limit the analysis to purely fiscal measures, it will be assumed that the deficit is financed by the sale of government securities to the public and that the amount of money outstanding remains constant.

Suppose that the government borrowed a billion dollars from individuals and enterprises and spent the proceeds on public works. The propensity to invest, including government expenditure as investment, would be temporarily increased. At the same time, the public borrowing would reduce the propensity to hold money. In a sense, the government would be "taking idle money and putting it to work." But in a more realistic sense, the money the government obtained would be no more "idle" than other money. It would be satisfying the desire of the holder to possess assets in that form. For the government to obtain this money in exchange for its securities it would have to offer inducements such as patriotism or higher interest rates. By these inducements it would persuade individuals and enterprises to be content with smaller money holdings at the initial level of incomes and activity. This would constitute a reduction in the public's propensity to hold money.[3] Indeed, if the borrowing action of the government did not force down the propensity to hold money, there would be no *net* increase in aggregate demand as a result of government spending. For example, if individuals, in order to buy government securities, were to curtail their expenditures on consumption instead of reducing their cash balances, the government expenditure would be offset by an equal contraction in private expenditure and there would be no net change in aggregate demand. Provided, however, that there was a decline in the propensity to hold money, the level of aggregate demand would be increased while the government was borrowing and spending.

The level of incomes during this process would be determined by the extent to which the propensity to hold money was reduced. The government having reduced the propensity to hold money by its borrowing activity and having put the money it borrowed back into circulation, the level of incomes and employment would have to rise until the community with its reduced propensity to hold money was willing and just willing to hold the stock of money outstanding. So long as the borrowing and spending went on, this "process" effect of a reduced propensity to hold money would be maintained and the levels of income and employment would be raised.[4]

The same sort of a conclusion would arise also in the case of a government deficit arising from reduced taxes and financed by public borrowing. The extra income in the hands of individuals and enterprises could be expected to lead to greater expenditure on consumption and investment, while the government borrowing would reduce the propensity to hold money. And, as in the case of public spending, the level of income would be determined at that level at which the stock of money just satisfied the reduced propensity to hold money.

In addition to this process effect, a government deficit financed by borrowing could also be expected to have an effect on aggregate demand and employment that would continue after the deficit process came to an end. The government selling of securities would add to the net assets of individuals and enterprises. This, according to the monetary theory of employment, would tend to increase the propensities to consume, to invest, and to hold money. As a result, the level of aggregate demand maintained *after* the government spending program had been completed would be higher or lower than before the program started, depending on which propensity-change dominated, the increased propensity to spend on goods or the increased propensity to hold money. The two types of propensity-change might just offset each other, so that a deficit financed by public borrowing would only have the process effect. But the more likely development would be a small continuing effect lifting the level of aggregate demand over the initial level, since the effect of the increased assets on the propensity to hold money is likely to be small compared with its effect on the propensity to spend on goods.

Any such continuing effect would be cumulative, so that, with each successive unit of deficit financed by public borrowing, the effect would become more important. It would presumably be insignificant at the beginning of any deficit program, but might become significant as the program continued. Deficit financing of the magnitude incurred during World War II could be expected to have a considerable effect. However, under ordinary circumstances, the magnitude of the increase in public holdings of government securities as a result of deficit financing is not likely to be so great, and the process effect is likely to be the major effect.

Monetary Expansion

In contrast to such fiscal action, monetary expansion could be expected to have a more important continuing effect than process effect. Thus, if the banking system bought securities in the open market and thereby increased the stock of money outstanding, the process of putting the money into circulation would not involve any direct purchase of goods, as in the case of public works, or increase of private disposable incomes, as in the case of tax reduction. However, the monetary expansion would permanently increase the money holdings of the public and could be expected to increase also the total real value of the assets held by the public. Both of these would, according to the monetary theory, tend to increase aggregate demand and could be expected to more than offset any decline in the propensity to hold money that resulted from reduced interest rates. Thus, a simple monetary expansion could be expected to result in a net continuing increase in aggregate demand.

This can be seen more clearly by considering a concrete example. Suppose that the banking system purchased a billion dollars of securities in the open market, and thereby increased the stock of money outstanding by a billion dollars. Individuals and enterprises would have surrendered one billion dollars worth of securities and would possess an extra billion dollars of money. Because of its greater liquidity, the extra money could be expected to increase the propensities to consume and invest more than these propensities were reduced by the surrender of securities. Furthermore, the bank purchase of securities would force up the level of security prices. *Thus, the value of securities remaining in the hands of the public would not shrink as much as the public's money holdings increased; indeed, might not shrink at all.* As a result, the total value of assets in the hands of the public would increase, a result also tending to increase the propensities to consume and invest. On the other hand, the higher value of assets would tend to increase the propensity to hold money. Also, interest rates could be expected to fall sufficiently so that the public was willing to hold the extra billion dollars of money rather than make additional loans. This would constitute a continuing support to the higher level of security prices, but would also mean an increased propensity to hold money. The new condition of equilibrium to be expected *after* the money supply had been increased would be one in which the propensity to hold money had been increased, but not by as much as the increase in the money outstanding. The difference would be reflected in higher propensities to consume and invest, so that the level of aggregate demand would be greater than before the money expansion. And like the continuing effect in the case of fiscal action, the results would be cumulative. Each additional billion dollars of money could be expected to increase further the level of aggregate demand.

The process effect of expanding the money supply in the above fashion is probably not great. The main difference would be the change in the opportunities to save in the form of money rather than in other forms. So long as the money stock is constant, it is impossible for the public in the aggregate to save in the form of money. Some individuals or enterprises could save in this form, but only if others reduced their savings held in this form. But the process of adding to the stock of money makes it possible, *while the process continues,* for the public in the aggregate to save in the form of money. The process of bank purchases of securities also reduces the public's opportunity to save in the form of securities. This shift in saving opportunities can be expected to cause some shift in the equilibrium adjustment while monetary expansion is under way. But there is no reason to think that these effects are very significant.

The process effect of monetary expansion could be significant if it took place through increased bank loans to businesses *and* the latter made investment expenditures that they otherwise would not have made. The process would thus include current expenditure on goods as well as increase in the stock of money. But under the usual peacetime conditions, the opportunities for expansion of bank loans to business for investment purposes are likely to be limited at the very time that monetary expansion is needed. When there is extensive unemployment, business loans tend to be more precarious and the demand for the type of investment funds that banks can appropriately supply is likely to be small. So far as full employment policy is concerned, it is the expansion of money through the purchase of securities that is the significant action.

Combined Fiscal and Monetary Action

The advantages of both important process effects and important continuing effects could be obtained by combining fiscal and monetary action. A federal deficit financed by expanding the stock of money could be expected to have a greater process effect while the deficit was being incurred than if securities were sold to the public, and perhaps also a greater continuing effect than a simple monetary expansion. Aggregate demand would be increased in the process of running a deficit, without the damping effect of selling securities to the public and thereby reducing the value of outstanding securities and raising interest rates. Also, the continuing effects of monetary expansion would result without the damping effect of reducing the securities in the hands of the public. Thus, the combined fiscal and monetary action would be the most potent in raising aggregate demand and in sustaining it.

Choice between Fiscal and Monetary Policies

In actual practice, the three types of fiscal and monetary action can each serve a special purpose. If there were a serious deficiency in aggregate demand, but it was believed that the deficiency was temporary, fiscal action without monetary expansion could give the temporary lift to demand without raising the level of demand significantly after the temporary condition had passed. On the other hand, a deficiency of demand arising from secular growth in the capacity to produce could more appropriately be met by monetary expansion without any increase in federal debt. In an intermediate situation, in which there was a serious deficiency in aggregate demand and it was expected that the deficiency would continue more or less indefinitely if not corrected, a situation such as presumably existed in the early 1930s, the combined fiscal and monetary action, if sufficiently large, could give a rapid recovery and lay the basis for a sustained high level of aggregate demand without the necessity of further deficits. Furthermore, if the government was heavily in debt, a program of debt reduction which would be deflationary in itself could be combined with monetary expansion, so that the continuing effect of a large stock of money would offset the depressing process effect of running a continuous surplus to finance debt reduction.

Other Measures

Fiscal and monetary measures are not the only measures that could reduce the demand for money relative to the outstanding stock, and thus stimulate employment. In every depression, a crop of recovery proposals are made that aim to reduce the demand for money. Taxes on money balances, stamped money that has to be spent to avoid a loss in value, and many other similar plans are offered to make money turn over faster. In effect, they are proposals to reduce the propensity to hold money, so that a higher level of incomes and employment would be necessary in order to induce the community to hold and just hold the outstanding stock of money. And since such measures would reduce the demand for money without a contraction in the stock of money outstanding, there is no reason to question their effectiveness in stimulating employment. The higher the tax or other disadvantage from holding money, the higher the level of incomes and employment required to induce the community to hold the whole of the outstanding stock of money. But such measures involve serious administrative difficulties, and because they rely on one or another form of taxation, they would tend to be inflexible in operation. One could not know beforehand just how heavy a tax to place on the holding of money, and one could not revise the rates too frequently. If fiscal and monetary action were not simpler, such measures would deserve serious consideration.

Another method of changing the relation between the demand and the stock of money would be a forced downward revision of all prices and wage rates. Such a general revision would reduce money incomes, though not real incomes, and would thereby reduce the propensity to hold money. With the stock of money unchanged, this could be expected to increase the level of aggregate [demand]. Such a measure was successfully tried in Australia in the early 1930s, but their problem was complicated by the dominant role played in their economy by foreign trade. Under more ordinary circumstances, the administrative difficulties make such a forced price–wage revision difficult and a device to be resorted to, if at all, only in an emergency.

A third device frequently discussed is a more even distribution of income. A relatively even distribution of income would presumably discourage enterprise, and so increase the propensity to hold money as individuals sought security rather than risking their money in enterprise. On the other hand, a very uneven distribution is likely also to increase the propensity to hold money, as those with large incomes accumulate large money balances. Presumably, there is an area somewhere between an even and a very uneven distribution of income at which the propensity to hold money is at a minimum. From the point of view of maintaining full employment, such a distribution of income would be desirable. But the effects of a departure from this optimum could presumably be offset by monetary expansion. Social considerations might therefore play a greater role in determining the most desirable income distribution. In any event, changes in income distribution could not be brought about quickly and could only provide a background for other policies aimed at achieving and maintaining full employment.

Still other methods of stimulating employment might be considered, but the main purpose of this chapter has been served in showing how fiscal and monetary measures could be used to increase aggregate demand, and thereby stimulate employment if prices and wage rates were rigid.

Notes

1. For practical purposes, it would be sufficient to assume no quick-acting forces, which would lift employment close to full employment. Forces that would operate only slowly and might ultimately result in full employment would still leave a short-run equilibrium at less than full employment.

2. For example, if wage rates were so high relative to prices that the differential cost of each item was equal to or greater than its price, no amount of increase in aggregate demand could be expected to increase production and employment. In the above discussion, this sort of situation is disregarded, because it would be a most unlikely one if prices and wage rates were rigid *and the initial condition was equilibrium at partial employment*. The latter condition implies price–wage relationships for a large number of products, which did give inducement to supply whatever demand developed, at least within the limits of existing capacity.

3. It should be noted that the term "propensity to hold money" refers to the schedule representing the amount of money the community would choose to hold at each possible level of income, just as the "propensity to consume" refers to the amount that would be spent on consumption at each possible level of income.

4. The above analysis assumes that the government itself does not accumulate additions to its cash balances, but is spending as fast as it borrows.

15

The Problem of Inflation

In the two preceding chapters, the problem of inflation has been post-poned. Both the maintenance and the achieving of full employment have been discussed on the assumption that prices and wage rates were stable. But in practice, an increase in aggregate demand aimed at in-creasing employment may actually spend itself in price and wage in-creases and, even if full employment were reached, an aggregate demand sufficient to maintain full employment at stable prices and wage rates might actually lead to price and wage increases and unemployment. Measures aimed at achieving or maintaining full em-ployment must, therefore, take account of these possibilities.

Appropriate Price and Wage Movements

In an economy in which prices range from the highly sensitive to the highly insensitive, a rotating increase in the more sensitive prices would be an appropriate result of an increase in aggregate demands aimed at increasing employment. To some extent, such price increases would negate a part of the increase in aggregate demand. Full employ-ment could be reached with a smaller increase in demand if *all* prices were stable. However, the resultant pattern of prices would almost certainly be seriously out of balance. A rise in sensitive prices would not prevent an increase in employment from being produced by an increase in aggregate demand, so long as insensitive prices did not increase, and, because it brings about a better balance in the price struc-ture, it would be a desirable result of the rise in aggregate demand.

Wage rates tend, in the short run, to follow an intermediate course parallel to that of the cost of living. As a rise in sensitive prices increased the cost of living, it would be appropriate for wage rates to rise also. In such a recovery, some wage rates could be expected to rise more than others, rotating in a fashion similar to but less extreme than the rotation of prices. This type of wage increase would thus keep wage rates as a whole in line with the cost of living and reduce the dispersion in wage rates. It also would be a desirable result of a rise in aggregate demand. Up to the point of full employment there is no reason to regard such rotating price and wage increases as inflationary.

Even if an excess in aggregate demand were to cause a rotation of prices above a balanced relation, there is some question as to whether it would be seriously harmful. Suppose that an excess of demand were generated. If the effect on prices were solely that of rotation, sensitive prices would rise above a balanced relation to insensitive prices, while there would tend to be overemployment in the insensitive-price industries reflected in excessive overtime, labor shortage, and rationing through excessive waits between orders and delivery. A subsequent decline in aggregate demand could then bring demand in the insensitive-price industries into closer balance with capacity and bring sensitive prices back into balance with insensitive prices. The excessive rise and subsequent fall in sensitive prices could take place more or less automatically as an excess in aggregate demand was generated and then eliminated. It need have no seriously harmful effects.[1]

Harmful Price and Wage Increases

Price and wage increases would be harmful to the objective of full employment, however, if insensitive prices rose along with sensitive prices. If all groups of prices went up in proportion to an increase in aggregate demand, there would be no increase in real demand and therefore no increase in employment. This means that the crucial problem in attaining full employment is to make sure that the insensitive prices do not move up as aggregate demand is increased, and that intermediately sensitive prices move up only to an intermediate degree.

There are two important conditions that are likely to lead to an increase of insensitive prices: (1) a high level of demand in relation to capacity, and (2) excessive wage increases.

The Effects of Capacity Operation

So long as there is a great deal of excess capacity in an industry, a rise in sales is not likely to lead to a serious increase in insensitive prices. Increased volume will reduce overhead costs per unit, and even though there is some increase in the costs of raw materials and labor, profit margins are likely to increase so that total profits are likely to increase more than in proportion to the increase in sales. In such a situation, there is good reason for "not rocking the boat." But when capacity is fully utilized and orders are piled up for months in advance, the pressure to increase prices is likely to be great.

Just how much pressure is needed to bring about a rise of insensitive prices is one of the things about which little is known. At the beginning of World War I the United States was close to full employment, and the huge demand for goods from abroad and the prosperity at home led to a rise in both sensitive and insensitive prices. There was inflation in the traditional sense, but many peacetime examples could be found of individual companies or industries with insensitive prices, which had not raised prices when the demand at the current prices was far larger than they were capable of supplying. During World War II, insensitive prices in the United States were, on the whole, kept relatively stable.[2] After the war, when price controls were removed, insensitive prices rose somewhat. But to anyone brought up in the tradition that prices adjust to equate supply and demand, the remarkable part is not that insensitive prices such as steel, automobiles, and agricultural implements rose, but that they rose so little. Insensitive prices were kept down in spite of demands far in excess of capacity. More needs to be known about the relation of capacity to insensitive price increases before the danger to full employment from this arbitrary power of management can be properly appraised.

The Effects of Wage Pressures

A second danger to full employment lies in labor pressure for increased wage rates. It has already been indicated that some increases in wage rates are appropriate in a recovery as living costs go up. Increases in real wage rates are also to be expected as labor shares in the gain from technical improvement. Finally, if profit margins are too high in relation to wage rates, wage increases or lower prices are in order. But labor may have the power to force wage increases in excess of those called for by living costs, productivity, and a reasonable balance between profit margins and wage rates. Such excessive wage increases are almost certain to lead to increases in insensitive prices. How great a threat to full employment lies in the arbitrary power of a labor [union] remains to be seen. This country has had little peacetime experience with strong labor organization, and the leaders of the latter are as little used to exercising economic statesmanship as are the leaders of big business.

This labor threat to full employment would be intensified if a serious difference of opinion developed between labor and management as to what constitutes a fair balance between profit margins and wage rates. If labor believes that profit margins are too high in relation to wage rates, it will try to squeeze profit margins by forcing up wage rates. But with increased wage rates, management is usually in a position to raise prices and thus maintains its profit margin. This would certainly be true in the case of a monopoly. It would also be true in a semi-competitive industry if the increase in wage rates applied to the industry as a whole. The more widespread the excessive increase in wage rates, the more certain that the individual producer could protect his or her margin by raising prices. Thus, wage pressure could not force a reduction in profit margins but would simply result in successive increases in insensitive prices.

No attempt can be made in this book to determine how serious these threats to full employment might be in practice. In the author's own opinion, their danger can easily be exaggerated. It seems quite possible that, once the peculiar conditions resulting from the war have ceased to dominate the economy, an excess of aggregate demand of 5 percent or even possibly 10 percent could be maintained for a number of months without a serious rise in insensitive prices. This possibility would be strengthened if the excess in demand were regarded as quite temporary, and if appeal were made to business and labor leaders to help maintain price stability.[3] If such an excess demand could be incurred without serious increases of insensitive prices, then the inflationary problem in more normal times would be quite secondary. It would be something to be watched, but not a dangerous threat to achieving and maintaining full employment.

On the other hand, if serious increases of insensitive prices begin to occur before or as soon as full employment is reached, either as a result of arbitrary price action by management or as a result of arbitrary wage increases forced by labor, the inflationary problem is a serious one. Unless ways could be found for dealing with it, the maintenance of reasonably full employment and a free enterprise system might prove to be incompatible.

Notes

1. The price rise in the summer and fall of 1946 was largely of this sort, and resulted in sensitive prices too high in relation to insensitive prices and with an overdemand for a large group of insensitive-priced goods.

2. Sensitive prices rose into balance in the first part of the war period and were then frozen, but rose above a balanced relation to insensitive prices after the war.

3. There are various reasons that would reinforce such an appeal. Raising steel prices makes it more difficult to resist a corresponding wage increase, and much of a price increase might be dissipated in higher wages, lower sales, and loss of public approval.

16

Dynamic Problems

The problem of employment has been discussed so far in terms of equilibrium adjustments because of the author's belief in their crucial importance. Yet actual policy must take into account the dynamic forces affecting the demand for money and employment as well as equilibrium forces. This chapter will consider the different types of changes that need to be taken into account, and will suggest how they complicate but do not fundamentally alter the problem of adjustment already considered in the equilibrium analysis.

Equilibrium Changes

It must be clear from the foregoing discussion that the equilibrium analysis is not restricted to static conditions. It can take some account of change. A moving equilibrium could reflect slow-moving changes such as population growth, technical improvement, and gradual change in tastes or preferences. It could also reflect slow-moving changes in the stock of money or other factors subject to policy. In these cases, equilibrium could be reached under successively different conditions so gradually that dynamic forces were not significant. Such a development would require no departure from equilibrium analysis.

In practice, however, there are three types of dynamic effects that need to be taken into account in any program to reduce business fluctuations: the effects of change itself, the effects of the *rate* of change, and the effects of oscillating change.

Effects of Change

Probably the most important single direct effect of change is to be found in capital gains and losses. If security prices have risen, the owners of securities will have profits, at least on paper, which may temporarily increase both their propensity to consume and their propensity to invest. These profits tend to be treated in part as if they were a form of current income. As a result, individuals may be led to spend more out of their current income than they otherwise would. The willingness to buy that new car can be increased by a 10-point profit on one's favorite stock. Similar capital gains are also possible in real estate and business transactions, as well as capital losses that work in the opposite direction. Such windfall gains or losses are in addition to the continuing effect of high asset values as against low asset values, or the reverse. They are a product of the change in asset values itself, and therefore occur only within (or as an outgrowth of) the period of change.

The presence of such windfall gains or losses means that a change in asset values can be expected to have a stronger *initial* effect in stimulating or depressing demand and employment than its equilibrium effect alone. If the equilibrium effect of a given increase in asset values would be sufficient to shift an equilibrium at less than full employment to one of full employment, the combined equilibrium and dynamic effect of a smaller rise would be sufficient in an initial period, while further increases would be necessary in subsequent periods until the whole burden was carried by the equilibrium effect.

The same conclusion would apply to a money-financed government deficit. A smaller deficit would presumably be needed in an initial period than equilibrium considerations alone would suggest because of the capital gains created by the rise of security prices. But for the same reason, subsequent periods would require some deficits that could be expected to taper off rapidly, as the equilibrium effect of the larger money stock provided the necessary level of aggregate demand.

A second and probably less important effect of change is the lag in the adjustment of living standards to changes in income. It is generally agreed that, if a typical group of families has an increase in incomes, there will be a considerable delay before their level of living has been raised to correspond with the new level of incomes. This is often taken to mean that as incomes go up there will be a lag in the upward adjustment of expenditures on consumption. However, while there is likely to be a lag in the expenditures on nondurable goods, even a small increase in the level of living is likely to require a more than proportionate expenditure on durable goods—a sort of capital outlay to obtain the services of durable goods consistent with the increased level of living in other directions. Only factual studies can determine whether the extra outlay on durable goods is likely to be more or less than the lag in expenditures on nondurables. Very possibly, the offset is sufficiently close to make this effect of changed incomes of secondary importance, except as it shifts the character of aggregate demand temporarily in the direction of durable goods.

Other direct effects of change would also have to be taken into account in any policy aimed at reducing business fluctuations. The psychological effects of unexpected change whether favorable or unfavorable; the adverse effects on investment of innovations in policy that run counter to the mores of the business community, however appropriate the policy may be; these and a host of other effects of change must play a part in any actual program, but need not receive further attention in this basic theoretical analysis.

Effects of the Rate of Change

The more important effects of the *rate* of change occur in connection with the more sensitive prices, including security prices. It is well recognized that a sufficiently rapid rise in security prices tends to bring speculators into the market on a large scale, who are buying, not because of the intrinsic value of the particular securities, but because they expect their prices to go higher before they go down.

The result of this kind of speculation is to force excessive price adjustments, with consequent effects on demand. Prices that are moving up to an equilibrium level may be forced to rise above that level and, unless forces bring about a change in the level that would constitute equilibrium, a subsequent collapse could be expected, with prices breaking back toward and even through the equilibrium level. In the goods market, a rapid rise in prices can engender speculation for the rise and inventory accumulation. Similarly, in the security markets, to the extent that security prices rise temporarily above the equilibrium point, the higher value of security assets and the paper windfall gains may overstimulate the demand for goods, while the subsequent collapse could damp the demand for goods.

This tendency for a *rapid* price rise or fall to create speculative momentum would be of secondary importance if a stabilizing policy were able to keep activity on a fairly even keel. Rapid price changes for particular products, or more general price changes of a minor sort, would not generate momentums that were serious for the economy as a whole. However, if a rapid general price change gets underway, its own momentum does create a serious problem. Efforts to bring it to a halt, if successful, may cause a violent reversal. Yet if the change is allowed to run its own course, the reversal is likely to be even more violent. A stabilizing policy would have to deal with difficult problems of timing and magnitude once a price change had acquired speculative momentum. So far as the prices of goods are concerned, if full employment has already been achieved, the main objective should be to prevent rapid and widespread changes in prices by maintaining the level of aggregate demand reasonably constant.[1] Rapid swings in security prices are likely to be more difficult to prevent, but also less harmful if they are not allowed to go to extremes. They do, however, present a major problem of policy on which more attention needs to be focused.

If the policy problem is not one of maintaining full employment, but of achieving it, a price rise at the more sensitive end of the goods price scale and an intermediate rise in wage rates would presumably be part of the recovery process. In this case, there would be a problem of controlling the expansion in the stock of money and in demand so as to obtain the most rapid rate of recovery, short of generating dangerous momentum in the price rise itself.

Oscillating Changes

Finally, there are important changes in activity that tend to set up oscillating changes in the demand for goods and the demand for money.[2] The housing cycle is a familiar example. Once a serious deficiency of housing has developed, the process of catching up means a period of heavy construction, and necessitates a rate of building greater than can be permanently maintained. Then, when the catching up is complete, and even if there has been no overbuilding, the high proportion of relatively new houses is likely to force building below what would represent a stable level. Any overbuilding would add to the subsequent underbuilding and help to create a new deficiency in housing. Similar, though less important, are cycles in the clothing industry, as inventories are built up to excessive levels and then excessively reduced; in potato raising, as excessive production follows a high price and subsequently forces the prices to an excessive low with subsequent underproduction; and quite possibly in the case of automobiles the low war production and the heavy postwar reduction may establish such an uneven age distribution of cars in use, that future replacement demand will tend to bunch in particular periods and result in a pattern of production with a more or less permanent oscillation. To these should be added the oscillating effects of the momentums arising from rapid price change, which have already been discussed.

Stabilizing policy can focus primarily on compensatory action that aims to prevent these oscillating activities from causing oscillations in total demand and employment, thus localizing their effect, or it can combine such action with action to reduce these local oscillations. To the extent that government construction can expand when private construction falls off, the oscillation in construction activity could be reduced. Credit controls through government aids to the financing of new construction provide a second approach to the damping of the construction cycle. Whatever can be done to stabilize the construction industry would reduce the compensatory action necessary to maintain full employment.

Other oscillations originating in specific changes in demand or production seem to be of secondary importance so far as the full employment problem is concerned. The potato cycle is certainly minor. So also is that of textile inventories. The possibility of a serious auto cycle arising from the effects of war on production is a problem for the future that may not materialize. Other comparable oscillations may develop or be discovered, but that in the construction industry appears to be far and away the most important.[3]

The oscillations arising out of the momentums of rapid price change are of a more general character. As has already been suggested, the problem is to avoid, so far as possible, conditions that lead to rapid changes in the level of goods prices and to broad rapid movements in the level of security prices. However, insofar as they occur, the harmful effects of such movements so far as employment is concerned are likely to be primarily in changing the level of aggregate demand. Here, compensating action of the types discussed in the equilibrium chapters would be appropriate.

Conclusion

Altogether it would appear that the dynamic factors complicate the execution of any policy aimed at maintaining full employment, but do not alter its general character. The objective of maintaining the necessary level of aggregate demand through monetary and fiscal policy remains basic. Capital gains and losses complicate but do not alter the basic problem. The objective of avoiding such rapid changes in aggregate demand [so] as to cause rapid changes in goods prices or wide rapid swings in security prices would be added. So also would be added the objective of damping oscillating swings of a more local character, particularly in the case of the construction industry. But underlying these problems would be the problem of maintaining the appropriate level of aggregate demand by adjusting the outstanding stock of money as nearly as possible to the amount the community would wish to hold as a store of buying power at full employment.

Notes

1. This presupposes free markets.

2. Some authors tend to make business fluctuations themselves a matter of oscillation, with each change in direction forced by what has already preceded. Statistical studies support neither the theory that fluctuations are essentially cyclical in character, nor the theory that they are essentially random. The statistics do appear consistent with random fluctuations combined with some oscillating elements in the economy, such as housing construction, textile inventories, and speculative momentums.

3. It should be pointed out that from the point of view of aggregate employment, a policy which maintained aggregate demand at the level necessary for full employment would be sufficient. But if there were great swings in construction activity, full employment would require correspondingly great shifts of workers and capital back and forth between the construction industry and other activities, a most inefficient use of resources. Also a more stable construction industry would reduce the difficulty of maintaining a relatively stable level of aggregate demand.

17

Certain International Implications of the Monetary Theory

Up to this point, the monetary theory and its implications have been developed without reference to international relationships. Yet the theory has important implication for the adjustment of trade among nations. It can explain why an international gold standard has proved so unsatisfactory, and throw light on the probable working of other mechanisms for maintaining a balance of payments between nations. These are problems of basic importance, both for the achievement of full employment within countries and for the maintenance of stable economic relationships within the world economy. This book cannot hope to deal extensively with these problems, but it can point to certain more significant conclusions as to international trade adjustments suggested by the monetary theory.

The Weakness of the Gold Standard

The essentials of the gold standard were relatively simple:

1. Each country conforming to the standard arranged that its currency should be convertible into gold (and the reverse) at a fixed rate.
2. Each country conforming to the standard had such monetary institutions that its total stock of money bore a fairly determinate ratio to that part of the stock of gold within its borders that was not used in the arts.

3. Gold could be shipped from country to country.

This system had the great advantage that the currencies of the different countries were made to exchange for each other at ratios that were relatively fixed. The value of one currency in terms of another could never depart very far from that indicated by their fixed ratios to gold. If too much of a discrepancy arose, it would pay to ship gold from one country to the other, and thus a major departure would be prevented.

The Classical Gold-Flow Mechanism of Trade Adjustment

The gold standard was also justified by its advocates on the ground that it provided an almost painless mechanism of adjustment for balancing payments between countries. If Country A was buying too much from other countries, so that it had an adverse balance of payments, gold would flow out of Country A. Because Country A had lost gold, its total money stock would contract and bring a contraction of aggregate demand at the initial level of prices. This in turn would, according to traditional theory, force a decline in the price–wage level within Country A so that other countries would be stimulated to buy more goods in Country A than before. At the same time, the shipment of gold of other countries would lead to an expansion in their money stock and in their aggregate demand. This was expected to produce higher prices within these other countries, and thus discourage the people in Country A from buying abroad. As a result, Country A would sell more abroad and buy less, so that the adverse balance of payments would be reduced. Indeed, according to the theory, gold flow and the process of adjustment could be expected to continue until a close balance of payments had been established.[1] Thus, under the gold standard, the classical writers expected that a reasonable balance in payments would be maintained between countries through adjustments in their internal price levels.

The Gold-Flow Mechanism with Insensitive Prices

But this mechanism of adjustment depended on the classical assumption that the price–wage levels in the different countries were highly sensitive. Quite a different mechanism of adjustment could be envisaged if the gold standard applied to countries with rigid prices and wage rates. If Country A were faced with an adverse balance of payments, an outflow of gold could be expected as in the case of sensitive prices, with the same effect in contracting both the stock of money and aggregate demand in Country A and expanding the money stock and aggregate demand in other countries. But at this point the similarity to the classical mechanism stops. If prices in Country A were rigid, the contraction in aggregate demand would not produce a fall in the price–wage level, but a fall in employment and incomes for the reasons already set forth in earlier chapters. And as a result of the reduction of incomes and scale of living, the people of Country A would buy less goods from other countries. At the same time, the countries receiving gold and having an expansion in their aggregate demand would have an expansion in employment and incomes, and therefore spend more in Country A as well as at home. Thus, Country A's sales abroad would be increased. This process of adjustment could be expected to continue until international payments were brought into approximate balance. In this case, the gold flow mechanism would operate, not through changes in relative price levels, but through changes in the level of production and employment in the different countries.

Since prices are not likely to be all sensitive or all insensitive, a more realistic gold-flow mechanism would be one in which part of the adjustment came through changes in prices and part through changes in employment. For example, if gold flowed out of Country A, sensitive prices in that country would fall, while in the case of insensitive prices production and employment would fall, and for prices that were intermediately sensitive the adjustment would be partly one of price and partly one of employment. The gold-receiving countries could be expected to have a comparable price–employment rise.[2] Thus, the adjustment would be one of depression in one country and boom in others, combined with distortions in price relationships in each country.

To be truly realistic, the mechanism of adjustment would have to be made much more elaborate to take account of such things as international capital movements, differential interest rates, international security speculation, the different role of sensitive and insensitive prices in different countries, and many other factors. But it is the belief of the present author that when this is done it will be found that the central core of the mechanism of international trade adjustment under the gold standard is not a matter of relatively familiar price level adjustments, but rather one of depression and boom.

The Gold Standard and the Transmission of Business Fluctuations

The same mechanism of adjustment could also explain the international transmission of business fluctuations under the gold standard. Suppose that initially all countries were prosperous and the payments between countries were in balance. Then assume that a serious depression developed in one country because of purely internal factors.[3] The resultant reduction of incomes would lead to a contraction of purchases from other countries. If the depression would not lead the latter to reduce their purchases in the depressed country, they would be faced with an adverse balance of payments. Under the gold standard, gold would flow from the other countries to the depressed country. This would lead to monetary contraction and depression in other countries, and monetary expansion and partial recovery in the initially depressed country. A new balance in payments would be reached when depression was so distributed between countries that the reduction in the foreign demand of the initially depressed country, taking account of the partial recovery, was just equal to the reduction in foreign demand on the part of other countries as a result of their depressions. The gold-flow mechanism would thus force a sharing of depressions even if no other factors made for sharing. Similarly, the mechanism would lead a recovery initiated in one country to spread to other countries.[4]

The monetary theory thus leads to the conclusion that, except for countries with highly sensitive prices, the gold standard could be expected to operate to adjust the balance of trade between countries through depression and boom, and to be a means of spreading business fluctuations between countries. If this is in fact the case, it is obvious that the gold standard is far from a satisfactory basis for linking the currencies of the world.

The Gold Exchange Standard

In the reconstruction period after the first World War, the gold exchange standard was adopted in many countries. Under this standard, currencies were convertible into gold (and the reverse) at fixed ratios, and gold could be shipped from country to country. But the third element of the gold standard was lacking. The money stocks of the different countries bore no close relation to their monetary gold. Under this standard, gold could flow between countries without producing major changes in the stock of money outstanding. It provided relative fixed exchange rates for the currencies of different countries, and there is reason to believe that it reduced, though it did not eliminate, international transmission of business fluctuations.[5] But it did not provide even a bad mechanism for adjusting the balance of international payments, as is testified to by the steadily rising gold holdings of the United States between the two wars. It largely avoided the depression– boom mechanism of adjustment inherent in the gold standard, but it provided no substitute mechanism of adjusting the balance of payments. It could not survive the cumulative effects of this lack of adjustment.

Flexible Exchange Rates

A third simple method of relating the currencies of different countries is through the market alone. If each country maintained its own currency with no common link between them, the relative values of the different currencies could be worked out through the offering of and the demand for each currency in exchange for others. Under these conditions, the depression-boom mechanism of adjustment would be largely avoided, but exchange rates would be unstable. Any unbalance in payments could be corrected through changes in exchange rates.[6] For example, if Country A had an adverse balance of payments, its currency would be offered in exchange for other currencies in a volume greater than was demanded, and the value of the currency could be expected to fall relative to that of other currencies. This would mean that, at the new exchange rates, the people in Country A would have to pay more in their own currency for the goods of other countries, and so would tend to buy less from abroad. At the same time, the people of other countries would not have to pay as much in their own currencies for the goods of Country A, and so would tend to buy more. In this way, the initial unbalance would tend to be corrected.[7] The adjustment would not need to affect significantly the levels of activity within the different countries, but only the relative values of their currencies.

Similarly, there would be no serious tendency for business fluctuations to be transmitted from country to country through this mechanism of trade adjustment. If a depression developed in Country A, it would affect the relation between the value of its money and that of other countries, but would not cause depression abroad except possibly in a very minor degree. Thus, suppose that Country A, before its depression, was spending ten billion dollars a year for the goods of Country B and selling ten billion dollars worth to Country B. With an exchange rate of five dollars for one pound this would mean that Country B was importing two million pounds worth of goods from Country A and exporting the same amount to Country A. Then assume that depression developed in Country A, that its prices remained the same but money incomes dropped and, as a result of the lower incomes, its demand for the goods of Country B dropped to eight billion dollars. Since the depression would not presumably initially affect the demand of Country B for the product of Country A, Country A would develop a favorable balance of payments. As a result, more pounds would be offered for dollars than the reverse, and the exchange rate could be expected to shift in favor of Country A and against Country B.

The effects of this change in exchange rates would depend on the character of demand in Country B. If Country B had a fixed monetary demand for the goods of Country A, its worsened exchange rate would not alter *the amount of pounds* offered for the goods of Country A, but only reduce the physical quantity of goods obtained for the outlay. Since, by this assumption, two billion pounds would be offered regardless of the exchange rate, the rate would have to fall until it was favorable enough to Country A to induce it to take two billion pounds worth of the products of Country B. The greater the elasticity of County A's demand for the products of Country B, the smaller the change in the exchange rate necessary to reinstate the initial level of physical exports for Country B. But whatever the character of Country A's demand, Country B would have no reduction in its physical exports, and therefore no reduction in production and employment as a result of the adjustment. Its standard of living would be reduced to the extent of the smaller quantity of the goods of Country A it obtained, but Country A's depression would not extend to it.

By much the same kind of reasoning, it could be expected that Country B would share, but only to a very minor degree, in Country A's depression if its demand for Country A's products was elastic, and would incur a very minor boom if its demand were inelastic. If its demand were elastic, this would mean that as the exchange rate became less favorable, its aggregate demand for Country A's goods in terms of pounds would decline, say to one point eight billion pounds. The exchange rate would only have to adjust to the point where Country A was buying one point eight billion pounds worth of Country B's products. This would mean a physical reduction of one-point-eight billion pounds in Country B's exports, and thus lead to reduced production and employment in Country B. However, this would be offset to a considerable extent by the expenditure on home-produced goods made possible by the .2 billion pounds not spent on imports. The net effect would be likely to be mildly depressing.

Similarly, if Country B had an inelastic demand for the goods of Country A, it would spend more pounds on imports from Country A as the exchange rate went against it. This means that the exchange rate would have to adjust until Country B's physical exports were greater than before. This would be a stimulus to production and employment, but it would be partly offset by the shift of expenditure within Country B away from home-produced goods as more was spent on imports. The net effect would be likely to be a very minor stimulus to total production and employment within Country B.

It should be recognized that the above analysis leaves out of account international capital movements, speculation, some degree of price sensitivity (except for imported goods), and many other factors that would need to be taken into account in a more realistic analysis. Its sole purpose has been to show that the mechanism of exchange rate adjustment could be expected to maintain a balance of payments between countries, without serious transmittal of business fluctuations, if only ordinary trade were involved.

Orderly Adjustment of Exchange Rates

The foregoing analysis indicates that fixed exchange rates are likely to be a serious impediment to the maintenance of full employment within a country. On the other hand, exchange rates free to adjust to the ebb and flow of demand are subject to speculation and likely to hinder international trade and investment. The least unsatisfactory compromise between evils might be one in which exchange rates were held stable or at least predictable over short periods of time, but adjusted over longer periods so as to maintain the balance of payments between countries on an even keel.

The World [sic] Monetary Fund appears to be designed to carry out such an orderly adjustment of exchange rates. It is in a position to prevent an unbalance in payments between countries from having an immediate depression–boom effect, just as could be done under the gold exchange standard. And while the depression–boom adjustment is being postponed, remedial action may be worked out that does not involve a change in exchange rates. However, if the unbalance in payments is more than temporary, exchange rates can be changed. Thus, a considerable measure of exchange rate stability could be combined with orderly adjustments sufficient to allow a fundamental balance in payments to be maintained. Such a procedure, if it can be effectively carried out, would leave individual countries relatively free to control the level of aggregate demand within their borders, and at the same time would provide a considerable degree of exchange stability required for the maximum volume of trade between countries.

Notes

1. The above gives only the bare bones of the classical mechanism of trade adjustment under the gold standard. Amplifications and modifications of this basic mechanism have been developed over the years, but these are not relevant to the more general analysis of this book.

2. The above analysis assumes that the gold-receiving countries have sufficient unused resources to allow for a significant expansion in employment. However, as the limit of productive resources was approached, more and more of the adjustment to increased demand could be expected to take the form of price increases.

3. A simple depression-initiating assumption would be that, because of increased uncertainty, the people of the country wanted to hold more money at the initial level of prices and incomes.

4. Undoubtedly, under the gold standard, other factors than gold flow contributed to the international spreading of business fluctuations. For example, fears that caused business contraction in one country might spread to other countries without any gold flow. The significant conclusion here is that the gold flow mechanism would spread fluctuations if other influences did not.

5. The theoretical reasons for this expectation can be exemplified as follows: If depression developed in Country A for internal reasons, its demand for the products of other countries could be expected to fall, while the depression would not immediately reduce the demand of other countries for the products of country A. The unbalance of payments would lead to gold movement without significant change in the money stocks of different countries, but the contraction in Country A's physical imports would mean a contraction in production and employment in other countries unless the loss in sales could be made up from other sources. The

magnitudes involved would probably be much less than under the gold standard. In practice, the U.S. action in "sterilizing" the gold inflow from 1926 helped to prevent the export of British depression to the United States, at least prior to 1930.

6. An important exception to this statement needs to be made. If a country has an adverse balance because of heavy debt obligations *that are determined in terms of currencies other than its own,* a fall in the value of its currency will tend to exaggerate the unbalance, not correct it.

7. In actual practice, the adjustment would be likely to be much more complex as speculative factors, capital movements, interest rates, and the like, are taken into account. But the underlying mechanism of adjustment would be operative, tending to correct any net unbalance arising.

18

Toward a Positive Program

The monetary theory of employment cannot only provide an explanation of unemployment, but can also point to the direction that remedial action can take to maintain reasonably full employment in an insensitive-price economy. The central focus of such a program must obviously be the maintenance of an adequate stock of money outstanding at all times. But how such a program should be carried out is a much more complex matter, which has to take into account the complexities of our actual economy and the institutions that already exist. All that can be done here is to suggest the main steps that need be taken in developing a positive program for maintaining reasonably full employment.

Examine the Validity of the Monetary Theory

The first step toward a positive program is to examine the validity of the monetary theory itself. How far does it provide the explanation of business fluctuations and mass unemployment in our actual economy? What modifications and amendments are necessary to make it fit the actual situation more closely? Some steps for testing the theory have already been outlined. These and others should be taken as a prelude to the use of the theory as a basis for policy.

Establish a Better Statistical Basis for Action

The second step toward a positive program is to lay a better statistical basis for policy. This must cover the ownership and flow of money in our economic system, and provide better figures on such items as the holding of assets other than money, plans for new real investment, and consumer behavior.

Though the whole economic system operates on the basis of money, it is only in very recent years that periodical figures have been compiled as to the ownership of bank deposits, and even less is known as to who holds currency. If the monetary theory of employment is found to be valid, figures on what groups hold how much money and the changes in the holdings are of vital importance for policy formation. At the very least, annual figures on the ownership of deposits should be obtained from all banks, and monthly or weekly figures from reporting member banks. Likewise, sampling studies of the ownership of currency should be established on a regular periodic basis. The rise and fall in the money holdings of different groups may provide a key to the need for action before that need becomes apparent in the figures of production and employment.

Of parallel importance with information on the holdings of money is a clear picture of the flow of money through the economic system. Figures on the magnitude and sources of national income have become a standard part of economic policy making, but they give only a partial picture of the total flow of money within the system. At the present time, the National Bureau of Economic Research is conducting a pilot study to develop an overall picture of money flow in the United States. The results should show the main elements of the picture, but on some matters basic statistics are lacking. Once a satisfactory basis has been developed for organizing data on money flows, whatever new statistical series are needed should be established, and regular compilations made, to show the whole picture of money flows at least quarterly, perhaps monthly.

Also, there is need to improve the statistical information in other directions. The monetary theory places considerable emphasis on assets other than money. Regular compilations are needed of the holdings of different types of securities, real estate, inventories, and other assets held by different economic groups, and the more significant changes in the market value of these assets. Inventory figures should be compiled in such a way that changes in inventory values due to changes in prices and to changes in quantities can be distinguished. The development of policy is likely to indicate other statistical lacks that will need to be filled.

Finally, there is surprisingly little factual information on why people and enterprises hold the amount of money that they do and why they choose to alter their holdings. Even techniques for discovering answers to these questions have not been developed. Monetary literature is full of such phrases as the transaction motive, the hoarding motive, and similar motivations for holding money, but these concepts bear no measurable relation to real behavior.[1] It is more likely that sampling studies of individual and business behavior (and perhaps of attitudes) with respect to money holdings will provide a more significant aid to policy making.

More extensive analysis of the material indicated above and similar material should disclose some of the magnitudes with which policy would have to deal. It should be possible to discover, at least crudely, the extent to which the demand for money is increased by a given reduction in interest rates; by a given rise in real income; by a given rise in money prices; by a given shift in income distribution; and by other significant influences. Also, analysis of such data should throw light on the magnitude of the effects on interest rates, prices, real income, and so forth, of a given increase in the stock of money put into circulation by various methods; and on the trends of change and the magnitude of change in the demand for money arising from sources outside of the immediate economic forces. These and similar analyses, plus an adequate and adequately organized flow of information on current developments, should provide the factual basis necessary for a stabilizing policy.

Effective Monetary Control

The third step in a positive program is to provide a positive control over the total monetary stock. At the present time, the Governors of the Federal Reserve Bank and the Federal Treasury, in combination, can exercise a considerable influence over the amount of money in the hands of the public, but this control is for the most part indirect and tends to fail at the times it is most needed. Thus, in a depression, Reserve authorities may have the power to force a contraction in the money supply that would be harmful, but are not in a position to bring about the needed expansion in the stock of money. Also, conditions could arise such that when the stock of money needed to be contracted, the Reserve authorities could allow further expansion but could not force contraction. As a result, the present banking arrangements give a very far from positive control over the quantity of money outstanding.

Just how the banking system should be modified so as to provide this positive control will not be discussed here. It is possible that some way could be found to provide the necessary control with only a relatively minor expansion in the powers of the Federal Reserve Board. Or it might be necessary to make more drastic changes in the banking system. It would be desirable if some kind of automatic control could be established so that the quantity of money would expand or contract to the extent required by the economy and without any central control, but this seems unlikely, at least in the near future. Much attention should be devoted to the question of the most satisfactory method for (1) establishing a positive control over the quantity of money outstanding; and (2) an exercise of this control in such a way as to meet both the short-run and the longer-run fluctuations in the community's demand for money as a store of buying power.

Fiscal Policy

A fourth step in a positive program is the clarification of the role of fiscal policy. Many advocates of the use of federal fiscal policy as a method of maintaining full employment consider it the only important short-run method of adjustment. But, under the monetary theory, fiscal policy plays a role secondary to monetary policy. A government deficit financed by monetary expansion could be one of the more stimulating methods of putting additional money into circulation. But it is by no means the only method.

Of even more importance is the conclusion that under the monetary theory, budget balance (or even a budget surplus) over a period of years is consistent with the use of a budget deficit to stimulate employment in particular years. If a budget deficit financed by monetary expansion is used in a particular year to maintain full employment, it will increase the money supply both in that year *and in subsequent years.* This will mean that in the next year a smaller deficit or perhaps no deficit at all will be needed to maintain full employment. A further monetary expansion, either by deficit financing or by bank expansion without a deficit, could so expand the money supply as to allow the government in subsequent years to run a surplus and yet maintain full employment. Thus, a proper balance between fiscal and nonfiscal methods of adjusting the money supply could maintain reasonably full employment without a net deficit over a period of years, but with the advantages of the more swiftly acting fiscal measures to meet more serious short-run situations.

The conclusion therefore seems reasonable that fiscal policy should be employed as one of the short-run instruments for maintaining full employment, but that it should be so combined with monetary policy that, *over a period of years,* the budget would balance or depart from balance in a manner decided upon in advance as, for example, through a planned reduction in the public debt.

Secular Expansion in the Stock of Money

A fifth step in a positive program is a reconsideration of the methods for bringing about a secular expansion in the stock of money. In a growing economy, such as that of the United States, there is usually a secular increase in the demand for money as a store of buying power. As a result, the stock of money must show a rising trend if full employment at a reasonably stable price level is to be maintained. In the United States, the average annual increase required might amount to as much as two or three billion dollars a year. To some extent this secular increase might reflect simply a desire to exchange securities for larger cash balances, but to the extent that it involved goods it would mean that individuals and enterprises were choosing to exchange more goods for money than they were choosing to exchange money for goods. Whoever created the net addition to the stock of money would determine who made use of this excess of goods offered for money.

Under a commercial banking system, the use of the extra goods would be made available to business through an expansion of bank loans. Thus, the real savings resulting from the desire to hold larger money balances would tend to be added to the real capital of business, with the banks acting as intermediaries. In an economy in which a major requisite is an expansion of capital, this would be an appropriate development. But in an economy in which the expansion of consumption is a prime requisite, some mechanism that converted the expansion of the money stock into increased consumption would be a more suitable arrangement.

Fiscal policy could provide a mechanism for converting an expansion in the stock of money into increased current consumption. For example, if tax rates were reduced and the resulting reduction in revenues were financed by government issue of additional money, the addition to the stock of money would be matched by an increase in that part of the incomes of tax payers remaining in their hands after the payment of taxes. A large part of this extra disposable income would presumably be spent on extra consumption, the amount depending in part on just how tax rates were reduced. Or the government might put the extra money into circulation directly by expanding its expenditure. Thus, adjustments in tax rates and government expenditures could make available to the community at large the goods that are released by the secular increase in the demand for money.

Intermediate between the secular expansion in the stock of money through financing federal expenditure, lies the possibility of increasing the stock of money by a progressive monetization of the existing public debt. To the extent that banks add to their total portfolio of loans and securities by buying additional government bonds in the open market, they thereby create additional money. At the same time, this method of expanding the stock of money would probably increase the demand for money as a store of value, at least to the extent that lower interest rates increased the willingness to hold money rather than other assets. As a result, a larger increase in the stock of money would be required to meet the secular increase in demand, if additional money were put into circulation by monetization of a part of the government debt, than by a government deficit or by an expansion in loans to business.

The question of how far it is desirable to meet the secular increase in the demand for money through increasing the funds available for business borrowing, how far by monetization of the public debt, and how far by reducing taxes or increasing the funds available for government use should be given serious consideration.

The Federal Debt

A sixth step in a positive program is a revision of thinking and policy with respect to the public debt. According to the monetary theory, the great increase in the public debt during the war should make it much more easy to maintain full employment after the war than before. The debt, instead of being a drag on business and the community, as so many people assume, should provide a positive stimulus to production and employment.

The reason for this is that the huge Federal debt can be expected to increase both the propensity to consume and the propensity to invest. The evidence is reasonably clear that in the decade before the war, the low level of investment was in reasonable balance with the low level of consumption, but the sum of the two fell far short of supporting full employment and full production.[2] Both the propensity to consume and the propensity to invest were low. But the high government debt should increase both propensities. Because consumers have increased their assets, it can be expected that they will spend a larger proportion of any given income on consumption. The necessity to save for the future will be somewhat reduced because individuals have already accumulated more savings.[3] Likewise, the increase in assets can be expected to stimulate investment. The enterprise with a large block of government bonds is more likely to make full use of its opportunities for expansion than one without this extra asset. Even if it does not sell the bonds to finance expansion it can obtain other funds for expansion more easily.

If the extra assets of the enterprise are in the form of money, the stimulating effect is likely to be even greater. But in either case the high increase in government debt can be expected to increase both the propensity to consume and that to invest, and thus make simpler the postwar problem of maintaining full employment. It should overcome to a considerable degree, and perhaps wholly, the lowness of the propensities to consume and invest in the 1930s.[4]

Perhaps the debt should never be paid off. This possibility is made explicit in the British Consols.[5] There is no reason to expect that all the *money* outstanding will be retired. It is necessary to have a large stock of money to satisfy the desire of the community to hold money, and its retirement would be disastrous. Government debt has some of these same characteristics. It may well be that a large government debt is the easiest way to maintain the high level in the basic propensities to consume and invest that are needed to maintain full employment. The big government debt can provide the basic lift in spending propensities, which is needed as compared with the prewar period, while smaller adjustments in fiscal and monetary policy could meet the temporary fluctuations in the demand for money. The government debt would thus provide a storehouse for savings to the extent that this could not be provided by the real assets needed to carry on production and distribution.[6] Individuals could have claims against future production without the necessity of the building up of current *physical* assets to an equal extent.

Once the large public debt is regarded as contributing to the maintenance of full employment, the problem of policy with respect to it takes on quite a different character. The problem of reduction or increase of the federal debt becomes one primarily of short-run adjustments as a result of a stabilizing monetary and fiscal policy, and one of handling the interest burden, rather than one of major debt reduction as such.

Preventing Inflation

The seventh step in a positive program concerns the problem of inflation. A full employment program should be based on the prevailing level of insensitive prices. A rise of insensitive prices as a group could defeat such a program. This could happen if, in the more concentrated industries, price administrators took a high level of demand as an opportunity to increase profit margins through raising prices, or if labor organizations took the same high demand as an opportunity to force up wage rates beyond the level justified by increased productivity, thereby forcing up insensitive prices. A very gradual rise in the price–wage level would be consistent with full employment but undesirable for other reasons. A more rapid rise could be a serious threat to full employment.

The national action necessary to maintain the relative stability of insensitive prices may be only one of education and a certain amount of national leadership. Enlightened business and labor leaders can be expected to work for insensitive price stability once the importance of such stability is recognized. Government backing in resisting arbitrary lifting of wage rates or insensitive prices might in practice be sufficient to maintain reasonable stability in the level of insensitive prices. Until such measures have been thoroughly tested under more normal peacetime conditions, and in the presence of aggregate demand sufficient but not much more than sufficient to support full employment, there is no necessity for adopting more positive measures of control.[7]

Improvement in Business Practices

The eighth step in a positive program would be a thorough investigation into ways by which business—particularly big business—could contribute to stability at full employment. There are undoubtedly many shifts in policy that individual business units could make, which would contribute to economic stability without reducing their long-run profits. For many big businesses, a well-designed program for capital expansion could result in a fairly stable outlay on new plant and equipment, and thus reduce this source of fluctuation in total demand. Greater stability in inventories might be achieved. Improved accounting techniques could somewhat reduce fluctuation in reported profits,[8] and consideration of the monetary impact of new security issues and changes in cash holdings might lead to less disrupting policy in these fields. Altogether, as individual businesses and particularly big businesses become more responsible toward the public interest, they should be able to make many shifts toward a more stabilizing policy consistent with their long-run interest in profits.

The Process of Policy Making

The ninth step in a positive program to maintain full employment is to make sure that there is adequate organization for establishing the necessary national policy. At the present time there is a newly created Joint Committee of Congress, which is explicitly concerned with the problem of full employment and all policies relating to this objective. Likewise, the President has a newly created Council of Economic Advisors concerned with the problem of full employment. But at the present time there is no agency on the administrative side specifically responsible for integrating fiscal policy and monetary policy into a single unitary policy. The Council of Economic Advisors can make constructive suggestions. Joint consultation between the Treasury and the Federal Reserve can iron out some difficulties. But none of these is sufficient to provide the unitary monetary and fiscal policy that is required.

There are various ways in which this difficulty could be met. Responsibility for coordinating fiscal and monetary policy might be placed specifically on the Council of Economic Advisors, but this responsibility would be difficult to carry out since it would interfere with the sovereignty of two important agencies that would have to carry out policy. The responsibility might be placed with a special Monetary and Fiscal Board consisting, say, of the Secretary of the Treasury, the Chairman of the Board of Governors of the Federal Reserve, and the Chairman of the Council of Economic Advisors. Or a new cabinet post of Secretary for Monetary and Fiscal Policy might be created with responsibility not only with respect to such policy, but also for certain of the administrative functions now carried on by the Treasury and the Federal Reserve so that policy making and policy execution would be more clearly tied together and unified.

These suggestions are made only to indicate the character of the problem. Unified monetary and fiscal policy would appear to be essential to a positive program for maintaining full employment. What arrangements are made to insure such a unified policy again lies outside the scope of this book.

Full Employment Policy

The essential steps toward a positive program for full employment have been outlined, but the operation of such a program has not been clearly indicated. If the various steps outlined were taken, we would presumably find ourselves in this situation. The monetary theory would have been discussed, tested, and accepted in general as a basis for policy. A more adequate statistical basis for policy would have been laid. A positive control over the quantity of money outstanding would have been established, so that the stock of money could be expanded or contracted according to the requirements of full employment policy. Fiscal policy and the public debt would have been accepted as important elements in a full employment policy. Efforts would be underway to determine the area of optimum balance between prices and wage rates, and to encourage business and labor to develop price–wage relations that fall in this area and avoid actions that lead to a price–wage spiral. Business, particularly big business, would be encouraged to seek greater stability in new construction, in physical inventories, and in financing. Arrangements would have been adopted to bring about unified monetary and fiscal policy.

In this situation, measures for maintaining full employment could be divided into three groups.

Most basic are the longer-run measures that aim to improve the general working of the economy. These would include measures to improve the price- and wage-making processes, such as clarification and enforcement of antitrust policy; measures to increase the mobility of resources, such as improved labor exchanges; measures to stimulate greater stability in business actions; and measures to establish long-run objectives with respect to the national debt.

The second group of measures are those aimed at maintaining full employment in the immediate future—a year or more—*insofar as this future can be foreseen.* This group of measures involves the general character of the budgeted expenditures and revenues of government, the current balance between prices and wage rates, the general objective with respect to the money supply, and similar matters, which are not subject to quick readjustment but whose initial adjustment could lead to full employment *if the future could be foreseen with sufficient accuracy.*

The third group of measures consists of the shorter-run actions that aim to make up for the deficiencies in foresight. These would include open market operations of the banking system to expand or contract the money supply to a greater or lesser extent than was planned in the intermediate group of measures, to expand or contract public works and other government expenditure or revenues, and similar actions that could be taken rapidly and with fairly rapid effects on demand and employment.

The locus of responsibility for these different types of action would presumably be different. The longer-run measures to help the workings of the economy involve many other considerations besides those of full employment. They often raise basic problems of national policy, and as such should be determined by the Congress. The administrative agencies responsible for maintaining full employment should be in a position to make recommendations as to such policy, but not to determine policy.

So long as the executive arm of government is given primary responsibility for maintaining full employment, the determination on the intermediate group of measures should be partly legislative and partly executive. The system of policies represented by the budget, the handling of the public debt, and the monetary supply must be such that, in the light of reasonable expectations, they *can* result in full employment. To this extent they are more an executive than a legislative matter. But insofar as there are various combinations of measures, any one of which could result in full employment under the expected conditions, the choices among these alternatives is essentially a legislative matter.

The shorter-run adjustments to make up for inability to foresee should be almost entirely an executive matter. Timing is often of the essence of such measures. The legislature can authorize such action and set limits to it, but the actual decision within these limits must be an executive responsibility. Today, large discretion lies with the monetary authorities. Perhaps larger executive discretion should also be allowed with respect to certain items in fiscal policy. This would seem to be essential if the monetary theory of employment is accepted as a basis for full employment policy, and monetary and fiscal measures are to be used as the means for maintaining reasonably full employment in a free society.

Notes

1. Some economists have given a semblance of measurability by *assuming* that money holdings *due to the transaction motive* bear a constant ratio to transac-

tions, and holdings above this amount are due to other motivation. Since the underlying assumption here is not capable of verification, the resulting measurements would seem to be of doubtful significance.

2. The proponents of the saving–investment theory would say that investment at full employment would be insufficient to offset all the saving that would occur at full employment. This places the emphasis on investment as the corrective, rather than giving equal emphasis to consumption and investment as is done in the text above.

3. This more or less permanent effect should not be confused with the temporary stimulus to consumption as savings are spent on consumption. The latter presumably comes to an end when savings have shifted from weak to strong hands.

4. How far the increased debt will overcome the lowness of the propensities of the 1930s will depend largely on what happens to insensitive prices in the first two or three years after the war. The first year and a half after the war, the total demand for goods has been greater than could be supplied, but part of this discrepancy arose from temporarily low production and part from temporarily high postwar replacement and catching up demand. It could happen that *insensitive* prices would rise under this temporary excess of demand over supply to such an extent that the increase in debt was negated. However, no such rise has yet taken place and seems fairly unlikely. The large rise of sensitive prices will presumably be reversed when the temporary stimulus to demand has disappeared.

5. Obligations to pay interest in perpetuity but without obligation to repay the principal.

6. Essentially this same argument was made by Alexander Hamilton as one of the reasons for advocating federal assumption of state debts arising from the revolutionary war. His emphasis, however, was on a big federal debt as an aid to investment, in that the businessperson could put funds in government when they were not needed in his or her business, and could take them out when he or she had the opportunity to use them.

7. It is notable that even under the *excessive* demand following the war, insensitive prices were not too unstable.

8. For example, the last-in-first-out method of inventory valuation tends to reduce "artificial" profits and losses due to price changes. Likewise, the allocation of depreciation on the basis of units produced rather than on a time basis, tends to reduce fluctuations in unit costs due to fluctuations in volume, and thereby reduce apparent fluctuations in profits.

Index

A

AAA. *See* Agricultural Adjustment Administration

Administered prices, xix-xxiii, 33–31, 69–71, 161, 167
  by buyers, 93*n.11*
  economic efficiency of, 69–71
  stability of, 71–72

Aggregate demand, xix-xx, xxxi, 95–109, 143, 161, 189
  determinants of, 135–40
  money as, 139–40
  savings versus money balance additions, 135–39
  effect of differences in, 166
  effect of increase in, 108
  excess in, 209, 211
  and full employment, 200, 203–204
  and government spending, 201–203, 205
  and inflation, 207
  in insensitive-price economy, 103–06
  and intermediately sensitive prices, 99–103
  monetary theory of, xxxii
  and money, 163–65, 166–68

  nonmonetary assets and, 165
  and sensitive and rigid prices, 96–99

Agricultural Adjustment Administration (AAA), xvii

Agriculture, 160

Assets, 145–46, 149, 181
  and aggregate demand, 165
  buying power of, 4
  and economic management, 127–33
  holdings of, 229
  marginal utility of, 156*n.1*
  and money demand, 116–19
  shifting into money, 149–51
  values and proportioning, 132–33, 214
  See also Capital

Automobile industry, 217

B

Balance of payments, 220, 222, 223
Bank accounts, 137–38
Banking system, xxi, 179, 182–83, 186, 192, 194, 230–31
Bank liquidation, 190
Bank reserves, 190–91

About the Author

Gardiner C. Means (1896–1988) was the co-author, with Adolf A. Berle, Jr., of *The Modern Corporation and Private Property* (1932) and, with James C. Bonbright, of *The Holding Company: Its Public Significance and Its Regulation* (1932). Although an academic outsider, he worked for a number of federal government agencies, most notably the U.S. Department of Agriculture and the National Resources Committee; and for the Committee for Economic Development and the Fund for the Republic. He wrote or edited numerous other volumes. He emphasized administered pricing by corporations and the resultant tendency to inflation as both an accurate description of reality and a basis for policy.

About the Editors

Warren J. Samuels is Professor of Economics at Michigan State University, East Lansing, Michigan. He specializes in the history of economic thought, the economic role of government, and methodology. He is author of *The Classical Theory of Economic Policy* and *Pareto on Policy,* a co-author of *Gardiner C. Means: Institutionalist and Post Keynesian,* co-editor of *The Elgar Companion to Institutional and Evolutionary Economics* and *Research in the History of Economic Thought and Methodology,* and the author of numerous articles and book reviews. He has been president of the History of Economics Society and the Association for Social Economics.

Frederic S. Lee is a Reader in Economics at DeMontfort University, Leicester, England. His areas of interest include Post Keynesian price theory, history of economics, and the Industrial Workers of the World. He is a co-editor of *The Heterodox Economics of Gardiner C. Means,* and has written articles on Means that have appeared in the *Review of Social Economy,* the *Journal of Economic Issues,* and the *Journal of Policy History.* His other published articles have appeared in the *Journal of Post Keynesian Economics,* the *Review of Political Economy,* and the *History of Political Economy.*

For Product Safety Concerns and Information please contact our EU
representative GPSR@taylorandfrancis.com
Taylor & Francis Verlag GmbH, Kaufingerstraße 24, 80331 München, Germany